Skateboarding and Philosophy

Skateboarding and Philosophy

Essays Concerning the Life of the Grind

Edited by Joshua Heter *and* Josef Thomas Simpson

McFarland & Company, Inc., Publishers
Jefferson, North Carolina

This book has undergone peer review.

ISBN (print) 978-1-4766-9544-0
ISBN (ebook) 978-1-4766-5568-0

LIBRARY OF CONGRESS CATALOGING DATA ARE AVAILABLE

© 2025 Joshua Heter and Josef Thomas Simpson. All rights reserved

No part of this book may be reproduced or transmitted in any form or by any means, electronic or mechanical, including photocopying or recording, or by any information storage and retrieval system, without permission in writing from the publisher.

Front cover images: © ninetysevenproject/cassava99/Shutterstock

Printed in the United States of America

*McFarland & Company, Inc., Publishers
Box 611, Jefferson, North Carolina 28640
www.mcfarlandpub.com*

Acknowledgments

If you'd told us as kids that we'd one day publish a philosophy book about skateboarding (or anything else), we probably wouldn't have known what to think. We didn't really project as scholars in our youth. Regardless, working on this book has very much been a pleasure as we've long held a great interest in and appreciation for both skateboarding and philosophy. We'd like to thank Dré Person and everyone at McFarland for their help making this volume a reality. We are also indebted to the School of Humanities at Jefferson College and the Center for Academic Success at the Catholic University of America as well as all of our families, friends, and colleagues for their support during our work on this project. We'd also like to thank Tim Simpson and Ben Crackle for getting us into skating so many years ago. And, of course, we would very much like to thank the gifted authors whose work comprises this book and without which it would not exist.

Table of Contents

Acknowledgments — v

Thinking Is Not a Crime
    JOSHUA HETER *and* JOSEF THOMAS SIMPSON — 1

I. Skateboarding Fundamentals

Skateboarding Is (in a Sense) a Sport
    JOSHUA HETER — 7

What We Talk About When We Talk About Skateboarding Tricks
    WILLIAM GIOVANNI JIMÉNEZ SENZANO — 15

If You're a Sellout, You're Not a Skateboarder
    MATTHEW J. CULL — 25

II. Skating Values

The Problem of the Poseur
    JOSHUA HETER — 37

Skateboarding *Is* a Crime
    BRADLEY ELICKER — 46

The Aesthetics of Skateboarding
    HECTOR QUINTERO — 54

Skateboarding Judgments
    JOSHUA HETER — 62

III. Ancient Wisdom on Four Wheels

De on Display
    CASEY RENTMEESTER — 73

Kierke-Grinding
    MICHAEL J. REGIER   82

The Journey of the Stoic Skater
    GLAVA SOFIA   91

Skating Toward the Good Life
    EMILY STEFL   101

The Sound of One Deck Snapping
    SETH M. WALKER   111

IV. Why Skate?

The Risk *Is* the Reward
    BRIAN HARDING   121

Skate and Destroy Capitalism
    THUNDER STORM HETER   131

The Serious Beauty of Skateboarding
    JOHN BECKER   141

The Girls Are Shredding It
    ELLY VINTIADIS   149

V. The Skater's Mind

Knowing How to Kickflip
    JOSEF THOMAS SIMPSON   161

Gleaming the Cube or Destroying the World
    MUKASA MUBIRUMUSOKE   169

The Skater's Eye
    BRIAN GLENNEY   179

Skateboarding Glossary   189
About the Contributors   193
Index   197

Thinking Is Not a Crime

JOSHUA HETER *and* JOSEF THOMAS SIMPSON

Skateboarding and philosophy have more in common than you might realize.

Skateboarding had a fairly inauspicious start. The first skateboards appeared on American streets in the late 1940s and '50s as somewhat crude, homemade inventions: thin wooden boards with roller skate wheels, often attached to wooden crates for steering (making them more analogous to Razor Scooters as opposed to modern-day skateboards). It wasn't until 1959 that the first commercially manufactured skateboard was made, it too being a pale comparison to its eventual, contemporary successors.

In the 1970s and '80s, skateboarding slowly started to gain more widespread popularity at least in part because advancements in hardware (such as grip tape, specialized trucks, and polyurethane wheels) brought about a virtual revolution in the field. No longer confined to taking part in downhill races or casual rides along beachfront bike paths, skaters were now in a position to experiment and innovate. They were able to make use of the vertical walls of the pools of southern California (a hotbed for skating) and to begin to invent the various tricks that street skating is known so well for today.

However, it was also during and perhaps because of this period that skateboarding garnered something of a reputation for rebelliousness and anti-authoritarianism. It wasn't long before a number of municipalities throughout the United States had ordinances against and bans of skateboarding. Skaters were seen as a menace, and the relatively new pastime they cherished was viewed as little more than a destructive element to public spaces and to the peace as a whole.

Of course, like most elements of counterculture, skateboarding would come to be accepted if not somewhat embraced by the culture at large. Heroes of blockbuster movies like *Back to the Future* were boarders, some of the most high-profile skaters found themselves front and center in

2   Thinking Is Not a Crime

celebrity culture, and in 2016, the International Olympic Committee even voted to make skateboarding a medal sport at the 2020 Summer Games. That said, while skating has come a long way in achieving broader acceptance, it is still fairly niche in its draw of both participants and fans. While skateboarding and skateboarders no longer suffer the same stigma they once did, they aren't exactly fully mainstream either. Skating has (and will likely continue to have) something of an outsider status in the world of sports if not society generally.

As it turns out, the history of philosophy is not entirely dissimilar from the history of skateboarding. Philosophy (at least in the West) is thought to have arisen somewhat organically in the seventh century BC in Asia Minor (what is modern-day Turkey) where well-worn trade routes brought a variety of disparate cultures and worldviews into contact with one another. The natural development then, so the story goes, was—for those holding incompatible views—to attempt to settle their ideological conflicts with reason and argumentation.

It didn't take long for what is recognizably philosophy today to spread throughout the ancient world. Philosophers during this period raised questions about the nature of reality, man's relation to the gods, the nature of justice, and what it means to live the good life. And, of course, long before the scientific revolution, philosophers were planting the seeds that would blossom into disciplines like modern cosmology, evolutionary biology, and even computer science. Indeed, this initial heyday for philosophy was important not only to the history of ideas but also to humanity as a whole.

However, philosophers have been (not unlike skateboarders), on occasion, labeled as outsiders, misfits, and anti-authoritarian troublemakers. It is perhaps the very nature of philosophy to question authority and established thought, and it is just this sort of activity that has—from time to time—led philosophers to be met with derision and even malice. Perhaps the most notable instance of this happened not too long after philosophy's inception. In 399 BC, Socrates (often described as the founding father of Western philosophy) was sentenced to death for the crimes of impiety and corrupting the youth: what essentially amounted to questioning the authority of Athenian society and teaching young folks to do the same.

Thankfully, philosophy and philosophers have not been permanently condemned to fates like that of Socrates, but they are often enough burdened with a sort of cautious, kept-at-arm's-length status and thought of as somehow less than ordinary. From the founding of the great universities of the medieval period to today, philosophy has been seen as a fundamentally important part of academia and a life of inquiry, and many philosophers throughout history have been rightfully credited with contributing to the founding of democracy, the fundamentals of science, and a host of other advancements important to the modern world. However, much like skating, philosophy has not entirely shed its outsider, not-*quite*-mainstream status. To many, the discipline of philosophy is odd and mysterious. It is not something to be mocked or dismissed, but it is something seen as taken up by those on the fringes, by those with a penchant for questioning the status quo in a perhaps not so useful if not counterproductive manner.

With all that skateboarding and philosophy have in common, it is only natural that the two should meet with a philosophical investigation of skating. And this is what the book you now hold in your hands attempts to do. There are, as it turns out, a great deal of interesting philosophical questions that arise when we take even a moment to reflect on the topic: is skateboarding a sport (and does it matter whether it is)? What compels skateboarders to attempt to perfect their craft through all the failure and injuries; is the risk worth the reward? Is skateboarding an art (and can it be beautiful)? What would thinkers from the ancient and medieval worlds make of skateboarding; could they help us think more carefully about it? Is skating inherently rebellious, or has it gained that reputation due to bad luck? What exactly does it mean to be a poseur (and should I care if I am one)?

Many of the authors whose work composes this book (and the all-too-fortunate editors who were able to bring them together) have spent their fair share of time both skating as well as studying, teaching, and composing philosophy. With that in mind, they invite you to read on and critically reflect on skateboarding with the same boldness and abandon that might lead you to launch yourself on a thin piece of wood on four synthetic wheels whether or not you have permission from the proper authorities. Should anyone give you any trouble for asking deep, thoughtful questions (about skating or anything else), just remember, much like the subject matter of this book, thinking is not a crime!

I
Skateboarding Fundamentals

Skateboarding Is (in a Sense) a Sport

Joshua Heter

Is skateboarding a sport? This seemingly straightforward question is (as you may have anticipated) more complicated than one might appreciate at first glance. This is due *in part* to the fact that its answer relies on two more fundamental questions: what is skateboarding? And what is sport? To the former question, we needn't devote a substantial amount of attention, because a fairly elementary definition of skateboarding will satisfy most of the relevant discussion on the matter, and I take it that much of the criticism of this definition that could be mounted will lead us into territory that is largely uninteresting. Skateboarding is simply the activity of riding a skateboard.

That said, one potential criticism of this definition is that not all skateboarding involves riding. If a skater simply stands atop his stationary board, performs a kickflip, and lands exactly where he began, there is perhaps some sense in which he is skateboarding even though he is not "riding" his skateboard. However, this objection relies on an overly narrow conception of what it is to ride. To ride an object (e.g., a horse, a scooter, a skateboard, etc.), one needn't traverse any particular distance on the object. To ride an object in the relevant sense is to control the movement of that object while on or in it. And while there are likely additional criticisms that could be leveled against our definition of skateboarding here,[1] they will only serve to further illustrate the point that what is most important (or at least of most interest) about the question of whether skateboarding is a sport is again the question, what is sport?

Beyond these two more fundamental questions which are important to determining whether skateboarding is a sport, an additional complicating factor is perhaps the surprising complexity of the language surrounding the question or the complexity of language *generally*. The term "sport" is used in a variety of ways. As such, as it turns out, there is at least one important sense in which skateboarding is *not* a sport and yet another sense in which it is.

Skateboarding Is (in a Sense) Not a Sport

It has been common in philosophy to take a concept or phenomenon that is utterly familiar to us and ask, what is the nature of that thing? Or, what is its definition? This is part of what we do when we raise questions in the philosophy of science. We know or at least have a reasonable idea of what science is. Chemistry and astronomy are sciences; crystal healing and astrology are not. But trying to give a truly precise, counterexample-free definition of science can be a real challenge. When a definition of science *is* proposed, it allows (or forces) us to rule on difficult cases. For instance, some (though not all) definitions of science do not count mathematics or even theoretical physics as sciences, because they do not produce falsifiable results.

This has been the traditional undertaking when we ask a question like what is sport? We know, or at least have a reasonable idea of what a sport is. Greco-Roman wrestling and basketball are sports; picnicking and watching paint dry are not. And much like the attempt to define science, defining sport has proven to be a somewhat difficult task as it has been observed for well over a century that "there are few words in the English language which have such a multiplicity of divergent meanings as the word sport."[2] Nevertheless, as our inquiry into whether skateboarding is a sport depends upon the nature or definition of sport, it is a question we are obliged to attempt to answer. Because of this, as we evaluate potential definitions of the term, we will be able (or forced) to rule on whether skateboarding is a sport.

With all of this in mind, consider the definition of sport offered by Bernard Suits (which has received more attention from philosophers of sport than perhaps any other definition of the term).

> [A sport is a game of physical skill in which participants] attempt to achieve a specific state of affairs, using only means permitted by the rules, where the rules prohibit use of more efficient in favor of less efficient means, and where the rules are accepted just because they make possible such activity.[3]

For instance, the sport of basketball involves a set of participants (i.e., a team) attempting to achieve a state of affairs (i.e., putting a ball through a hoop as many times as possible while allowing a different set of participants [i.e., the other team] to put the same ball through a hoop as few times as possible). However, the teams limit the methods by which they attempt to accomplish this task in various ways even though doing so makes it more difficult to accomplish the task in question (e.g., when in possession of the ball, a basketball player only moves along the playing surface while bouncing the ball, he does not use a step ladder to get closer to the hoop, he does not tackle opposing players, etc.). And the reason participants follow these seemingly arbitrary conventions, of course, is simply because doing so allows them to play basketball.

The first thing to notice about Suits's definition is that it could be interpreted in at least two ways. This is perhaps a minor point, but it will remind us of an important notion that will be of use to us later. It is simply that a single term (such as "sport") can be used in a variety of different but *interconnected* ways. Again, defining sport as a game of physical skill could have at least two meanings. In one sense, a game (and by extension, a sport) is an abstract set of rules that would exist whether or not anyone actually ever plays the game. In this sense, basketball is simply identical to the *rules* of basketball. As such, in this sense, basketball would be a sport whether or not anyone ever played a game of basketball.

However, there is another sense of the term; there is a sense in which a sport is an actual event of the rules of the game being used in order to "make possible [the] activity" of playing the game. This is the sense of the term to which philosopher of sport John W. Loy, Jr., refers when he calls sport a "game occurrence."[4] In this sense, a sport is the event in which participants conform their goal-oriented behavior to the rules of a game of physical skill for the purposes of playing the game.

Nevertheless, whether we interpret "sport" as an abstract set of rules which allows for an event in which a sport is played, or we define the term as the event itself, there is a problem for Suits's definition, and it is one of which he is aware. It is simply that there are a number of sports that are not games in the way that Suits suggests. Often called "judged" (or "aesthetic") sports, certain sports do not involve participants attempting to "achieve a state of affairs" (e.g., putting a ball through a hoop) "using only means permitted by the rules, where the rules prohibit use of more efficient in favor of less efficient means." On the contrary, certain sports are merely sets of competing athletic *performances*.[5]

For instance, Olympic figure skating is a sport, but the goal of a participant in a figure skating competition is simply to skate *well*. And the winner of any particular figure skating competition is simply the skater who is judged to have skated the best. In the face of this objection, Suits offers a definition of sport which is much broader than his original definition.

> [A sport is a] competitive [event] involving a variety of physical (usually in combination with other) human skills, where the superior participant is judged to have exhibited those skills in a superior way.[6]

Again, this much broader definition seems to encompass sports which are both games as well as those which are made up mere athletic performances. A game of basketball as well as a figure skating competition are both events involving a variety of skills in which the superior (set of) participant(s) is (or are) judged to have exhibited those skills in a superior way.

Now, the point is this. Potential problems for this subsequent definition notwithstanding,[7] we are now in a position to consider whether skateboarding is a sport. It is not. Or, at the very least, there is a straightforward sense in which skateboarding is not a sport according to our two (particularly influential) definitions from Suits. Again, skateboarding is merely the activity of riding a skateboard, and there is nothing *fundamentally* competitive about such an activity. Put differently, competition or competitiveness is not *inherent* to skateboarding. Skateboarding can be and often is done for leisure, for fun, or simply for transportation. And while Suits's definitions are far from the only attempts philosophers have made to define sport,[8] I take it the one element that should be present in any definition of the term is that sport—by its very nature—is competitive. In contrast to skateboarding, basketball is a sport because basketball—by *its* very nature—is competitive; basketball (by definition) is a game at least in the way Suits outlines in his initial definition of "sport."[9] For these reasons, we should conclude that skateboarding is not a sport, at least in what we will call the *primary* use of the term.

Skateboarding Is *a Sport (in a Sense)*

According to the definitions we've considered, skateboarding is not a sport. However, recall an important feature of the discussion thus far that a single term can be used in a number of distinct but *interconnected* ways. Because of this, though it would seem to be a mistake to say that skateboarding is a sport in the primary sense of the term, there is perhaps a second, important sense in which we may correctly label skateboarding as a sport.

One manner in which a single term can be used in a multiplicity of distinct but interconnected ways is through the use of figurative (as opposed to literal) language. To use a term figuratively is to use the term in a way that goes *beyond* its most basic sense by employing allegory or metaphor; to use a term literally is to use it precisely in its most basic sense *without* the use of allegory or metaphor.[10] For instance, the sense of "stoked" to which skateboarders are probably most familiar is the figurative sense of the term. To be stoked in the figurative sense is to be exceedingly enthusiastic or excited. However, the literal use of "stoked" expresses something quite different. For something to be literally stoked is for it to have had fuel (which is often simply just oxygen) added to it so that it will burn hotter or more intensely. And, of course, it isn't difficult to appreciate the underlying metaphor; in the figurative use of the term, someone who is "stoked" is enthusiastic or excited in a lively way that is akin to the liveliness of a well-burning fire which has been literally stoked.

However, this is not the only manner in which a single term can be used in two different, interconnected ways. As we've alluded, a single term can be used in a primary sense as well as in any number of *secondary* senses.[11] To use a term in its primary sense is to use it in its most important or fundamental sense. To use a term in a secondary sense is to use it in a way that is a natural *extension* of the primary sense; it is to use it to refer to things related in relevant ways to that which is referred to by the primary sense of the term. However, the secondary sense of a term does not employ metaphor or allegory as in cases in which a term is used figuratively.

Recall that not unlike the term or concept of sport, philosophers have attempted to offer a definition or set of criteria for science. In its primary sense, "science" is (something like) the *procedure* of collecting data, formulating and testing hypotheses, etc. This is the sense of the term which is expressed in a claim such as "The age of the universe has been estimated to be 13.7 billion years through the science of cosmology." However, a secondary use of the term might be one in which we think of "science" as the *results* of or the body of knowledge obtained through the *procedure* of science. This is the sense of the term that is expressed by a claim such as "If you want to lose weight, it helps to learn the science of nutrition." It seems unlikely that one making such a claim is encouraging those who wish to lose weight to become a dietitian or to learn how to do experiments in nutritional biology. Rather, what is meant is that those hoping to lose weight would be well-advised to learn what dietitians and nutritional biologists have discovered through science.

There are additional secondary senses of "science." Beyond science as a *body of knowledge* (which is again a secondary use of the term) arrived at through the *procedure* of science (which is again the primary use of the term), philosophers of science occasionally refer to the *institution* of science (i.e., the hierarchies or social connections among those who do science).[12] The point here is simply that a variety of different types of things (e.g., procedures, bodies of knowledge, institutions, etc.) can all be labeled with the same term because each referent of the term (e.g., a procedure, a body of knowledge, an institution, etc.) is connected to the other distinct but related referents in some important way.

What does any of this have to do with whether skateboarding is a sport? Arguably, the primary use of "sport" is (something like) one of Suits's definitions we considered in the previous section. In the primary sense of the term, a sport is a competitive event, involving a variety of physical skills, where the participants enter into the event for the purpose of being judged as superior in regard to those competition-relevant skills. However, there are a variety of secondary uses of the term, and it is here that we will find an important (secondary) sense in which we can label skateboarding as a sport.

While skateboarding *itself* is not a sport in the primary sense of the term, it nevertheless may be the principal activity constituting a sport. That is, according to the primary use of the term, skateboarding is not a sport, but a game of SKATE (modeled after the basketball game HORSE, in which skaters attempt to match each other's tricks until one skater fails enough to earn each letter of the word "SKATE") *is* a sport as it is an event which is competitive, which involves a variety of physical skills, and which participants enter into for the purpose of being judged as superior (often simply by one another) in regard to those skills. Similarly, while skateboarding itself is not a sport in the primary sense of the term, the X Games is a collection of sports, a number of which make use of skateboarding as their principal constitutive activity (e.g., the men's or women's vert final). Because of this, we might call skateboarding a *sport-conducive activity*. A sport-conducive activity is any activity which can be easily (or is frequently enough) used as the principal activity constituting a sport. And it is natural and perhaps correct to label sport-conducive activities as sports in a secondary sense of the term.

This is the sense in which we might call running, kayaking, or cheerleading sports. None of these activities themselves qualify as sports in the primary sense of the term as they are not fundamentally competitions or because competition is not inherent to them. People run for all sorts of reasons that (when so doing) do not qualify as sports in the primary sense of the term: to get in shape, because they are being chased, because they are late for a meeting, etc. Similarly, even though cheerleaders are athletes, it seems like it would be a mistake to say that what they do on the sidelines of a basketball game is itself a sport (again) in the primary sense of the term (even when what they are doing is athletically impressive). However, as both running and cheerleading are sport-conducive activities, it would *not* be a mistake to label them as sports because they are sports in a secondary sense of the term; they are sport-conducive activities. This is the sense of the term that is being used if one claims "Bill has taken up the sport of running." even when Bill only runs in the morning before work in order to get in shape. And this perhaps in part explains the rather passionate stance advocates take in regard to cheerleading: that it is a sport, even when it isn't being done competitively.

This is the sense in which skateboarding is a sport. Skateboarding competitions (of various kinds) are sports in the primary sense the term. Skateboarding *itself* is a sport in a secondary sense, because it is a sport-conducive activity; it can easily be and often enough is used as the principal activity constituting a sport.

The familiar but all too easily forgotten lesson here—for skaters and non-skaters alike—is simple. When wandering into any philosophical debate, it's paramount to define your terms. As we have seen, language can be much more complicated than we might recognize pre-reflectively. But with a few careful, precise definitions, we can make progress on (and maybe even begin to answer) difficult questions like whether skateboarding is a sport. Skateboarding is a sport, at least in one important sense of the term.[13]

Notes

1. For instance, consider the following objection. If we define skateboarding as the activity of riding a skateboard, and if we define riding in terms of controlling the movement of the board while on it, then it would follow that the skater momentarily stops skateboarding in the middle of certain tricks when he is (for a short time) no longer on the skateboard (e.g., during the midpoint of a kickflip).

2. Graves, H. 1900. "A Philosophy of Sport." *Contemporary Review*, Vol. 78, 877–893.

3. Suits, Bernard. 1973. "The Elements of Sport." *The Philosophy of Sport: A Collection of Essays*, 48–64. Osterhoudt, R. (ed.).

4. Loy, John W., Jr. 1968. "The Nature of Sport: A Definitional Effort." *Quest*, Vol. 10, No. 1, 1–15.

5. Hurka, Thomas. 2015. "On Judged Sports." *Journal of Philosophy of Sport*, Vol. 42, No. 3, 317–325. Taylor & Francis.

6. Suits, Bernard. 1988. "Tricky Triad: Games, Play, and Sport." *Journal of the Philosophy of Sport*, Vol. 15, No. 1, 1–9.

7. One additional (fairly familiar but contentious) objection to Suits's definition(s) involves games with a high degree of *mental* skill. According to both definitions, a necessary condition of sport is that it requires some amount of *physical* skill. In spite of this, it has been argued that certain games such as chess or poker should be considered sports as well (perhaps "mind sports"). Suits's definition could be altered to accommodate such examples by dropping the condition that a sport is a game (or requires some degree) of physical skill, but doing so would have the perhaps counterintuitive result that all (or at least, most) games would then be considered sports. See Kobiela, Filip. 2018. "Should Chess and Other Mind Sports Be Regarded as Sports?" *Journal of the Philosophy of Sport*, Vol. 45, No. 3, 279–295. A second potential objection that applies only to Suits's latter, more broad definition is that there are athletic competitions which involve a variety of human skills that are not sports (e.g., a bar room brawl or a war) even when the "superior participant is judged to have exhibited those skills in a superior way." However, Suits could avoid these counterexamples by adding a condition which is essentially present in his original definition: that the participants must be entering the competition *for the purpose* of being judged as exhibiting their competition-relevant skills as superior.

8. For a variety of issues important to defining sport, see Klein, Shawn E. (ed.). 2018. *Defining Sport: Conceptions and Borderlines*. Lexington Books.

9. While someone merely "shooting hoops" or a team running basketball *drills* might

be thought to be playing basketball (even though they are not playing a *game* of basketball), it would be more accurate to say that in such cases, participants are merely engaged in basketball-related activities.

    10. Heter, Joshua. 2021. *Logic: A Guided Introduction*. Independently Published. 58–61.

    11. The most important thinker to distinguish between the primary and secondary sense of a term was Wittgenstein. However, his employment of this distinction is quite different and more ambitious than my employment of it here. See Wittgenstein, Ludwig. 1953. *Philosophical Investigations*. Anscombe, G.E.M. (trans.). Basil Blackwell. 216–217.

    12. Hartung, Frank E. 1951. "Science as an Institution." *Philosophy of Science*, Vol. 18, No. 1, 35–54. We began this discussion by defining skateboarding as simply the activity of riding a skateboard. However, we are now in a position to recognize that this is perhaps only the primary use of the term. In a way that is analogous to "science," there is a secondary sense of "skateboarding" which refers to the *institution* or the *culture* of skateboarders.

    13. Thank you to my students at Jefferson College for giving me helpful feedback on this project.

What We Talk About When We Talk About Skateboarding Tricks

WILLIAM GIOVANNI JIMÉNEZ SENZANO

Of all the sports that emphasize artistry and technical skill, none may require as much creativity as skateboarding. It's not just that skaters perform dizzying jumps, spins, tailslides, and the like; much of that can be done in a number of other sports (e.g., biking, surfing, figure skating, etc.). In the world of extreme sports, only skateboarding has been able to continually evolve at such an unprecedented rate, generation after generation, with little to no sign of slowing down.

Since its modern debut, skateboarding has left its distinct mark on popular culture through its contribution to fashion, film, music, graphic design, urban planning, and even language. And at the center of this pop culture phenomenon is the skateboarding *trick*. Without tricks, skating would exist only in its utilitarian form as a portable method of transportation. Fortunately, skating persists in exciting new ways through skaters' ever-evolving use of tricks in each generation, while other extreme sports have been comparatively stagnant in regard to their artistry.[1]

But just what exactly is a skateboarding trick? What are skaters trying to do on those occasions when they end up losing their balance on a ledge or handrail and break an appendage? They are clearly laboring toward some task (and taking heavy beatings in the process), but it's not exactly clear what that task is exactly. This is the concern of this essay; it's to try to figure out what (if anything) each of these instances have in common. It is to arrive at a clear understanding of what a skateboarding trick actually is.

Generally speaking, *any maneuver that begins and ends on a skateboard* could be considered a skateboarding trick. Of course, offering any such definition will be vulnerable to critique. I would argue that the best answer to the question of what counts as a skateboarding trick is one that may be at least somewhat vague. Nevertheless, by thinking carefully about the question of what counts as a skateboarding trick, we can exercise some of the same critical faculties used in similar philosophical questions and ultimately arrive at a conclusion about what it is exactly that makes a trick *a trick*, while retaining the same artistic freedom that makes skateboarding so special. With all that out of the way, we can head out bravely onto the pavement to see which definitional approaches might safely land.

A First Attempt

Trying to define the concept of a skateboarding trick is similar to trying to define the concept of art. There are a variety of ways to define the concept—and countless fringe cases to challenge each definition—but (not unlike defining pornography) perhaps the most reasonable approach is to simply employ a "I know it when I see it" sort of methodology.

In any particular instance, it really just seems fairly obvious whether a trick has (or hasn't) taken place. We might say that there's plenty of *prima facie* evidence to determine whether a trick has (successfully) occurred: the presence of a skateboard, the lack of blood or broken bones, a skater who used to be *here* but is now *there*, and other skaters or onlookers are momentarily losing their minds. These can all be used as reasonable pieces of evidence to infer that a skater just successfully performed a trick. As such, we can take tricks apart piece-by-piece to see how the whole process operates, beginning with how a skater initiates each new attempt.

A trick usually begins with the skater adjusting their body in anticipation. By their posture, it's clear that they are about to attempt *something*. Context clues in the environment can provide helpful information ahead of time (e.g., if the skater is approaching a rail, they'll likely grind on it), but so far, we already have two essential pieces of the puzzle: a skateboard and a skater who *does something with their body* on or near said skateboard. So, it should be uncontroversial to claim at this point that a skate trick is some kind of a *maneuver* involving a skateboard and that it begins when a skater shifts from a casual skateboarding stance to preparing their body to undergo some motion along with their board.

The middle portion of a trick thus involves some kind of intentional action that almost always includes a window of time spent airborne, though this is not essential. There are plenty of tricks (e.g., rail grinds, ledge stalls, primo slides, etc.) which require complete contact with a surface, and these are just as important to the discussion regardless of whether we are discussing "vert" skating (which requires skaters to be airborne at one point or another) or else "freestyle" skating with all of the artistic liberties it has to offer.[2]

For the most part, then, every trick's intermediate section will see the skater achieve some kind of posture or motion before it's been completed. This is a subtle point, but in order for the trick to be thought of as having been successfully completed (i.e., for it to "count"), there has to be some kind of "there and back again" aspect where the skater leaves the comfort of casual skating for something uncomfortable.

A trick is usually said to be complete when the skater (1) lands on their board before (2) relaxing their posture and riding off (or when they revert to being "at ease" on their board). Landing is therefore the bookend matching a skater's departure from casual riding. It isn't necessary, of course, that they revert to the same *exact* position as they begin (i.e., tricks that involve 180° spins have the skater beginning and ending in mirror-image opposite orientations along the length of the board), but for the most part, the trick can be said to be complete only when the skater returns to a position of comfort or ease.

And, just like that, we've landed our first definition of a skateboarding trick:

> A skateboarding trick is a (sequence of) maneuver(s) undertaken by a person beginning and ending on a skateboard with some kind of motion(s) comprising the middle.

Depending on how challenging or dangerous a maneuver is, the accomplishment of a trick is typically accompanied by the collective validation of fellow skaters.[3] This last detail adds an interesting social element to the potential answers of what might count as a trick: the kind of thing *other skaters would recognize as a trick*. This is more of a *socio-aesthetic* approach to defining a skateboarding trick that privileges the opinion of skaters over non-skaters.[4] This is similar to gathering artists, critics, and scholars for them all to decide for themselves what counts as a piece of art. It's important to remind ourselves that structures exist to support and evolve these concepts and to consider the views found in skate culture more broadly.

This is also where skate culture becomes an invaluable part of the discussion: skate tricks don't exist in isolation, and if you're looking to understand them you'd do best to spend more time riding a board or being among skaters rather than reading some philosophical essay. It takes a complex social process of incremental change and acceptance to define a human activity as unique as skateboarding. There are familiar philosophical problems of language regarding sense and reference at play here, but for now I'll shelve this kind of talk to get our first-pass definition off the ground.

Trick Taxonomy

With at least a preliminary attempt at understanding what constitutes a skateboarding trick, we can dig deeper. Consider how the traditional trick takes one of only a surprisingly few forms. Pretty much every trick skaters attempt can be classified under one of six categories: ollies, flips, grabs, grinds, balance tricks, and ground tricks.

The "ollie" label encompasses any trick where the principal aim is for the skater to achieve air-time. While airborne, the skater can then *rotate* their board (flip tricks) with their feet or else *grip it* (grab tricks) with their hands before returning to the ground. They can also land and continue to move across some surface like a ledge or rail in a variety of different stances (grinds), or else stop moving completely and hold their position in a stall. Stalls have enough in common with the manual (a "wheelie" in another context) to share the title of "balance trick," a catch-all term for any kind of maneuver requiring balance as the skater holds their pose as long as spatiotemporally possible before returning to a casual stance. Similarly, the label of "ground tricks" exists as another catch-all term for any trick where the board remains on the ground and the skater completes some maneuver with or around it. This is where tricks like powerslides, hippie jumps, or even "hill bombing" comfortably reside: the goal isn't to have the wheels detach from the ground, but rather for interesting things to happen while the board is still rolling.

Trying to find exceptions to these classifications will usually lead to an exercise in reduction. Consider the following examples, though this by no means constitutes a final say on the matter. A "no comply" or "boneless" reduces to an ollie trick because it takes the skater into the air from the ground (same with "wallrides" even though the skater is moving along a surface). Tricks in the "primo" or "casper" stance reduce to balance tricks since they rely on the skater's ability to maintain certain board positions (though if the skater begins in these positions rather than moving into them, they may reduce to ground tricks). The "caveman" or "bomb drop" is more complicated because they both begin with one's feet on the ground (asymmetric to how the trick ends on a board), but since they each involve an airborne maneuver relying on the skater's grip, both can be reduced to grab tricks.

Admittedly, at this point, some readers might understandably scoff at what they might perceive as an eye-roll inducing, overly-academic attempt to analyze a concept like a skateboarding trick: something which is produced through free-form artistry and non-conformity. I began by comparing skate tricks to works of art, and now it seems like I'm backtracking by claiming that there are really only a small handful of tricks that can be done. Wouldn't this be like insisting that all art reduces to painting, sculpture, photography, and other traditional mediums? Admittedly, critics are right to point out that there's so much more to art and skating than what can be described by a handful of categories, just like how reducing dancing to a varying handful of basic moves sucks the individuality and cultural relevance out of any given piece of choreography.

However, to these critics, I would suggest to not get too caught up in the seriousness with which these questions are being considered. At present, I'm only interested in essentializing elements of traditional tricks to get the conversation off the ground. In what follows, we'll take on the more exciting project of rebelling against such an analysis and pondering the socio-aesthetic status of non-traditional skateboarding tricks. Even with that said, it's not as if the idea that all *new* tricks are really just variations of old tricks is really all that radical; most skaters will gladly be able to accept this.[5] So (for now, anyway), we can enjoy a quantum unit for skateboarding tricks as any one of six different genres,[6] and with this one, we can start throwing variations and extensions on any of these tricks in whichever way our hearts desire.

It'll turn out this gets 99 percent of skaters extremely far, creatively speaking. Take a regular kickflip and combine it with a (backside) shove-it, and you've got a *varial kickflip*. Perform the shove-it in the opposite (frontside instead of backside) direction, and you've got a *hard flip*. Perform the kickflip in the opposite (a "heel" flip instead of a "kick" flip) direction and that's a *laser flip*. Rotate your body 360° and your hard flip becomes a *diamond flip*. Perform any of these tricks in your opposite ("regular" or "goofy") skate stance and append the "switch" qualifier to the front of the name. Do the trick by popping the nose of your board instead of the tail, and you've done the "nollie" (nose ollie) version, or else assume the switch position and perform the same "nollie" trick to achieve the trick in its "fakie" modification. The variations and combinations are practically endless, and any small variation can make any plain skateboarding trick considerably more interesting to pull off.

When these tricks are strung together, they form combos or lines. This is where the act of performing skateboarding tricks (along with their variations) becomes a truly inspiring thing to witness. These maneuvers gain context and artistry in ways that can only be hinted at in isolation. This is also where many skating competitions begin to emerge: give skaters a block of time to string together any number of tricks in any number of interesting ways, and a panel of judges can rate them against each other. As in dance or gymnastics, successful skateboarding will require technical ability as well as creative instincts in reacting to one's surroundings. A kickflip alone is surely an impressive thing, but a kickflip *into a grind* is truly something noteworthy. If you can tack on a third trick after the grind, it's all the more impressive.

The surroundings of a skater (particularly relevant to the *street* or *freestyle* skater) are going to factor into these combos as well. Stairs, benches, handrails, and ramps will all change the context of a given trick. The significance of "gaps" (tricks executed between two significantly spatially-separate locations) also deserves mention: there's a difference between performing an ollie over a cement crack in a driveway versus doing one over the Great Wall of China.[7] The trick itself is technically indistinguishable in either case, but it gains clear aesthetic relevance when we modify the trick along dimensions of length, gap, foot placement, body rotation, and so on. So, what has started as a humble kickflip now contains the potential to be something much more interesting and contextually satisfying, and this applies to any move in skateboarding we can think of.

Go crazy: 540 nollie backside McTwist? Darkslide handstand to fakie manual? Russian boneless frontside shove-it? As long as the conceptual schema of the trick is compatible with the laws of physics, you can make up any trick you want and give it a funny name.[8] If you've ever spent time laboring behind the screen of the Create-A-Trick menu in *Tony Hawk's Underground*, you know that "inventing a new trick" in this capacity really just amounts to stringing together a bunch of existing trick animations in a cool way. As it turns out, this is a pretty decent way at capturing what kind of a thing counts as a trick.

Bailing Out

Despite what we've said thus far, there really is so much more to skateboarding tricks than (for instance) the things you can do in *Tony Hawk's Underground*. Just as the avant-garde can challenge traditional definitions of art, there are any variety of skateboarding maneuvers that might challenge relatively straightforward definitions of a skateboarding trick.

Sometimes a trick involves simply riding a skateboard normally except that it's doused in gasoline and catches fire when the skater grinds. Sometimes a trick is a skater laying on their back, using the skateboard as a luge. Sometimes a trick is tying shoelaces to a board and flinging it along the ground in circles like a Skip-It toy from the 1990s.[9] Sometimes in a trick, the skateboard is only an afterthought, a vessel to carry the skater's momentum forward after they've performed a totally unrelated move and need to use the board as a getaway.

Sometimes there are multiple boards or skaters involved; have you ever tried to land a skateboard on top of another skateboard? Have you ever tried riding two boards, one on each foot like skis? What about stacking three skaters on top of each other's shoulders like a scene in *Little Rascals*? Or, jumping up in the air while a fellow skater flips the board underneath you? The board itself can also be a vehicle for modification in a trick: swap out your plain old donut wheels with tank threads or ice skates and turn your skateboard into an all-terrain vehicle. Chop your board in half and bolt a rod along the length so both hemispheres can rotate freely. What should we even call something like this (other than totally awesome)?

Sure, you *could* try to turn any one of these things into a series of the previously listed maneuvers. However, it's at least arguable that this defeats the spirit of creativity and free expression that skating naturally calls for. To reduce the "northern hemisphere board flip" described in the preceding digression as belonging to the "flip" genre is perhaps technically defensible, but doing so would come at the cost of something extremely important about its ingenuity and evasion of traditional trick taxonomy. Here, the socio-aesthetic relevance of skater-approval reemerges: what's more important with these non-traditional tricks is that other skaters recognize and validate the maneuver (whatever it may be) and *not* that it's classifiable based on anything anyone has seen before. Skater-approval aside, we've entered a brave new world of skate tricks largely ungoverned by genre or convention, and in the spirit of the Socratic tradition, it's paramount that we embrace the fresh air outside every allegorical cave we find ourselves escaping.

With this in mind, I propose that we loosen our definition for what counts as a trick and begin to accept *most any intentional maneuver involving a skateboard in some capacity* as constituting a skateboarding trick. The most important aspects are that (1) at least one skateboard is involved but also that (2) the skater (or skaters) *lands their maneuver* and rides away largely unharmed.[10] As long as these elements are satisfied, what you've got is a skateboarding trick. This throws our first attempted definition out the window the same way the avant-garde does to traditional definitions of art. Arguably, this is only a good thing.

This ensures that skating never gets stale and that the world around skaters remains an inspiration (or even a *challenge*) for anyone crazy enough to try, for instance, nailing a fakie big spin down a 10-stair while eating a slice of birthday cake. Not only should this count as a trick, it should be at the *forefront* of the discussion. An artform should be *exemplified* by its avant-garde fringe cases, and as such, no conversation is complete without serious contemplation of these boundary-pushing instances.

Beyond our initial attempts to define the concept, and bearing in mind any number of the fringe examples, we might now make the case that the concept of a skateboarding trick is best captured by a "family resemblance" sort of notion. The 20th-century philosopher Ludwig Wittgenstein proposed that we can understand certain concepts as being part of a recognizable category not by every member of the category sharing certain necessary features, but rather, by the members of the category being part of a web of overlapping similarities which connects them all to some degree.[11]

For example, it is arguable that there is no one thing (or set of things) that makes something a game. Rather, a particular game may share certain features with certain other games but not all games (e.g., being a game of chance as opposed to a game of skill) while another particular game may share some of *its* features with some but not all of a subset *other* games (e.g., having a winner or not). The point again is that on the family resemblance understanding of the concept of a game, there is no one thing (or set of things) that all games share, but any particular game can be thought of as being in an interconnected web of overlapping similarities which in total encompass all things which fall under the category of games.

Perhaps this is the right way to think of the concept of a skateboarding trick. Perhaps there is no one thing (or set of things) which all skateboarding tricks share necessarily (or essentially), but rather, any particular skateboarding trick can be thought of as sharing some of its features with certain other (but not all) skateboarding tricks. If this is correct, we should ditch the notion that there's any essentialized idea of what counts as a skateboarding trick and instead gesture toward many vague strands of similarity among a sea of common usage. We should be able to recognize that for every definition which seeks to identify the necessary and sufficient conditions of a skateboarding trick, there will always be counterexamples that land us right back where we started. As it turns out, there was never any one thing (or set of things) which makes something a skateboarding trick in the first place. Perhaps we'd gotten so comfortable talking about tricks that we pretended as if we knew what one was, but taking this idea seriously has revealed this to be a mistake. Whatever the case, we should find value in *thinking about* skateboarding tricks and focus less on having a maximally precise understanding of the concept itself. This has led me to defend an answer without an essential definition of a skateboarding trick. Again, this is a good thing.

This gets the job done with the added benefit of enabling liberal practice and (as a result) maximizing artistic freedom. Now that we've pondered skateboarding philosophically and reached a point where the discussion has been made more clear, we can knock down the ladder of dogma and take to the streets of Dogtown and apply our definitions in practice. We can focus on things more important than nailing a trick on the page and instead nail the trick in the streets, where it actually counts. Take this as an invitation, then, for you to put down the text, leave the plush comfort of armchair theorizing, and to go skate.

Notes

1. Have you tried watching a surfing or snowboarding video lately? They're not terribly different from videos that have been around since the '80s (excluding, of course, changes in cinematography and technology) because the sports themselves don't have as much creative room to grow: surfing and snowboarding continue to evolve *athletically* (attempting bigger jumps and faster flips, like how each new generation of gymnasts "raises the bar" just a little bit higher than the last), whereas skateboarding also evolves *aesthetically*. This makes a lot of sense when you consider differences in each sport's topography: even though surfing and snowboarding (and any other board-and-body-centric sports) employ tricks that are *functionally* similar to skateboard tricks, they lack the modular urban context that privileges skaters to rethink their relationships to their boards in non-traditional ways. As such, there can never be as many staircases to jump or ledges to grind (or cops or Karens to escape) in the ocean as there are in the city, and so skaters enjoy near-limitless freedom in creating content because their environment is so much more adaptable (and because they aren't *physically bound* to their boards) than that of their snow-or-water-riding progenitors.

2. This already brings up the taxonomic question that I attempt in the following section: how can you separate the "grind" from the ollie that precedes it? At what point does a kickflip become a "late flip" (an initial ollie with a subsequent flip added on later)? It might not be clear that we actually *want* to distinguish between these things and instead treat the whole process as a singular unit, which is where I end up taking the discussion later in the second section.

3. If a kickflip happens and nobody's around to see it, *was the gnar still shredded?* Of course, the skater who performed the trick will say "no doubt," but surely the shredding of the gnar depends somewhat on the existence (or else the *approval*) of an audience.

4. Kind of like how we might want to understand members of a social group through *second-order* validation: a "liberal," for example, is not just someone who self-identifies as one, but who is also someone who other self-identified liberals would they themselves identify as being a liberal.

5. Rodney Mullen himself—the undisputed godfather of freestyle skating—has said as much in his own TED talk on the subject. See Mullen, Rodney. 2015. *Pop Ollie and Innovate*. TED Conferences. YouTube. Does his own taxonomy make skateboarding any less interesting or liberating? It's not for me (or any one person or institution) to say, but if one of the originators of an art form has thoughts regarding the operating rules of said artform then it's definitely worth hearing them out.

6. One can say the "trick state" enjoys *six degrees of freedom* or is composed of *six orthogonal basis-vectors in skateboard-Hilbert space to* abuse my analogy to quantum mechanics.

7. Danny Way did exactly this in 2005 with a literal broken ankle.

8. As far as I can tell, the proper grammar for giving a trick description goes "Angle Measure" (always multiples of 180) + "Qualifier" (nollie/switch/fakie/etc.) + "Spin Direction" (frontside or backside) + "Base Trick Name." So, it's a *180 Frontside Shifty* and not a *Shifty Frontside 180* or anything else in that vein. Metaphysically speaking, this signals a departure from the implicit form of a thing being modified: a *180 Frontside Melon* Grab is not the same as a *Melon Grab*. This seemingly small distinction actually carries significant philosophical weight since there are other areas in language where adjectives merely complement rather than alter the noun being described: a "big red truck," for instance, could appropriately be called "a truck." It could be big and red or small and green for all one cares, but nothing about the object has changed as a result of using a different reference. Skateboard tricks, however, operate differently, and so it would be inappropriate to

leave out preceding adjectives when giving a description because you would be referring to a totally different trick.

    9. These are the kinds of tricks I suggest the reader view for themselves in the "Everything Counts" videos by Braille Skateboarding, or else in any of the numerous visual triumphs produced by the Fancy Lad skate company (of which *Is This Skateboarding?* most directly inspired the creation of this essay). See Fancy Lad Skateboards. 2019. *JENKEM—Matt Tomasello in* "Rodney Mullen on Bath Salts: Round Three." YouTube. Jenkem Magazine.

    10. That is, unharmed by their latest attempt, they will no doubt carry battle harms from past failures on their path to glory.

    11. Wittgenstein, Ludwig. 1953. *Philosophical Investigations*. Anscombe, G.E. (trans.). Basil Blackwell.

If You're a Sellout, You're Not a Skateboarder

Matthew J. Cull

What is it to be a skateboarder? Who counts as a member of the kind *skateboarder*, and who doesn't? What is the definition of "skateboarder"? At first blush, these questions seem to have fairly obvious answers: a skateboarder is one who skateboards. Everyone who skateboards, from Tony Hawk and Elissa Steamer to Tillman the skateboarding bulldog[1] and that grandparent who once rolled around on their driveway all count as members of the kind *skateboarder*. The term "skateboarder" simply refers to everyone who has taken the time to step on a board.

This easy approach to answering these questions is nice for a number of reasons: it's very inclusive and makes being a skateboarder something that most people can achieve without much effort. Moreover, it's pretty clear cut: it gives us a really easy way of figuring out who the members of the kind *skateboarder* are—we just go and find out who has skateboarded.[2] Of course, you might think this is a bit *too* inclusive: Granddad only tried skateboarding *once*, and I haven't stepped on a board in the past 10 years, so we shouldn't *really* count as skateboarders. Right? In light of this sort of objection, we might refine our easy approach: a skateboarder is someone who skateboards *regularly*.[3]

However, these easy definitions seem to be missing something. While useful for certain purposes, the easy definitions of "skateboarder" miss out on an important aspect of skating culture which, in certain circumstances, we want to capture and which present us with a much more exclusive definition of the term. This *punk* aspect of skating culture would reject the easy definition of "skateboarder": being a skateboarder means more than just standing on a board one time. No, being a skateboarder is a lifestyle, dude.

Being a Skateboarder as a Way of Life

This punk aspect of skate culture tells us that *real, authentic* skateboarding is rebellious and rowdy. It isn't a sport; it's a way of life. A real skateboarder doesn't sell out to corporate sponsors, and they always tell The Man to "fuck off." Proper skateboarding exists in an antagonistic relationship with authority. These conflicts with authority range from local conflicts with police and security guards while trying to skate a spot, to grand ideological struggles against models of the good life under late capitalism.

According to this aspect of skateboarding culture, when someone threads a line under the despairing arms of a security guard to tre-flip down a private stair set, that's *being a skateboarder*. When someone gives up the opportunity of having a secure corporate job in order to have more time to skate, that's *being a skateboarder*. Meanwhile, if you take a sponsorship from a big company, you've sold out, and you're not a *real* skateboarder. If you settle down with a secure job and a family in the suburbs, it doesn't matter that you occasionally still come to the park: you're not a real skateboarder.

We see this aspect of skate culture explicitly in much of the media surrounding skating. Consider the film, *Lords of Dogtown*, Catherine Hardwicke's 2005 fictional depiction of the Zephyr team (better known as the Z-boys), a group of California skateboarders which included the likes of Stacy Peralta, Tony Alva, and Jay Adams.[4] Hardwicke's plot in part turns around the fictionalized version of Adams rejecting the increasing commercialization of skateboarding and what he perceives as its move away from its authentic roots as a hobby for working-class kids when the waves weren't big enough to surf. Rejecting the comfortable bourgeois life offered to him by corporate sponsors, Hardwicke's Adams walks away.[5]

That these skate cultures also had their roots in '70s surfing communities also seems to have been crucial to the development of a more exclusive conception of what it is to be a skateboarder. The Venice Beach surf culture that gave birth to the Z-Boys was a hotbed of locals-only activism, with outsiders being forcibly evicted from the most desirable surfing spots until they had "proven" themselves. In Peralta's own documentary on the period, *Dog Town and Z-Boys*, one of the Z-boys, Jim Muir, recalls how such a locals-only policy was enforced in forceful and yet mischievous ways:

> JIM MUIR: Best thing I ever saw was someone paddled out in the water with the [outsider]'s carburetor on top of his board and goes "Hey does this belong to you?" and dropped it in the water.[6]

When the Z-boys began attending skateboarding competitions, this authentic sense of "skateboarder" that excluded many of their fellow competitors seems to already have been at work. *Dogtown and Z-Boys* describes their attendance at the Del Mar National Skateboard Championships:

NARRATOR: Del Mar would be the team's first introduction to the world of organized skateboarding. Their unconventional skating and disorderly presence marked them as outsiders right from the start.
BOB BINIAK: It was like a hockey team going to a figure-skating festival.
PEGGY OKI: The difference between us and them felt very real.[7]

Elsewhere, if we look at the skate videos put out by skateboarders to this day, we see a general "screw The Man," devil-may-care attitude. Many, if not most, skate videos put out feature (alongside skateboarding) skateboarders getting up to various nefarious deeds such as graffiti and vandalism, the over-indulgence in controlled substances, and pulling pranks.[8]

When not pulled on The Man, such pranks are often played on one another, a practice that was taken to new heights in the *Jackass* movies and TV show.[9] While sometimes dismissed as mere destructiveness, such rule-breaking can also be constructive. On the one hand, it is constructive of skateboarder identity, creating the norms of behavior acceptable in various skating cultures; on the other, it is constructive in a very literal sense: skaters will find disused parts of the city to hand-build ramps and rails.[10] Breaking the rules of property and trespass law, skateboarders take the spaces left behind by projects of urban redevelopment and make art. As is also now widely recognized in urban and architectural theory, skateboarders are rule-breakers in another sense: they break the rules for how one is "supposed to" move through the city, constructing new uses for and ways of moving through urban space.

Such novel uses of space, from grinds to graffiti, are often illegal or against the wishes of the bourgeois property owning class. Thus, conflicts with authority figures are almost inevitable. As such, sticking it to the security guard who wants to try to stop you from landing that one trick by doing it under their nose before getting away, pulling one last hand plant on the DIY bowl before the bulldozers roll in to tear it down, quitting your restrictive office job to drop out and drop in: this is what a real skateboarder does.[11]

In this sense, if you want to be a skateboarder, it's not just enough to skate; you need to live out a certain way of life. That way of life involves rejecting another lifestyle: comfortable, law-abiding bourgeois life in the suburbs with a steady corporate job, where one is married and has 2.5 kids and a dog.

Critical Social Kinds

How should we make sense of this way of thinking about what it is to be a skateboarder? This aspect of skateboarding culture seems to understand being a skateboarder as in part involving a resistance to the mainstream, The Man, and the good life as often understood under 20th and 21st-century capitalism. One resource that might help us here comes from Robin Dembroff's work on what they call "critical gender kinds" in transgender philosophy. Dembroff contends that we can understand *genderqueer* as a critical *gender* kind:

> Critical Gender Kinds: For a given kind X, X is a *critical gender kind* relative to a given society [if and only if] X's members collectively destabilize one or more core elements of the dominant gender ideology in that society.[12]

"Genderqueer" can be read in a few different senses, but the one that Dembroff highlights is one that traces its history back to queer cultures of 1990s and 2000s in the United States, where people such as trans activist and theorist Riki Wilchins began identifying as genderqueer in order to capture how they were rejected by society as "gendertrash" and how they in turn rejected the repressive gender order of mainstream society.[13] *Genderqueer* as a critical gender kind involves rejecting key parts of the ideology of that repressive gender order's ideology.[14] Crucially, Dembroff contends that genderqueer people destabilize the binary axis of mainstream gender.

> **The binary axis:** The genders *men* and *women* are binary, discrete, immutable, exclusive, and exhaustive.[15]

By existing in ways that insist that they are neither men, nor women, but rather some other thing(s), genderqueer people destabilize this ideological axis. *Genderqueer*, then (at least in this sense) is a critical gender kind for Dembroff.[16] It is a kind centered on a way of living that rejects and destabilizes a key part of a dominant gender ideology.

Skateboarder as Critical Social Kind

Now, *skateboarder* isn't a gender; as such, skateboarder isn't a critical *gender* kind, but why not think that there are other types of critical kinds out there? There is, of course, no reason to think the dominant gender ideology is the only ideology which might be in need of destabilization, so we can posit that there may be other critical social kinds: those kinds whose members destabilize one or more core elements of some dominant ideology in their society.

Following the law, getting a secure job, working for The Man—we might say that these are all aspects of *bourgeois* ideology. That is, if you want to live the good life under capitalism, you ought (according to this ideology) work hard to live a cushy middle-class lifestyle. Anyone who steps outside of these lines is rejecting this model of the good life: they are telling the dominant bourgeois ideology to screw itself.

So, here's the main thought: central to skateboarding culture is a notion of skateboarder as a *critical social kind*.[17] We can define critical social kinds generally following Dembroff:

> Critical Social Kinds: For a given kind X, X is a *critical social kind* relative to a given society if and only if X's members collectively destabilize one or more core elements of the dominant ideologies in that society.

If we understand *skateboarder* in line with the easy approach set out at the start of this essay (in which almost anyone who has stepped on a board even once is a skateboarder), *skateboarder* is not a critical social kind. Right now, at least in the UK (where I'm writing this essay) merely skateboarding itself (even doing so regularly) is not enough to destabilize core elements of any dominant ideology.

However, suppose instead that we understand *skateboarder* as a kind which is, at its heart, about the rejection of the bourgeois way of life, which offers a lifestyle centered on rebellion and an alternative to selling out. Here, it looks a lot like *skateboarder* is a critical social kind. The assumptions of bourgeois ideology—that one will abide by the law and get a secure corporate job—are destabilized in the practice of being a *skateboarder* in this sense. It's also disrupted in a second way; the kind *skateboarder* offers a way of living outside of the expectations of bourgeois ideology, which tends to (falsely) posit that living according to its standards is the only valuable way to live.[18]

So, *skateboarder*, in this sense at least, is a political kind. As a critical social kind, it is based on resistance to a dominant ideology, one whose members reject various aspects of bourgeois capitalist and family ideology. The skateboarder destabilizes the central models for life under bourgeois capitalism, rejecting the authority of the family, the police, and a host of other institutions.

The Bones Brigade and Other Apparent Non-Skateboarders

The critical social kind understanding of *skateboarder* sheds light on an important way that the term "skateboarder" gets thrown around and used as a badge of identity in skate cultures. It tells us what standards are at work when groups of skaters complain that this or that person isn't a proper skateboarder anymore—not after they sold out to The Man! Those who skate but fail to live up to this promise of rebellion are not skateboarders in the critical social kind sense.

This, one might contend, gives us some rather counterintuitive results: one might make the case that (say) some members of the Bones Brigade are no longer skateboarders in the critical social kind sense. Take Tony Hawk: you could argue that by doing things like licensing a huge video game franchise, accepting an invite from the President of the United States to skate at the White House, and appearing in countless TV shows and movies, Hawk has sold out. Far from destabilizing bourgeois ideology, this line of argument goes, Hawk fits into that ideology's bosom rather snugly. If that's right, then according to the critical social kind account of what it is to be a *skateboarder*, Tony Hawk is not a skateboarder!

Normally, this sort of thing would be a problem for an account of a kind. If your account of what it is to be a *vehicle* excludes paradigm vehicles like (for instance) a car, then something has gone wrong with your account or definition of *vehicle*. So too here: ordinary intuition tells us that if *anyone* is a skateboarder, surely Tony Hawk is a skateboarder.

However, things are not so simple when it comes to critical social kinds. Note that, much like Dembroff's *genderqueer*, *skateboarder* as critical social kind doesn't pretend to aim at matching ordinary intuitions about who is and who is not a member of the kind in question. If we want an account that matches ordinary intuitions, we have things like the easy definition of "skateboarder" considered at the opening of this essay. No, *skateboarder* as critical social kind is supposed to capture a different set of intuitions about who counts as a skateboarder: those intuitions of the punk skater complaining that a sellout isn't a proper skater anymore because they've given up on the rebellious spirit of skateboarding.[19]

So, it's not a problem for this conception of what it is to be a skateboarder that certain people who are usually taken to be paradigm examples of skateboarders aren't skateboarders. The person using this kind of understanding of *skateboarder* is making a political judgment that (despite appearances) this person isn't a skateboarder; they're just a sellout.

The "Animal Chin" Problem

The Bones Brigade may yet have their revenge on those who would call them sellouts, however—their classic film *The Search for Animal Chin* gives us a nice illustration of a tension at the heart of this way of thinking about what it is to be a skateboarder.[20]

The Search for Animal Chin centers around the search for the mythical skater Animal Chin, the original skateboarder who "represented everything good and pure about skateboarding."[21] The mythic Chin is opposed to the crass corporate vision of skateboarding represented by the market research department of fictional skate company *Slash Skates*.[22] Seeing themselves as true, hardcore skaters, faithful to the real spirit of being a skateboarder, the Bones Brigade embark on a trip in search of this ur-skateboarder figure. After skating spots across the United States in search of Chin, the Bones Brigade come to the conclusion that Chin isn't real, or if he is, he is embodied in the joy of skating.[23]

That Chin (this pure, essential figure of true skateboarding in its hardcore form) doesn't actually exist serves as a nice metaphor for an issue with the critical social kind account of *skateboarder*. That is, when we reflect on who is actually going to count as a skateboarder, if we buy this way of thinking about the kind, it looks as if no one actually meets the very high standards for being a skateboarder that the account sets.

Remember that on this account of the kind *skateboarder*, to be a skateboarder one must disrupt bourgeois ideology, rejecting the ways of life that are dominant under contemporary capitalism. But, when we consider what skateboarding actually looks like, and indeed what it has looked like since virtually its inception, we see a hobby that has been absorbed into the mainstream. Instead of being at odds with capitalist accumulation and the rejection of corporate authority, skateboarding is totally imbricated in the capitalist infrastructure, from the production of boards and shoes to the sponsorship models that govern the pro scene and the magazines that report and produce skate culture. No one hand-makes their own board from scratch. No one has dropped in and totally dropped out. No one—so it would seem—is a skateboarder.

At its heart, the problem is that the standards for being a skateboarder in the critical social kind sense are far too stringent, requiring a disruption of the systems and ideology that make skateboarding possible in the first place.

Skateboarder *as Regulative Ideal*

Does this mean that uses of "skateboarder" in the critical social kind sense are somehow incoherent? Perhaps! Maybe everyone using this sense of the term is being incoherent. However, even if the ideal presupposed by such language is an impossible ideal (which no one actually lives up to) the ideal of the skateboarder as critical social kind can still play a role in skate culture.

What is that role? Well, perhaps the most charitable reading of such uses of "skateboarder" is instead as a regulative ideal. That is: sure, no

32   I. Skateboarding Fundamentals

one can truly and completely be a skateboarder in this critical social kind sense, but one can act in ways that embody that way of living to a greater or lesser extent. So, when a skater criticizes someone by saying that "they're not a real skateboarder," the skater is expressing the idea that the person in question is a long way off from behaving as a skateboarder (in the critical social kind sense) ought to behave.

This is to treat the critical social kind *skateboarder* as a regulative ideal. Being a skateboarder, in this sense, is a goal—the way of living that one should strive toward if one wants to exist as a respected member of many skateboarding cultures. Failing to attempt to live in line with this ideal by selling out, treating skateboarding as a sport, and so on, is to open oneself up to criticism from other members of skateboarding cultures that one is not a "real" skateboarder. So, Animal Chin, the truly authentic skateboarder, may not exist. However, the idea of such a figure regulates acceptable kinds of behavior in many skate communities.

Notes

1. Tillman held the world record for fastest 100m by a dog on a skateboard, at 19.678 seconds. See https://www.guinnessworldrecords.com/news/2015/10/tillman-the-fastest-dog-on-a-skateboard-has-died-404387.

2. There's lots of debate in philosophy about what kinds are. Too much for a short essay like this to address! For our purposes, a kind is just a grouping of things—so all tigers are members of the kind *tiger*, all aeroplanes and trains are members of the kind *vehicle* and so on. Those interested in further reading might like to begin with Bird, Alexander, and Tobin, Emma, "Natural Kinds," *The Stanford Encyclopedia of Philosophy* (Spring 2023 Edition), Edward N. Zalta & Uri Nodelman (eds.), and Epstein, Brian, "Social Ontology," *The Stanford Encyclopedia of Philosophy* (Winter 2021 Edition), Edward N. Zalta (ed.).

3. Question: just how regularly? At least once a week? At least once a month? We can argue about how best to spell out "regularly" here, but note that this is refinement to the original easy approach makes our new definition less clear-cut.

4. Hardwicke, C. 2005. *Lords of Dogtown*. Sony Pictures Entertainment.

5. The Z-Boys' influence on skate culture can hardly be overstated. This is partially due to the likes of Peralta, who would found the company Powell-Peralta, but also due to some mythmaking in skateboarding media, not least a seminal series of articles in *Skateboarder Magazine* featuring photography by Craig Stecyk, and two films on the Z-Boys at the turn of the century.

6. Orsi, A., Peralta, S., Stecyk, C., & Penn, S. 2002. *Dogtown and Z-boys*. Special ed. Culver City, CA, Sony Pictures Classics.

7. *Ibid.*

8. This, combined with widespread misogyny in skateboarding communities, means that in many cases, skateboarding communities were and continue to be difficult places to be a woman.

9. Aside from the likes of Bam Margera, who were professional skateboarders in addition to being members of the *Jackass* team, the close ties between *Jackass* and skateboarding culture are exemplified in their inclusion in the videogame *Tony Hawk's Underground 2*. See Neversoft. 2004. *Tony Hawk's Underground 2*. Activision.

10. See, for instance, the parks constructed in Malmo as documented in perhaps the greatest arthouse skate video ever produced: Pontus Alv's *The Strongest of the Strange*. See Alv, Pontus. 2005. *The Strongest of the Strange* Klez Motion Pictures International.

11. According to this way of thinking about what it is to be a skateboarder, a *real* skateboarder would never support skateboarding becoming an Olympic sport, for instance. This would be to work with authority—not against it.

12. Dembroff, Robin. 2020. "Beyond Binary: Genderqueer as Critical Gender Kind." *Philosophers' Imprint* 20 (9): pp. 1–23, here p. 12.

13. Wilchins, R. 2017. *Burn the Binary! Selected Writings on the Politics of Trans, Genderqueer and Nonbinary*. Riverdale Avenue Books. p. 80.

14. "Ideology" is an even more contested term than "kind"! For our purposes here, it's enough to think about an ideology as a particular way of thinking about and representing the world, with accompanying rules for human behavior. Readers interested in a deeper dive on ideology might like to start with Sally Haslanger's first Hempel lecture: Haslanger, Sally. 2019. Ideology in Practice.

15. *Ibid.*, Dembroff. p. 15.

16. Just as there are lots of potential ways of spelling out what a skateboarder is, so too there are lots of different ways of going about spelling out what it is to be genderqueer, beyond the critical gender kind given by Dembroff. One closely related kind often referred to using the term "genderqueer" is an umbrella category, made up of everyone who is nonbinary, gender nonconforming, or otherwise queers their gender. Whilst this will share many members with *genderqueer* as critical gender kind, this umbrella kind account of *genderqueer* will include some people that Dembroff's kind will not.

17. Genders are social kinds, so critical gender kinds are just one type of critical social kind.

18. Those interested in this value-distorting aspect of ideology should consider Haslanger, Sally. 2016. "I-Culture and Critique." *Aristotelian Society Supplementary Volume 91* (1): pp. 149–173. A related phenomenon of the closing down of alternative is excellently described in Fisher, Mark. 2012. *Capitalist Realism: Is There No Alternative?* Zero Books.

19. Indeed, long before *Tony Hawk's Pro Skater*, Hawk and the other members of the Bones Brigade were already being criticized for failing to be proper skateboarders: wearing kneepads, not taking drugs or drinking heavily, and not having tattoos. As Willing et al. describe it, the Bones Brigade were seen as the nerdy boy scouts set against punk "bad boy" skateboarding contemporaries such as Christian Hosoi—see Willing, Indigo, Green, Ben, and Pavlidis Adele. 2020. "The 'boy scouts' and 'bad boys' of skateboarding: a thematic analysis of the bones brigade," *Sport in Society* 23 (5): pp. 832–846.

20. Peralta, Stacey. 1987. *The Search for Animal Chin*. Powell Peralta.

21. *Ibid.*

22. Chin himself is presented as a crude and rather racist Asian stereotype, the film buying into the racist trope of the "magical master from the far east" completely uncritically.

23. Yes, this film really does embody a meme: the real Animal Chin was the skateboarding we did along the way. The Bones Brigade even say this explicitly at one point, rapping in a convertible, "If we don't find him that's okay, 'cause we had a rad time anyway." Peralta, the film's director, has admitted that he's rather ashamed of how corny it is—see Zaleski, Luke. 2017. "Tony Hawk and the Bones Brigade Tell the Story of Legendary Skate Video 'Animal Chin.'" *gq.com*.

II
Skating Values

The Problem of the Poseur

Joshua Heter

That one or another person may be a poseur is an idea that can be found in any number of subcultures. However, next to artists and fans of punk rock,[1] the group for which the concept is perhaps most familiar is the skateboarding community. Skating seems to have been infiltrated, so the allegations suggest, by at least a handful of questionable if not altogether fraudulent individuals (i.e., poseurs). Anecdotally, the problem seems to be so pervasive, *Urban Dictionary* maintains dozens of entries dedicated to the concept of the poseur specifically within skateboarding.[2] And it would be difficult to spend any significant time skating without coming across the concept, if not hearing specific accusations that some alleged skater is really just a poseur.

What exactly is a poseur? Arguably, being a poseur is about more than merely pretending to be something that you're not. Bearing in mind that the concept isn't unique to skating, being a poseur is about representing oneself as the member of a group or merely representing oneself as being committed to that which the group is committed, because there is some benefit to doing so. We might then simply say that the essential mark of a poseur is portraying oneself as having a significantly deeper level of commitment than one actually has to the beliefs, values, or practices essential to a community's identity for the purpose of obtaining the social benefits which come from being seen as a member of that community (or from simply being seen as dedicated to that which the community is dedicated). The skateboarding poseur either doesn't skate at all or isn't really committed to the practice even though he speaks the language of the skater, wears a skater's garb, and perhaps makes disingenuous, halfhearted attempts at skating. The poseur *presents* as a skater, but he does so simply to acquire whatever social gains there are to be had by doing so.[3]

Nevertheless, with all of this in mind, it's worth asking, why do skaters (or members of any community) really care all that much about poseurs? Is the issue so serious that they should spend substantial energy trying to identify and call them out? Arguably, if there is to be any utility whatsoever in having membership in a community, there must be some effort made to ensure that only genuine or sincere members benefit from inclusion in the group. That said, while there are a number of such understandable if not justifiable reasons why the skating community would be on the lookout for disingenuous infiltrators, there is also, I'll attempt to argue, good reason why it would be advisable for skaters to de-emphasize their concern for (what we might call) the problem of the poseur.

Skating Concerns

Poseurs portray themselves as having a deeper level of commitment than they actually have in regard to the beliefs, values, or practices essential to a community's identity. Or, they misrepresent their place in that community. And the reason that they do this is to obtain the social benefits that come from maintaining such a facade. The skateboarding poseur isn't genuinely committed to skating, but he presents himself as if he is because being thought of as a skater comes with some sort of (real or perceived) reward.

There are a number of understandable if not justified interconnected reasons why skaters might care about this. The first is simply that it is natural and frankly quite useful to value authenticity to the point that we aim to identify those who are inauthentic. Someone who is inauthentic in regard to what *might* be fairly benign matters (e.g., exaggerating one's commitment to skating for increased popularity) may be more likely to be inauthentic in matters more material (e.g., pretending to be your friend in order to harm you in some substantial way). Thus, it is predictable if not advisable that we attempt to recognize inauthenticity in *any* form.

It's also worth pointing out that skating is disproportionately done by the young. With age often comes time-sucking responsibilities which make it painfully difficult to find time to skate. Age can also bring physical ailments which can make skating literally painful. As such, much of the culture surrounding skateboarding is disproportionately influenced by the concerns of youth which include an (arguably laudable) emphasis on personal authenticity. For a variety of reasons, young folks are (or at least claim to be) especially concerned with living in accordance with their own beliefs and values and associating with those who they perceive to be doing the same. Relatedly, perhaps yet another affliction that comes with age is the begrudging, pragmatic acceptance that plenty of people live their lives playing some sort of role that forces them to live in conflict with their authentic selves. Nevertheless, it is no real surprise that young people in general and skaters in particular are uniquely concerned with identifying (and possibly even calling out) poseurs.

Beyond a general concern for authenticity, a second and related reason to be concerned about the infiltration of poseurs is that it can seem as if the poseur is guilty of a certain type of theft. To be sure, the theft of which poseurs may be guilty is different than theft as we might typically think of it (e.g., taking a five-finger-discount by walking out of your local skate shop with some new gear without paying). But of course, this is not the only type of theft that exists. Thankfully, we have two helpful concepts which can allow us to articulate the type of theft poseurs may be committing.

First, to the dedicated skater, it can at least feel as if the poseur is guilty of cultural appropriation[4]: the "unacknowledged or inappropriate adoption of the customs, practices, and ideas of one people or society by members of another."[5] Of course, the cases of cultural appropriation which often seem to be the most egregious are those which involve theft across racial, ethnic, or nationalistic lines. However, insofar as there exists a culture of skateboarding, those who disingenuously or superficially take the signs, symbols, or artifacts of skateboarders as their own are arguably doing so inappropriately and may very well be guilty of a kind of cultural appropriation (and thereby guilty of a type of theft).

With this in mind, it's worth pointing out that the types of cultural appropriation crossing ethnic lines about which we tend to be the most concerned are those in which there exists a power imbalance between those who take cultural artifacts as their own and those whose cultural artifacts are taken. This may help us understand why the skater might be so concerned with the problem of the poseur; skating has been—at least historically—a pastime often taken up by those who are somewhat removed from centers of popularity or by young people who are less interested in more traditionally celebrated sports. It's an activity populated at least to a degree by misfits and outsiders. Because of this, it can seem particularly problematic for potential poseurs from more elevated social groups (e.g., preps, jocks, etc.) to artificially adopt the culture of skating (or aspects of it) as their own.

A second type of theft of which the poseur may be guilty (which explains the skater's emphasis on such a problem) is analogous to the phenomenon of stolen valor: the act of falsely claiming participation in military service or the earning of military awards. To be clear, stolen valor (as the phrase is typically used) in a military context is an immeasurably more serious and heinous offense. The point here is simply that there may be something at least somewhat analogous going on in the cases of skateboarding poseurs.

II. Skating Values

Skating is difficult. It takes significant dedication and effort to improve as a skater. And, as skaters are all too familiar, skating is rough. No one who has skated for any significant amount of time or in any serious way has done so without injury. While some injuries can be minor, many are not. Because of this, it isn't difficult to understand why one might view their participation in skating as something to take pride in; they see it as part of their identity and as something they've *earned*. You have to pay your dues to be a skater, and the dues aren't cheap. Thus, it's only natural for skaters to be concerned about poseurs, because poseurs are taking something important to skaters which they simply have not earned.

Finally, beyond a general concern for authenticity and theft (of various kinds), there is a third related reason why skaters may be understandably concerned about the problem of the poseur. The more poseurs infiltrate the skating community, the more it becomes diluted.[6] Skaters rightly (or at least, understandably) feel an ownership over skating culture, because it's something that's special and sets them apart. If a new wave of genuine, committed skaters takes up the practice, that's something to be accepted if not celebrated. However, if skateboarding culture gets appropriated, or if the status of being a skater can be carried by just anyone, then skating as a whole becomes less significant. The analogy between the dilution of skateboarding culture and *chemical* dilution (i.e., the lowering of the concentration of a solute by adding increasing amounts of solvent such as water) is apt. There is a sense in which the infiltration of poseurs makes skating or skating culture (weaker, less potent, or at the very least) less substantive.

Beware the [Skate]keepers

As we've seen, there are a variety of interconnected reasons skaters might be concerned with the problem of the poseur. In general, it is natural if not advisable to value authenticity and to flag those who are inauthentic. Poseurs may be guilty of one or another type of theft. And the proliferation of insincere or fraudulent members of the skating community dilutes what makes skateboarding (and what it means to be a skater) unique.

Nevertheless, while these may be real and genuine concerns, I want to make a call for temperance. That is, I want to at least attempt to make the case that skaters should turn their focus away from their worries about poseurs or that they should at least exercise a degree of modesty in regard to their identification of potential poseurs. Much like the explanation for why skaters might be understandably concerned about the issue, there are at least a handful of interconnected reasons that should give them pause in regard to their focus on and explicit labeling of poseurs.

First, it would be wise for skaters to exercise a degree of what philosophers call intellectual (or "epistemic") humility.[7] There are a variety of ways to think about the virtue of humility generally, but one of its important aspects is that the humble person does not have an overinflated or exaggerated view of their own powers and abilities. And even in the case where a humble person does in fact have significant or even extraordinary powers or abilities, they do not focus their attention on them needlessly, and they do not do so in any sort of overt or braggadocios manner. Thus, *intellectual* humility entails not having an overinflated or exaggerated view of one's own *cognitive or intellectual* powers and abilities, and the intellectually humble person does not unnecessarily draw attention to the cognitive or intellectual powers and abilities which they do have.

Many of us have skated with someone with an over-inflated view of their own ability as a skater. It's just a matter of time, they assure us, before they're discovered and offered a sponsorship. Perhaps just as frustratingly, we've all come across (or at times been guilty of being) that person with an over-inflated view of their own powers of perception, evidence-gathering, and reasoning. Every opinion such a person holds is a strongly held opinion that, they assure us, is so obviously correct that anyone who disagrees with them is either stupid or corrupt. But of course, there is a strong case to be made that we should want to avoid being such an intellectually arrogant person.

First, there is practical reason we should aim to exercise intellectual humility and avoid intellectual arrogance. It's simply annoying to be around intellectually arrogant people; it's a chore to spend time with those who are particularly closed-minded or who count themselves as some sort of special beacon of reason or source of information. A second reason to exercise intellectual humility (perhaps more relevant to our concern about the problem of the poseur) is that intellectual arrogance can put us in a precarious epistemic state. That is, it can lead us to arrive at more false (or at least more unjustified) beliefs.

No matter any individual's intellectual powers or abilities, everyone is subject to being deceived by their own biases. As much as we'd all like to think of ourselves as perfectly reliable gatherers and processors of evidence, in virtue of being human, the beliefs we form can be influenced by our desires: what we *hope* is true (as opposed to what we have good *reason* to believe). Likewise, our beliefs can be impacted by non-rational influences from our surroundings (e.g., what we perceive to be valued by the members of our community). This is why the exercise of at least a modest amount of intellectual humility is so important: it can help us avoid such mistakes. A key to avoiding being fooled by our biases is to recognize that they exist. And the partial reliance on the perspective and expertise of others (as opposed to a hyper-focus on one's own perspective or expertise) can act as a check or a safeguard against forming mistaken beliefs.

Now, the point is this. While there may be cases in which it is just obvious that someone is (or is not) a poseur, it would seem that most cases fall somewhere within these two extremes. In any case, the dedicated skater, committed to protecting the skating community from an infiltration of poseurs will have to make a judgment based on his perception or a set of evidence he's gathered about whether the *potential* poseur is an authentic and committed skater. And it is far from obvious (at least in a good number of cases) that we are in any sort of privileged position to make such a determination. The skater concerned with the problem of the poseur might have *some* reason to flag a potential poseur, but there always exists the possibility that his evidence gathering in regard to this question involved some error or that his weighing of that evidence is flawed in some way.

I would suggest that in many (if not most) cases, if we are exercising any reasonable amount of intellectual humility, the amount of evidence we have that someone is a poseur calls for us to *withhold* judgment (i.e., to conclude neither that the individual in question is a poseur nor that he isn't). In any given case, how confident can we be of someone's motives (e.g., for decking themselves out in new skateboarding gear) or of someone's level of commitment (e.g., in regard to their passion for skating)? And if the rational thing in a given case is to withhold judgment, then a modest sort of innocent-until-proven-guilty principle would seem to call for us to at least *treat* the individual in question as a non-poseur.

It should be noted that the call for intellectual humility here goes beyond the sort of skepticism which we could raise about almost *any* belief we might have (e.g., the belief that you're sitting here right now, reading this book, even though you *could* be dreaming or trapped in the Matrix). This is because a second, related reason to temper our focus on poseurs is that we can identify at least two specific biases we all plausibly have which could play a role in at least some instances in which someone is erroneously labeled a poseur.

The first such potential bias is our tendency toward tribalism. History and contemporary society are replete with examples of individuals drawing unnecessarily exclusionary boundaries around their communities. The tendency to sort ourselves into groups is innate. And it is unfortunately all too common for people to take this tendency to unreasonable (and sometimes scary) places.[8] The fact that we know that we have such a strong social-boundary-drawing proclivity (buried deep inside what makes us human) should at least give us pause when we are inclined to label someone as a poseur. Do we really have a rational basis for drawing such a conclusion? Or, are we arriving at this judgment for non-rational reasons, such as a hyper-intense, unreflective desire to protect the tribe from "outsiders"?

A second bias which may lead a skater to erroneously label another as a poseur is what psychologists call a self-serving bias: any cognitive process that fallaciously leads us to draw conclusions in order to enhance our own standing or self-esteem.[9] By labeling someone *else* as a poseur, we signal to others (and importantly, ourselves) that *we* are the *bona fide* article. We, of course, have the elevated status of being an authentic, genuine skater as opposed to the now-labeled fraudulent poseur. Again, when we draw such conclusions, it's at least worth asking: do we really have a rational basis for doing so? Or, do we arrive at such judgments in order to publicly buoy our own status (as genuine, authentic skaters) which can now be contrasted with the newly identified poseur?

Bearing in mind these potential biases, the dedicated skater who's committed to exercising intellectual humility has substantial reasons to take these questions seriously and perhaps even to withhold judgment about whether someone is a poseur and maybe even to afford them the benefit of the doubt. Put differently, heeding a call for intellectual humility along with a recognition that we may have biases which could lead us to label someone as a poseur when they are not should give the reasonable skater pause when identifying and labeling others as poseurs.

Admittedly, despite (our recognition of) our potential bias toward tribalism, it is not always irrational to flag someone as an outsider or even to explicitly label them with such a status. Similarly, despite (our recognition of) our potential self-serving biases, it is not always irrational to call out inauthenticity or fraudulent behavior in others. That said, it is nevertheless a non-trivial possibility that these biases, on occasion, can lead us to incorrectly label someone as a poseur. And, with this in mind, a final reason to heed a call for temperance (in regard to the focus on and explicit labeling of poseurs) is that making such a mistake really is something we should want to avoid.

Recall again that skating is disproportionately done by the young; certainly, most *new* skaters are young. And one thing you quickly come to appreciate after spending a significant amount of time around young people (as a parent, a skate instructor, or a college professor) is just how much or how often young people are, to put it crudely, just sort of trying stuff out. Youth really is a time for experimentation (and not just in regard to vice). It is natural and perhaps inevitable for adolescents and even young adults to try out a new hobby, enter into a new social arena, or even take on a new identity simply to sort of try it on and see how it fits. Because of this, it is all too easy to potentially drift into poseur territory with no real malice or forethought.

Because of this, there should be at least a modicum of latitude given to young and burgeoning skaters, so they don't have to worry about whether they'll cross the invisible boundary into being (labeled as) a poseur (in skating or anything else). And once we recognize that this is a reasonable accommodation that should be afforded to young and new skaters, perhaps it's something that can also be extended to older or even seasoned skaters. We shouldn't expect every single (beginning or even expert) skater's outward enthusiasm or professed love for skating to perfectly match their inward level of commitment or passion for skating. So, we shouldn't be quick on the draw in regard to thinking of someone or labeling them as a poseur.

While it is again natural if not advisable to keep skating from being diluted, we also don't want to be guilty of gatekeeping: the process of controlling access to some domain often by making determinations on another's claims of legitimacy to access that domain. And an overemphasis on the identification and labeling of poseurs can (at least potentially) put us in a position to be doing just that in regard to skating. As such, one final reason to heed this call for temperance is that if the focus on the problem of the poseur becomes pervasive enough, the authenticity or claim of legitimacy of the next skater that might be called into question is your own.

Notes

1. The topic of poseurs in punk rock has received some recent attention from philosophers. See Barry, Peter Brian. "The Paradox of the Poseur" (Chapter 7); Prinz; Jesse. "The Seven P's of Real Punk" (Chapter 9). 2022. *Punk Rock and Philosophy: Research and Destroy*. Heter, Joshua; Greene, Richard (eds.) Carus Books.
2. *Urban Dictionary*. 2023. "skate poser." https://www.urbandictionary.com/define.php?term=skate%20poser; "poser skater." https://www.urbandictionary.com/define.php?term=poser%20skater; "skater poser." https://www.urbandictionary.com/define.php?term=skater&page=21; "poser." https://www.urbandictionary.com/define.php?term=poser&page=6; "A poser." https://www.urbandictionary.com/define.php?term=a%20poser; "poseur." https://www.urbandictionary.com/define.php?term=poseur&page=2.
3. There is perhaps a slightly different, secondary use of the term "poseur" in a skating context. In certain cases, the accusation that some skater is a poseur seems to express that the alleged poseur is misrepresenting their *skill set* or level of *achievement* as a skater (i.e., they claim to be a better skater than they actually are). For instance, there could be a skateboarder who is completely dedicated and passionate about skating; he simply isn't particularly good at it. Embarrassed by this fact (or perhaps wanting to reap some reward for being thought of as a good skater), he misrepresents how good of a skater he is. There are at least some who might label such a person as a poseur. However, this is at least a slightly different use of the term, and (as such) comes with its own unique problem from that of the term as we are discussing it (which goes beyond the scope of this essay).
4. Prinz.

5. Oxford University Press. 2023. "Cultural Appropriation." *Oxford Living Dictionary.* https://en.oxforddictrionaries.com/definition/cultural_appropriation.
6. Prinz.
7. Roberts, Robert; Wood, Jay. 2003. "Humility and Epistemic Goods." *Intellectual Virtue: Perspectives from Ethics and Epistemology*, Depaul, M., and Zagzebski, L. (eds.), Oxford: Clarendon Press, 257–279.
8. Clark, Cory J.; Liu, Brittany S.; Winegard, Bo M.; Ditto, Peter H. 2019. "Tribalism is Human Nature." *Current Directions in Psychological Science*, Vol. 28, No. 6, 587–592. Association for Psychological Science.
9. Myers, D.G. 2015. *Exploring Social Psychology*, 7th Edition. McGraw Hill Education.

Skateboarding *Is* a Crime

Bradley Elicker

In 1988, the slogan "Skateboarding is not a crime" first appeared in Powell-Peralta's *Public Domain* as a graphic response to newly enacted efforts to curtail street skating through city ordinances and law enforcement pressure. A decade later, the phrase was copyrighted by Santa Cruz Skateboards after becoming ubiquitous on stickers, skate decks, t-shirts and a variety of other gear. In the interim, the number of ordinances and the severity of law enforcement pressure increased as street skating became the newest front in the decades long battle for control of the urban environment.

On the surface, business and civic leaders argued that such measures were needed for a number of reasons ranging from the destruction of public property to the risks of bodily harm to the very presence of those who utilize city spaces for skateboarding. However, these measures could also be interpreted as a struggle of ownership; a fight over who gets to use city spaces and in what ways. This claim is based on a view of the city as a "normative space" governed by certain societal rules. In other words, the city is not just a collection of buildings, roads, and other pieces of the urban landscape. These features—which in part make *up* the city—direct people to use the city in specific, predetermined ways, and it is the agents of business and government who dictate who may use urban space in ways that protect and further those interests.

The street skater threatens these interests by using the features of the urban environment in unsanctioned ways. Thus, the skateboarder is viewed by those agents of business and government as a dangerous, oppositional figure to the commercial interests of the city. Of course, it's worth noting that, although skating had existed for decades by this point, efforts to discourage the practice coincide with the reversal of white flight from American cities.

Nevertheless, comparisons here can be drawn between the street skater and the street *artist,* specifically in ways discussed by Michael Irvine in his essay on graffiti and street art "The Work on the Street: Street Art and Visual Culture." Like the street artist, the street skater challenges who owns and controls urban spaces. The street skater does both real and symbolic harm to the city's commercial interests. This creates relationships between skaters and law enforcement and businesses which are inherently adversarial. This can be seen in the ways that cities in the 1990s began enacting ordinances banning skateboarding specifically in commercial zones, the rise of hostile urban design to discourage this unsanctioned use, as well as violence (or at least the threat of it) taken against skaters as shown in contemporaneous skate videos by Birdhouse, Zero, and *Thrasher Magazine*.

All of these forces are designed to push skateboarders out of urban spaces and into designated areas cordoned off from the city (i.e., skate parks). Often, skate parks are viewed as a legitimization of skateboarding as a sport or pastime, as if they are created to prioritize the safety and interests of skaters. However, if my preceding account of the relationship between the street skater and urban interests is correct, I believe that such claims should be viewed with suspicion. Skate parks remove the skater from the urban environment in order to preserve the designated uses of urban spaces that protect commercial interests. Viewed in this way, the skate park begins to resemble the "free speech zones" which began to be used more frequently by state and federal law enforcement in the early 2000s as well as "legal graffiti areas" to manage urban visual spaces. Each takes a practice that is necessarily unsanctioned and subsumes it into the environment's regulated modes of operating. The skate park creates a space that is now a controlled, segregated area that protects commercial interests and reintroduces the skater into those predetermined roles of urban spaces. From the perspective of government and business and in order to protect their interests, skateboarding is (and must continue to be) a crime.

The City and Its Uses

The city is more than just buildings, roads, people, or pieces of urban architecture. It is an urban *system* that serves a normative function. Something performs a normative function if it encourages or instructs us toward or away from holding some belief or performing some action. In this sense, the features of the city encourage certain uses while discouraging others. This normative, urban system dictates that the city *should be* used in certain ways sanctioned by, and designed to, protect commercial interests. In "Walking in the City," Michel de Certeau argues that "the act of walking is to the urban system what the speech act is to language."[1]

Similar to the ways in which the definitions of words and the rules of a language guide the speaker's use of that language when speaking, the features of urban spaces guide and direct the pedestrian's use of the city. De Certeau refers to the prescribed uses of urban spaces as "ways of operating."[2] The objects and features of the urban environment connect to one another in sanctioned, predetermined ways of operating just as words relate to one another in sanctioned ways to create utterances. Streets, sidewalks, bike lanes and paths, as well as stairways and railings all direct and control urban traffic. Ledges, walls, gates, and fences divide and cordon off urban space in order to demonstrate and enforce ownership. Statues, sculptures, and other instances of public art reinforce cultural values. And billboards, storefronts, and street signs communicate governmental and commercial messages.

In his study of street art and visual culture, Michael Irvine views the city as a "protected zone" for commerce and industry.[3] The agents of commerce, industry, and government designate and enforce the "ways of operating" to protect and further their own interests. The regulated, controlled use of urban space allows for greater commerce. When pedestrians and those operating two and four-wheeled transportation use the city in these sanctioned ways, commerce in the city can thrive. And insofar as the city government benefits from increased commerce, the agents of the city such as law enforcement will strive to enforce this order. So, we can see these ways of operating being enforced against those who would use the urban environment in unsanctioned ways. This is exemplified in efforts to criminalize and discourage vagrancy, panhandling, busking, street performances, graffiti and street art, unlicensed street vendors and, more recently, drag racing as well as the use of ATVs and dirt bikes on city streets. All of these practices threaten the interests of the agents of the city by discouraging commerce.

Who Owns Urban Spaces?

Cities instruct agents to use the urban environment in predetermined ways that protect and expand commercial interests. Adversarial agents (e.g., street artists) violate these norms and reappropriate urban spaces for their own uses. In much the same way, the street skater uses the city in unsanctioned ways that challenge the notion of who owns urban spaces. Again, in their uses of and challenges to ownership of the urban environment, there are many similarities between the street skater and the street artist. With this in mind, Irvine argues that

> street art continually reveals that no urban space is neutral: walls and street topography are boundaries for socially constructed zones and territories, and

vertical space is regulated by regimes of visibility.... The artists understand that publicly viewable space, normally regulated by property and commercial regimes for controlling visibility, can be appropriated for unconstrained, uncontainable, antagonist acts.[4]

Just as the works of street artists challenge who gets "heard" in the urban visual landscape, the street skater challenges who can use urban physical space and in what ways. Features like benches, tables, stairways, railings, and public art all have different "meaning" to the street skater. Skating in the city reinterprets the ways in which the features of the urban landscape can be used and how they relate to one another in ways that challenge ownership of urban spaces. Thus, to the governmental and commercial agents of the city (and possibly inhabitants as well), the street skater is viewed as a dangerous, oppositional figure to their interests.

However, street skating is more threatening to the agents of the city than what would amount to a mere reinterpretation of urban space. In its rejection of these designated ways of operating, street skating does both real world and symbolic harm to those commercial interests. In symbolic ways, the street skater is a visible challenge to the governmental authority of the city while the presence of skaters is often said to cause a decrease in real-world commercial traffic. We might also say that street skating "leaves its mark" on the urban environment through scrapes, worn paint, and left-behind skate wax in a way that is both destructive and serves as a reminder that these spaces have been (and may again be) used by the skating community. The threat of harm to commercial interests (of which the city itself benefits) creates a confrontational and sometimes violent relationship between skaters, law enforcement, and business owners.

The responses to street skating from city government are similar to the responses to the other unsanctioned uses of urban spaces mentioned thus far. The agents of the city will seek to enforce the proper use of the city against street skaters through both city ordinances as well as hostile urban design. One of the first laws enacted against skateboarding in commercial areas came from the city of Los Angeles in 1993. The city council justified the ordinance as a way to protect pedestrians and shoppers. However, Deputy Dave Kolinski of the Los Angeles Sheriff's Department admitted that, at that time, there had been no reports filed of skateboarders injuring pedestrians. And, perhaps unsurprisingly, Mac Ausbon, president of the city's Chamber of Commerce, seems to have suggested that there was an altogether different motivation behind the ordnance, stating that "you don't want customers afraid to come into your place of business."[5] Businesses also began to take matters into their own hands by crafting or purchasing devices such as skatebumps that could be attached to railings and ledges to discourage any unsanctioned uses of them. The first commercially produced skatebump was created by Chris Loarie and his company, Skatestoppers, in 1998 in order to protect local businesses in San Diego County.[6]

Archival footage and promotional material from skateboarding companies from this period also demonstrate the lengths to which agents of urban environments were willing to go to discourage skating. Plan B's *Questionable* (1992) shows various instances of the harassment of skaters and the destruction and theft of skateboarders' property perpetrated by both members of the public and law enforcement. We see similar scenes in *Thrasher Magazine*'s *Search and Destroy* (1996) where skaters are threatened with law enforcement responses, chastised by business owners for non-existent property damage, reprimanded by security guards and law enforcement officers, and physically assaulted by several security guards. And Toy Machine's *Welcome to Hell* (1996) opens with footage of skaters interspersed with images of police officers and American flags. Over its thirty-minute run time, a skateboarder is told by a business owner "I hope you break your legs!" Another is shown being assaulted by a police officer. The piece ultimately concludes with a Catholic priest striking a skater and attempting to confiscate their camera for the offense of skating on church property.

The Skate Park

From hostile architecture to threats and acts of violence against skaters, the message is clear that the agents of the urban environment will go to great lengths to discourage skateboarding. All of these forces are designed to push skaters out of urban environments and into designated areas, cordoned off from the larger city. All of this brings us to the issue of the skate park and its role in protecting commercial interests.

Again, Michel de Certeau argues that the city becomes a "universal and anonymous subject" directed toward the production and protection of its own space. Thus, the agents of the city will expel anything abnormal or deviant to its interests. De Certeau calls these the city's "waste products."[7] After the demise of commercial "pay-to-play" skate parks in the 1970s, public skate parks emerged in the 1990s as skaters were being pushed out of the urban environment to protect commercial interests. Often, skate parks were pointed to as evidence of the *legitimizing* of skateboarding as a sport or pastime. The argument was that the skate park was a welcoming space where skaters could enjoy themselves in relative safety. However, when we take into account the relationship between street skating and the agents of the city as we've here described it, all of these positive, almost promotional skate park claims should (at the very least) be viewed with suspicion.

The skate park removes the skateboarder from the urban environment and neutralizes the threat that she poses for businesses and other commercial interests. Thus, it could be argued that cities and municipalities create skate parks, not for the benefit of the skateboarder, but to protect their ownership of (and to further their interests in) the urban environment. Of course, one might claim that cities can be motivated by protecting *both* commercial interests and the safety of skateboarders at the same time. However, the risk of injuries to skateboarders from hostile architecture as well as actual injuries from physical altercations with law enforcement call into question how seriously cities actually take the safety of skaters. Though skateboarder safety is certainly a potential benefit of skate parks, their predominant purpose seems to be to preserve the designated ways of operating in the city by removing the skateboarder from public, urban spaces.

In this way, we may again view skate parks similar to other spaces created to protect commercial and governmental interests such as the designated "free speech zones" which emerged in the early 2000s as well as "legal graffiti walls" which are beginning to appear in global urban centers. Designated free speech zones became prevalent after the infamous World Trade Organization protests in Seattle in 1999. They are now common during political speeches and conventions with the alleged goal of protecting and encouraging free speech. However, there is evidence to suggest that the true purpose of these zones is to remove and stifle protected speech from public view.[8]

Similarly, the stated purpose of legal graffiti walls is often to "manage" graffiti and discourage vandalism outside of these designated zones. Very rarely do any justifications for such areas take seriously the idea that they are attempts to beautify the city or to encourage street art as a legitimate art form.[9] Both free speech zones and legal graffiti areas take something spontaneous and unsanctioned only to subsume it into the urban zone's designated ways of operating. Skate parks do much the same. The skateboarder has been cordoned off from the city. Her power to challenge commercial interests and question who can use urban space and in what ways has been neutralized. The skateboarder has been silenced and the skate park has become another regulated, designated area of urban space that protects commerce.

Skate Park Funding and Self-Segregation

If the skate park serves the interest of those who have commercial and financial stakes in the urban environment, wouldn't we expect municipal governments to fund skate parks themselves as they do other urban spaces? If the skate park benefits the city, as opposed to benefiting the skater, why are most skate parks funded by skateboarders themselves? The cost of building a skate park can range from half a million dollars for a small, neighborhood park that could serve around 50 skaters to well over a million dollars for a larger regional park that could accommodate anywhere from 150 to 200 skateboarders.[10] Websites such as skatepark.org and publicskateparkguide.org have pages dedicated to ways that skaters might secure funding for skate parks. Given that skating is a recreational activity taken up most often by adolescents and young adults, securing such funding can often be difficult. Typically, these websites suggest direct crowd sourced funding, forming your own nonprofit, or partnering with and seeking grants through NGO nonprofits. Very rarely do we see cities and municipalities putting up the funding to remove skateboarders from the urban environment.

If skate parks serve the city rather than skateboarders, why do we see skaters themselves constructing their own segregated areas? The simple answer is that the agents of the city have left them no choice. The threat of sanctions and violence from law enforcement and the business community has forced skaters to fund their own self-segregation. The fact that the agents of the city push skaters out of the urban environment and into skate parks *while at the same time* getting skateboarders to pay for it themselves shows just how motivating these agents can be in their efforts to remove skaters from urban spaces.

As we've seen, the city is a normative space controlled by governmental and commercial interests. De Certeau writes that the city will seek to expel any "waste products" that threaten those interests and violate the cities designated ways of operating. In order to do so, challenges to those interests like skateboarding must continue to be a crime. Personally, I have lived and worked in the Philadelphia area for over 20 years and, for a time, taught across the street from Dilworth Plaza and Love Park. For decades, both were prized areas to the skateboarding community. Now, due to city ordinances, hostile architecture, and law enforcement pressure, they are essentially empty on most days save for the occasional tourist who will, presumably, be off to spend their money at one of the city's many commercial spaces. Unfortunately, this mostly just serves as a bit of additional evidence that (at least in the view of those in power) skateboarding really is a crime.

Notes

1. De Certeau, Michel, 1984. "Walking in the City," in *The Practice of Everyday Life*. Trans. Stephen F. Rendall. Berkeley: University of California Press, 91–110, here 97.
2. *Ibid.*, 100.

3. Irvine, Martin, 2012. "The Work on the Street: Street Art and Visual Culture," in *The Handbook of Visual Culture*. Eds. Barry Sandywell and Ian Haywood. London: Berg, 235–278, here 255.

4. *Ibid.*, 243.

5. See Helfand, Duke, 1993. "Skateboarding Prohibited in Business Areas: Safety: The City Council moves to protect shoppers and merchants," in *Los Angeles Times*, May 6, 1.

6. See Kelly, John, 2020. "It's a Grind: The birth of those metal ledge guards designed to deter skateboarders," in *Washington Post*, May 23.

7. De Certeau, 94–95.

8. See for instance, George W. Bush designating a "free speech zone" nearly half a mile away from his speech site in Pittsburgh, Pennsylvania, in 2002. See Bovard, James, 2003. "Free Speech Zone: The Administration Quarantines Dissent," in *The American Conservative*, December 15.

9. See McGhee, Tom, 2023. "Permission Walls Help Create a Canvas for Managing Graffiti," in *The Denver Post*, September 30.

10. This is calculated using a publicskateparkguide.org estimate of $40 per square foot and a size range of 8,000 to 30,000 square feet.

The Aesthetics of Skateboarding

Hector Quintero

Skateboarding emerged in the 1950s as surfers in California attempted to recreate their experience of riding a wave on land. The impetus to recreate experiences generally is an important idea in the work of philosopher John Dewey. According to Dewey, aesthetic experience is built on natural experience; our natural experience of the world involves a fundamental relationship that connects us to our environment related to our own survival (or what Dewey calls "rhythm"). Once we are attuned to our natural experience, the aesthetic experience emerges as a product of our imagination as a way to enjoy those things which go beyond our natural experience.

For Dewey, art resides in our aesthetic experiences, and this may include things like philosophy and even skateboarding. Although Dewey said nothing about it (that we know of), skateboarding qualifies as an aesthetic experience because it's a creative venture which seeks to express internal qualities of the skater. As we explore Dewey's naturalism, internalism, and how these apply to his philosophy of art, we'll be able to see that there is strong evidence that skateboarding in indeed a creative art (according to Dewey's criteria). Naturalism and internalism are technical terms defined by the relation that the aesthetic and natural experience share. Naturalism is defined by our common or ordinary experience of the world. Internalism, in contrast, is the view according to which aesthetic experience is one internal experience among many, yet it is one of the most significant and impactful.

The Natural Experience

Dewey's naturalism involves a variety of properties that can also be identified in skating: interaction, immersion, order, and disorder. Our interaction with an environment is a quality of natural experience. So, a skater's interaction is fundamental in intuiting the skateboard and its relationship to the environment. Naturalists and skaters alike share this connection to the environment. Dewey reminds us that "while man is other than bird and beast, he shares basic vital functions with them and has to make the same basal adjustments if he is to continue the process of living."[1]

For skaters, as for naturalists, engaging the landscape is an essential process that allows them to exercise creativity but also to continue the process of living. The analogy here is crucial in comprehending Dewey's naturalism since he suggests that we are grounded in the natural world. More importantly, we can conclude that skaters are in a state of interaction with the natural world.

It is significant to note that Dewey owes his understanding of naturalism to the discoveries proposed by Charles Darwin in *On the Origin of Species*. There, Darwin attempts to provide a natural explanation of how different species emerged. Here, we can draw a parallel between the evolution of animals and the evolution of tricks. Briefly, a skateboarding trick is a maneuver that the skater performs using the board in order to demonstrate technique. Similarly enough, what Darwin supposes is that animals change over time just as the environment changes, producing different species. Tricks also emerge and change with time. Some species become central in the development of other species while still other species die out. Millions of years ago, spineless life in the ocean gave rise to land-walking animals. So, too, some tricks become the backbone of the evolution of other tricks. Consider the relevance of the basic ollie as a foundational trick, whereas tricks like dolphin flips and nollie hard flips build on the ollie but may have died out due to their impracticality. In any case, Darwin reminds us that humans are simply one species among many. He may have rooted humanity in the natural world, but Dewey analyzes the philosophical implications of the starting point.

The other important attribute of natural experience, according to Dewey, is immersion. We become immersed when we eat, skate, or even think. For example, the skater is completely immersed as she nails a 50–50 for the first time. Immersion is therefore a significant element of natural experience. Examining skaters more closely, we can see that they develop a sense of immersion in the tricks they land and the feats they achieve only when they feel a sense of order and stability. If the skater is uncertain about their basic ollie, it is hard to not only find stability, but also to be fully immersed. They may constantly notice their missteps or reflect on what exactly went wrong. This can show that immersion occurs when the trick is executed naturally, without much thought. So, immersion is characteristic of experience.

With this in mind, Dewey asks us to imagine a world that is constantly unstable or always changing, a world in which "stability and rest would have no being."[2] In contrast to this, he imagines a world that is completely perfect and without change. These ideal worlds are devoid of natural experience (as well as skaters), according to Dewey. To say that the natural world is always changing may be a complicated claim. We can clearly see that some things in the world stay constant. Skating, for example, has been a constant phenomenon for some time. However, particular elements of skating have naturally changed. Overall, the natural experience gives rise to the aesthetic experience as creative projects like skating emerge.

Lastly, experience exhibits episodes of order and disorder as products of our relation to the environment. We can imagine that the order of the world can become chaotic, one in which skaters can never land a trick or even successfully get onto their boards. The disorder of this world can resolve or dissolve. The skater finally lands a basic ollie she's been practicing. It is through this process that aesthetic experience begins to emerge. When we adapt to our environment, we naturally produce things we need. Even in the age of prehistory, early humans developed ceramic bowls, stone axes, and primitive clothing. But these things may have not had any artistry to them. They were produced in order to serve our natural needs, our needs for basic human survival. Yet, when we examine ancient ceramic bowls or clothing, we can clearly see that early humans were attempting to reproduce those properties of the environment. The bowl exhibits an orderly composition even though we may have discovered only half of it. The piece of clothing displays interactive patterns that we recognize as artistic. In the end, it is this pull of necessity that gives emergence to the aesthetic experience from the natural experience.

The Aesthetic Experience

From the basic properties of interaction, immersion, and order and disorder, natural experience thus culminates in aesthetic experience. Although we may not be aware of it, we are in fact having aesthetic experiences all the time. Skaters, for example, are having an aesthetic experience when they successfully land a difficult trick or when they are first starting out and land *any* trick. But how are these experiences different from natural experiences?

First, it's worth pointing out that every experience is a natural experience, but not every natural experience is an aesthetic experience. The difference arises from the new qualities associated with what Dewey calls *an* experience. According to Dewey, "Such an experience is a whole and carries with it its own individualizing quality and self-sufficiency. It is *an* experience."[3] So, as the natural experience has intrinsic qualities like immersion and interaction, the aesthetic experience has unique properties which make it distinctive. The distinct features of an aesthetic event are dynamics, accumulation, intensity, resistance, rhythm, momentum, direction, and fulfillment. With this in mind, we can construct a vivid explanation of how skaters may internalize *an* experience.

One property of the aesthetic experience is that it is intrinsically dynamic. An experience is dynamic "because it takes time to complete."[4] Skaters may experience a dynamic event when they successfully perform a trick as they take off from the half-pipe. In contrast, a skater may have an incomplete experience when they fail to land a trick, causing them to suffer an injury. These relations to the environment can directly impact whether we have a complete experience or not. The dynamics of *an* experience resemble a natural experience, but the qualitative differences matter. A natural experience may be dynamic, but it may also be unmemorable. According to Dewey, "Experience in this vital sense is defined by those situations and episodes that we spontaneously refer to as being 'real experiences'; those things which we say in recalling them, 'that *was* an experience.'"[5] All in all, the emergent property of dynamics demarcates an aesthetic experience from a natural one.

Next, consider the notion of accumulation. Imagine it's your first time trying to ride a skateboard. Note the use of "first" here. In order for an experience to become *an* experience, the attempts need accumulate over time. So, it may not turn out to be a successful first effort, but you look forward to a second try. Your second attempt goes a little better; you are able to skate five or six feet, but you lose control. By your third or fourth attempt, you feel at least a bit more comfortable. You can skate a greater distance. All of a sudden, you have *an* experience. You may not recognize it as *an* experience, but you realize that something internal has just happened, and you reflect on how accomplished you feel. In other words, the accumulation of each attempt creates a series of events that form a kind of internal narrative. Natural experience, on the other hand, may lack this narrative structure. We tend to think that (for instance) a bird building nests does not reflect on the conclusion of their attempts. As Dewey puts it, "If a conclusion is reacted, it is that of a movement of anticipation and cumulation, one that finally comes to completion."[6] It is our sense of reflection that allows us to have *an* experience. Considering this, it would be worth reflecting on some of the other qualities that a skater undergoes as she attempts to skate for the first time.

Consider the qualities of intensity and resistance. As we consider the experience of someone skating for the first time, we can imagine that such an event can be intense as the skater encounters resistance. In fact, remembering Tony Hawk landing the first 900 (a trick which seemed essentially impossible at the time), we can also infer that the trick and the experience carried intensity and resistance. Whether it is your first or last trick, the intensity and resistance of an experience tend to be packed with emotional content. Again, as Dewey puts it, "Nevertheless, the experience itself has a satisfying emotional quality because it possesses internal integration and fulfillment reached through ordered and organized movement."[7] The resistance of *an* experience comes from the accumulated attempts that our skater has just underwent. While our skater is undergoing *an* experience, the last qualities to consider are rhythm, momentum, direction, and fulfillment.

The property of rhythm builds into the notion of momentum, direction, and fulfillment. Although our skater struggled at first, the rhythm of her experience built momentum and direction. The first attempt is the first beat, while the second attempt is the second beat and so on. Dewey states, "In an experience, flow is from something to something. As one part leads into another and as one part carries on what went before, each gains distinctness itself."[8] If our skater gave up after her first attempt, the aesthetic experience may not have happened. However, since she continued to try, the momentum and direction of the experience led her to feel fulfilled. Each phase or attempt is integral to the development of an experience. Natural experience, on the other hand, does not account for the summation of each phase. There seems to be no direction and momentum in natural experience. If there is no sense of rhythm in the experience, then it is difficult to say that the person is going to find fulfillment. The aesthetic experience is fulfilling because we recognize that our efforts can culminate into long-lasting memory. Without our capacity to reflect, the properties of *an* experience may have not been identified or felt.

Skateboarding History

The history of skateboarding can serve as a helpful illustration of how a natural experience becomes an aesthetic experience. Again, skateboarding emerges in the 1950s as surfers attempt to recreate the experience of riding a wave on land. So, it seems as if skateboarding owes its development (at least in part) to surfing. But of course, this naturally raises the question, how is it that *surfing* emerged (within the natural environment)? According to former professional surfer and writer Matt Warshaw, "Modern surfing was born in Hawaii, but for any ancestral society living on a temperate coastline, riding waves would likely have been a natural, perhaps intuitive act."[9] There is no general consensus as to when ancient surfing developed, but we can reasonably speculate (or at least imagine) the natural development in what follows.

Suppose a group of people are living along the coast where they depend on the fish at sea. The fishermen produce boards that allow them to coast along the beach so they can come close to the fish for an easy catch. A good example of what those early boarders looked like is provided by Warshaw. "Fishermen along the coast of what is now Peru were likely riding waves more than three thousand years ago using a woven-reed vessel called the *caballito*, or 'little horse.'"[10] The natural experience of ancient fishermen consisted of riding waves and catching fish along the coast. They may not have had *an* experience, but they may have laid the groundwork for surfing to develop. However, it is easy to imagine that after a hard day's work, fishermen could float freely back to the shore with a sense of fulfillment. Perhaps it was in these leisurely moments that *an* experience finally evolved.

As surfing established itself as a creative activity over the centuries, there came a time when California surfers got inventive. Somewhere around the 1950s "California surfers attached roller skate wheels to wooden planks to 'surf' the sidewalk when there were no waves."[11] We can see that early skaters were seeking *an* experience when surfing was not possible.

A now famous team of skaters known as the Z-Boys helped transform skating during this period. They were primarily a set of surfers, but with the mass production of skateboards throughout the 1960s, they remained in touch with the skateboarding scene. After the waves died down, the Z-Boys brought their surfing style to skating, eventually solidifying skating as an authentic and creative pursuit.

Dewey's emphasis on naturalism again provides an account of how *an* experience develops from our natural engagement with the world: "the outline of the common pattern is set by the fact that every experience is the result of interaction between a live creature and some aspect of the world in which he lives."[12] In our case, the ancient fisherman is the live creature, and the waves he rides in order to catch fish are the aspects of the world where he survives. Eventually, the ancient fishermen, like early skaters, may have had *an* experience which changes their whole orientation. They may seek to surf independently of fishing or recreate riding waves on land. What is significant is that the aesthetic experience is an internal quality that is not necessarily attached to creative work. In other words, it is not the creative work that has an aesthetic experience; it is you. So, we might say that the value of art is not in the artwork, but in the experience of it. Dewey opposes the view of art as something separate from everyday experience. Again, he wants to ground creativity in natural process, not something beyond nature. Through this brief history of surfing and skateboarding, we can see how our natural dealings with the environment lead to the enjoyment of aesthetic experiences.

Skateboarding and Aesthetics

With all of this in mind, with skateboarding being (or giving rise to) aesthetic experience, there is an argument to be made that skateboarding is a creative art according to Dewey's criteria. Although the natural and aesthetic experiences are internally realizable, according to Dewey there are "objective conditions" which fulfill aesthetic form. Those are conditions which help us differentiate between objects that are artistic and those that are not: "But where there is no administration of objective conditions, no shaping of materials in the interest of embodying the excitement, there is no expression."[13] Expression, therefore, is a feature that any object of art must conditionally meet. So, it is worth considering whether or to what degree skating resembles other forms of art. Consider the case of dance.

The prevailing common sense is, of course, that dance is an art. After all, it is an activity which spans human history, with each culture developing its own sense of style and worth. The same cannot be said of skateboarding. It may be for this reason (at least in part) that the question "Is skateboarding an art?" is so pressing. In fact, for a variety of reasons, we might be more inclined to consider skateboarding a sport.[14] That skateboarding is a sport seems to be accepted by the culture at large, but the focus of this argument is to justify why skateboarding is an art (such as dance). And, for what it's worth, there is no *prima facie* reason why something cannot be both a sport *as well as* a form of art. So, we can consider that the dancer seeks expression; she wants to understand the relation of the moving body parts in order to embody aesthetic form. By analogy, it seems that we can place the skater in a similar position.

The aesthetic form of skating has to do with the execution of tricks. Though two skaters may perform the same trick, the expression of it is unique to the style of the skater. Similarly, dancers perform the same dance, yet they realize it in their own way. As dancers have a repertoire of moves at their disposal, so too do skaters. A skater learns tricks as a dancer learns moves. So, the difference between the two is simply the medium in which the aesthetic form is realized. The medium for the skater is the board, whereas the medium of the dancer is the body. That said, one may argue that skaters use their bodies just as much as dancers. Regardless, it cannot be denied that the maneuvers of the skateboard help to draw in swathes of spectators and the admiration of other skaters. Skateboarding is an art because it gives rise to aesthetic experience, it represents aesthetic form, and it provides a medium for expression.

All things considered, Dewey's philosophy of art demonstrates how it is that art emerges from natural processes. Moreover, Dewey illustrates the different internal experiences we may have. As natural creatures of an environment, we have aesthetic experiences that come from the objects that symbolize aesthetic form. From the ancient fishermen who found it pleasurable to surf back to shore, to the surfers of California who first began skateboarding, the objects of aesthetic form are conceived by creatures like us. In the end, Dewey provides a philosophy which allows us to justify emerging arts, skateboarding being an important one of them.

NOTES

1. Dewey, John. 1934. *Art as Experience*. Perigee Books, 13.
2. *Ibid.*, 17.
3. *Ibid.*, 35.
4. *Ibid.*, 55.
5. *Ibid.*, 36.
6. *Ibid.*, 38.
7. *Ibid.*
8. *Ibid.*, 36.
9. Warshaw, Matt. 2017. *A Brief History of Surfing*. Chronicle Books, 18.
10. *Ibid.*
11. Snyder, J. Gregory. 2017. *Skateboarding LA: Inside Professional Street Skateboarding*. New York University Press, 35.
12. Dewey, 43.
13. *Ibid.*, 62.
14. See the first essay of this volume, "Skateboarding Is (in a Sense) a Sport."

Skateboarding Judgments
Joshua Heter

In *Philosophy and Human Movement,* David Best distinguishes two types of sports: purposive sports and aesthetic sports. A purposive sport is one in which "the purpose can be specified independently of the means of achieving [that purpose] as long as [those means conform] to the limits set by the rules or norms" of the sport in question.[1] That is, in a purposive sport, there is a specific, well-defined goal participants attempt to achieve, and there is a set of rules which marks the limits by which those participants may attempt to achieve that goal. But, beyond those factors, the manner or fashion in which the goal is achieved is irrelevant to the ultimate outcome of the contest (i.e., who wins and who loses). In other words, in purposive sports, you don't get any points for style.

Baseball is a purposive sport (as are most team sports), the purpose of which is to circle the bases and arrive safely at home. Beyond the rules which regulate the bounds in which a runner does this, whether he does in fact arrive safely at home is what matters, not whether he does so artfully or inartfully. If a runner successfully traverses the distance from third base to home by crab-walking, he is neither penalized nor rewarded for doing so.

However, aesthetic sports are a different matter. An aesthetic (sometimes called a "judged")[2] sport is one in which its "aim cannot be specified in isolation from the manner of achieving it."[3] So, in contrast to purposive sports, it is precisely the ways in which athletic performances are carried out that are the deciding factors in who wins and who loses. Olympic diving is an aesthetic sport. Though the purpose of Olympic diving is, of course, to dive, it is hardly noteworthy that any particular diver can successfully make it into the water from the dive platform. Rather, it is the grace, precision, and level of difficulty with which the diver achieves this that ultimately determines who ends up atop the medal stand.

Skateboarding Aesthetics

With rare exception, any particular athletic competition can be classified as either a purposive sport or an aesthetic sport.[4] Most (if not all) skateboarding competitions can be classified in this way. Some skateboarding competitions are purposive sports such as downhill or pump track races. The skateboarder who crosses the finish line first is the winner regardless of the grace, style, or manner of his skating, provided he does not break any of the rules or regulations of the race.

A game of SKATE (modeled after the basketball game HORSE)—in which competing skaters attempt to replicate each other's tricks and earn a letter of the word "skate" for each failed attempt until the eventual loser's word is complete—may also be considered a purposive sport. Though participants perform tricks (which perhaps calls to mind aesthetic matters such as performing well or gracefully), so long as a skater meets the sufficient or bare minimum conditions for completing a trick, he successfully avoids earning a letter, or he makes it such that his opponent must match his trick in order to avoid the same fate. In a game of SKATE, there is no advantage in performing the same trick as your opponent in a more artful manner, again, so long as the minimum conditions of the trick in question are met.

However, a great deal, perhaps a majority of skateboarding competitions, are aesthetic sports. For instance, the X Games street competition "features a street-inspired course that consists of stair sets, banks, manual pads, ledges, rails and quarterpipes" in which skaters perform a variety of trick, grind, and slide filled timed runs (at least partially analogous to figure skating programs) in which judges evaluate "the difficulty, execution, and originality of their tricks."[5] And, in this, as well as a number of similar skateboarding competitions, it is not that there is some goal competitors attempt to achieve that is irrelevant to the manner in which they achieve it. Rather, it is precisely the way in which the skaters perform—in regard to the difficulty, execution, and originality of their performance—which determines the victor.

Importantly, all such aesthetic competitions require a set of judges who are tasked with making a determination on the quality of each skater's performance as it relates to the specific, agreed-upon metrics. And their job is arguably quite different than that of an umpire in a baseball game or a referee in a pump track race whose jobs are primarily to ensure that participants do not break the rules of their given competitions and to give an official accounting of who has completed the purposive task in question (e.g., arriving at home safely or crossing the finish line). Beyond these concerns, and unlike their counterparts in aesthetic sports, officials in purposive sports are rightly indifferent to the manner in which participants achieve the stated ends of their competitions.

With this in mind, it may be natural to think that the outcomes of purposive sports are an "objective" matter, while the outcomes of aesthetic sports are merely "subjective." In the official rules for the street skating competition at the X Games, judges are instructed to "immediately assign a value between 1 to 100 to [a] run" based on five judging criteria: aggressive execution of maneuvers, degree of difficulty, variety of maneuvers, continuity of run, and originality and style.[6] But this of course raises the question, on what basis are judges to assign their scores if not their subjective impression or opinion? As such, perhaps another way to express the sentiment behind this question would be to say that while determining the winner of a purposive sport (e.g., a race) is a matter of *fact*, determining the winner of an aesthetic sport (e.g., a street skating event) is a matter of mere *opinion*.

Nevertheless, there is an argument to be made that this is not so. Or at least, there is a case to be made that there is an important way in which the outcome of aesthetic sports is not *merely* a "subjective" matter and that determining the winner of aesthetic sports is not a matter of mere opinion. As we will see, the case is built upon the idea that what it is for an issue to be an objective matter depends upon whether or not there are underlying truths about or an objective reality which constitutes the subject matter that judging officials attempt to gauge and upon which they award credit. And this is precisely the type of activity judges of aesthetic sports (such as street events in skateboarding) are able to engage in because there *is* such an objective reality that undergirds the skating competitions in question and constitutes the criteria upon which their winners are determined.

Of course, this issue is not *unique* to skating as it is perhaps just as much of a problem for any aesthetic sport, but it is an issue which is *important* to skating as so many skateboarding competitions are aesthetic in nature. So, skaters would be well advised to think carefully about it. Could it really be that the skating community is awarding the lion's share of its prizes (and all of the spoils that come with them) for purely subjective reasons? Is the issue of who should win and who should lose a matter of mere opinion?

Truth in Skating

Is deciding the winner of aesthetic skateboarding competitions (such as the street skating competition at the X Games) an objective or a purely *subjective* matter? Of course, answering this question depends upon what it is for an issue to be an objective (as opposed to a subjective) matter generally.

To say that a matter is objective is to say that there is an underlying truth or reality about the matter which does not depend upon any conscious awareness of it.[7] That is, a matter is objective if there is a *way that things are* about it irrespective of whether it is known, perceived, or even thought about. And when any person makes judgments *about* the matter, it is straightforwardly possible for those judgments to be wrong or incorrect when they do not accurately map onto the objective truth or underlying reality of the matter.

Most would agree that there are a host of issues in science that are objective matters. Whether or not there is gold on Mars is an objective matter because there is an underlying truth or reality about the matter whether it is ever known, perceived, or thought of. And if one concludes or sincerely believes that there *is* gold on Mars, but (as it turns out) there is not even a single atom of gold on or in Mars, then that person has an objectively false belief whether or not they know it (indeed, whether or not *anyone* knows it).

In contrast to this, whether or not mint chocolate chip is the tastiest ice cream is not an objective matter. It is a purely subjective matter because there is no underlying truth or objective reality about what the tastiest ice cream is independent of any conscious awareness of it. In fact, when one claims something like "Mint chocolate chip is the tastiest ice cream" what is most often meant is simply that the speaker *prefers it* the most. But of course, this is just the point, that when it comes to the matter of the tastiest ice cream, there is no reality about the issue independent of any conscious awareness of it. And unlike the example of the alleged gold on Mars, it is difficult to see how one could be incorrect about what the tastiest ice cream is, because there is no underlying reality or objective truth about what the tastiest ice cream is. For any individual ice cream taster, there is only what the tastiest ice cream is *for them*.

How can all of this help us answer the question of whether or not the outcomes of aesthetic skateboarding competitions are an objective matter? Recall the criteria used to judge the X Games street competition: aggressive execution of maneuvers, degree of difficulty, variety of maneuvers, continuity of run, and originality and style. The point is this: it is at least arguable that there is an underlying truth or objective reality about each criterion (or at least a number of them) which judges attempt to accurately assess and about which they can be incorrect. And, if this is the case, then the matter of who should win the competition is not a purely subjective matter; it is not a matter of mere opinion.

The Reality of the Criteria

Consider the second judged criterion for the X Games street competition: degree of difficulty. There is an objective truth about which tricks

66　II. Skating Values

are more or less difficult or that the degree of difficulty for any particular trick (or a set of tricks constituting a timed run) is a matter of fact. If a skateboarding run is constituted of nothing but ollies and manuals (tricks which even beginners can master) and is measured against a run filled with laser flips and backside tailslides (tricks which even proficient skaters might struggle with), then the X Games judge who awards more points on the criterion of difficulty for the former run than the latter run has made a mistake because it is objectively true that the latter run is more difficult than the former. This is because there is a reality (independent of any conscious awareness of it) about which tricks skateboarders struggle with and about which skateboarders master more easily.

If there *is* such an underlying reality about the level of difficulty of a skateboarding (trick, or more importantly) run, then what judges are doing when they award their score (from 1 to 100) is applying their expertise in an attempt to accurately gauge the objective truth about the underlying reality of the difficulty of the run in question. And to the degree to which an assigned score maps onto the reality of the actual, objective difficulty, the judge's score is correct or accurate.

Of course, it might here be objected that what is difficult for one skater may be easy for another. For instance, one skater could have the disposition or physical attributes which make landing tre flips easy despite the fact that his competitor struggles with them a great deal. And that same skater who has mastered tre flips may struggle with some aspect of his rail tricks, though his competitor has perfected all manner of grinds and rail slides with little to no effort. Thus, so the objection goes, there *is* no objective truth or reality about skating difficulty for judges to accurately or inaccurately assess. Rather, judges must give their subjective impression of what might seem most difficult *for them*. However, the conclusion of the argument here simply does not follow from its premises.

While it's true that there is a substantial amount of variation in what individual skaters find particularly difficult, the judged criterion of difficulty can be thought of as the degree of difficulty for skaters *generally*. What matters for the purpose of judging a skateboarding competition is the difficulty of tricks *on average* for the sum total of all skaters. The fact that an individual skater may find a particular trick easy (that almost all others struggle with) is largely irrelevant.

It is not difficult then for a seasoned judge to have a reasonable grasp of the proper ordering of tricks (based on their level of difficulty) and to award a score to a timed run on the difficulty criterion. Nevertheless, the relevant point here is that there is at least one important aspect of the criteria used to determine the winner of an aesthetic (skating) sport which is grounded in an objective reality. As such, there is at least one important way in which establishing the winner of such a competition is not a purely subjective matter or a matter of mere opinion.

In a similar vein, consider also the third judged criterion for the X Games street competition: variety of maneuvers. As is the case for the difficulty criterion, there is an argument to be made that the degree of variety of maneuvers in a skateboarding run is an objective matter; it is not a matter of mere opinion. This is because there is an underlying reality (independent of any conscious awareness of it) that some skateboarding maneuvers are more alike than others. An ollie kickflip is arguably a different trick than a kickback or a fingerflip. But it is *inarguable* that these tricks are more similar to one another (as they each primarily involve flipping the board 360° along its axis) than they are to a host of other tricks such as a backside tailslide (in which a skater ollies along a ledge or rail and slides his back tail along it).

Parsing the similarities and differences between a set of tricks is of little difference than determining the set of similarities and differences between the members of *any* set of things. Two skateboarding tricks are similar to the degree they share a set of properties (e.g., flipping the board 360° along its axis). Two skateboarding tricks are different the degree to which they have different properties (e.g., where one involves a grind and the other does not). Thus, a timed run should score high on the variety criterion only insofar as the sum total of tricks which constitute it are made up of a variety of different properties. And, for any timed run, there is an objective truth or underlying reality about the number of properties the tricks which constitute it share. This objective reality is what judges attempt to assess when they award a score on the variety of maneuvers criterion. The degree to which their score accurately maps onto that objective reality, their score is correct. As such, along with the difficulty criterion, we can now see that there are at least *two* important ways in which establishing the winner of an aesthetic skateboarding competition is not purely subjective; it is not a matter of *mere* opinion.

Judging Opinions

At least two of the five criteria judges use to determine the winner of the X Games street competition are grounded in an objective reality: level of difficulty and variety of maneuvers. I would argue that a similar case could be made for the remaining judged criteria: aggressive execution of maneuvers, continuity of run, and *even* originality and style. The degree to which maneuvers in a timed run are executed aggressively, to which a run is performed with a unifying continuity, and to which a run is original and even stylistic are all (again, arguably) objective matters which judges attempt to accurately assess with their awarded scores.

However, it would be beneficial here to answer a potentially obvious objection to the project as a whole. Again, the role of judges in aesthetic sports is quite different than the role of officials in purposive sports. The official's role in (for instance) a pump track race is to monitor the participants for rule violations and to give an official accounting of the order in which participants have completed the competition's purposive task (i.e., crossing the finish line). In contrast, the role of a judge in an aesthetic sport is—to put it simply—*to judge*. Whether or not there is an objective truth or an underlying reality about some or all aspects of the judging criteria, judges are nevertheless to give their personal, subjective assessment of a performance as it relates to those criteria. And, so the argument goes, this fundamental, constitutive aspect of aesthetic sports makes the task of determining their winners *nothing but* a matter of mere opinion.

While it is true that—in one important sense—judges of aesthetic competitions are being asked to give their opinion, it does not follow that the issue of determining the winner in such sports is a matter of *mere* opinion or that it is purely a subjective matter. This is because there are two important senses or ways in which something can be dependent upon a judge's subjective assessment. Put differently, there are two ways in which an issue can be considered to be a "matter of opinion."

In certain cases, to label something a "matter of opinion" is to say that there is no (objective) truth about the matter. This is what is meant when we say that the issue of the tastiest ice cream is a matter of opinion. There *is* no such thing as the tastiest ice cream. That is to say, there is no underlying reality about what the tastiest ice cream is independent of any conscious awareness of it. There is only what the tastiest ice cream is *for me* (or *for an individual*). We might say that for an issue to be a matter of opinion in the sense that there is no underlying objective truth or reality about the matter is to say that it is a matter of *subjective* opinion or a matter of *mere* opinion.

In contrast, in other cases, to label something as a "matter of opinion" is not to say that there is no objective truth about the matter but to say that there *is* an objective truth about the matter but that the truth of the matter is in dispute. Suppose two jurors are discussing the details of an ongoing murder trial. Many details of the case are relatively straightforward (e.g., that a murder did occur and how the murder took place), but the guilt or innocence of the defendant is still in question. If one juror claims "The defendant is guilty" or "I think the defendant is guilty," his fellow juror may respond "Well, that's your opinion" or "That's a matter of opinion." But of course, the most natural understanding of what is meant here is not that there is no (objective) truth about the guilt or innocence of the defendant. Either the defendant is the perpetrator of the crime, or he is not. Rather, what is meant is that the defendant's guilt or innocence is (at least at present) a matter of dispute or that in the context of the conversation it is publicly undecided whether or not the defendant is guilty. We might say that for an issue to be a matter of opinion in this second sense in which the objective truth about a matter is simply in dispute is to say that the issue is a matter of *disputed* opinion.

With this in mind, while it is again true that judges in aesthetic skateboarding competitions (as well judges in aesthetic sports generally) are—in *some sense*—asked to give their opinion, impression, or evaluation of an athletic performance, if there is an objective truth or underlying reality about the judging criteria (as it has here been argued), then the only sense in which the issue of determining the winner is a "matter of opinion" is that it is a matter of *disputed* opinion. It is not a matter of *subjective* or *mere* opinion.

It's worth pointing out that officials in purposive sports are, on occasion, asked to make rulings on matters of disputed opinion as well. Often referred to as "judgment calls," such issues appear with more regularity than we might appreciate. In American football, a pass interference penalty occurs when "any act by a player more than one yard beyond the line of scrimmage significantly hinders an eligible player's opportunity to catch the ball." Despite this, players are allowed to make "incidental contact by an opponent's hands, arms, or body when both players are competing for the ball or neither player is looking for the ball."[8] However, the concept of contact that is "incidental" is inherently vague. It is not and perhaps cannot be defined with any decisive precision. That said (it is at least arguable that), the vagueness of the concept of "incidental contact" does not change the underlying, objective reality that some contact between players is incidental and some is not.[9] Nevertheless, referees are required to occasionally deliver their opinion on whether or not some contact in particular is merely incidental and that no pass interference penalty should be called.

In the same way, there are concepts relevant to officiating baseball (e.g., the "deviation" from a runner's path),[10] hockey (e.g., a player's "premature" substitution),[11] as well as concepts important to officiating a host of other sports that are inherently vague and require officials to deliver their disputed (or disputable) opinions. However, I take it that the existence of such "judgment calls" does not make deciding the outcomes of these purposive contests purely subjective or matters of mere opinion.

Despite the fact that there is an objective truth or underlying reality about the criteria used to judge street skating competitions, that underlying reality is complicated. It is difficult to determine in any sort of precise, systematic way that one set of tricks is more difficult or contains more variety than another (though it does not follow from this fact that there are no objective truths about which sets are more difficult or contain more variety). Because of the complex nature of the issue, competitions such as those in the X Games rely on the expertise of judges to—as best they can—evaluate runs on these and similar criteria to determine a winner. The fact that, in so doing, judges express an opinion does not mean that the issue is a matter of *mere* opinion or that determining the winner of aesthetic skating competitions is a purely subjective matter.[12]

Notes

1. Best, David. 1978. *Philosophy and Human Movement*. Allen and Unwin.
2. Hurka, Thomas. 2015. "On Judged Sports." *Journal of Philosophy of Sport*, Vol. 42, No. 3, 317–325. Taylor & Francis.
3. Best.
4. There are a small number of sports which have both purposive and aesthetic elements. For instance, winter ski jumping competitions are judged by a combination of the distance jumped (which is a purposive matter) as well as the style of the jump (which is an aesthetic matter).
5. X Games. 2023. https://www.xgames.com/events/x-games-japan-2023/competitions/mens-skateboard-street-final.
6. X Games. 2023. https://xgamessportsandcomp.wordpress.com/rules-documents/skateboard-rules-final/.
7. Mulder, Dwayne H. 2023. "Objectivity." *The Internet Encyclopedia of Philosophy*.
8. National Football League. 2023. "Pass Interference." *Official Playing Rules of the National Football League*.
9. Of course, it could be argued that the issue of whether contact is "incidental" is a matter of *mere* opinion and not *disputed* opinion. However, even if this is the case, it would nevertheless be difficult to argue from the presence of mere opinion in regard to pass interference to the conclusion that deciding the winner of the game as a whole is a matter of mere opinion. As such, even *if* there are matters of mere opinion which play a role in elements of determining the winner of an aesthetic skateboarding competition, we might still deny the conclusion that determining the winner as a whole is a matter of mere opinion.
10. Major League Baseball. 2021. "6.01 Interference, Obstruction, and Catcher Collisions." *Official Baseball Rules*.
11. National Hockey League. 2022. "Rule 74—Too Many Men on the Ice." *National Hockey League Official Rules 2022*.
12. Thank you to my students at Jefferson College for giving me helpful feedback on this project.

III

Ancient Wisdom on Four Wheels

De on Display

CASEY RENTMEESTER

> "The beauty of skating is that everybody has a unique set of variables that they can put in place and express their individual identity."
>
> —Rodney Mullen

As one of the greatest skateboarders of all time, Tony Hawk has become a cultural staple whose influence has grown well beyond skateboarding. And yet, in his youth, Hawk identified very much as an outsider, a narrative which fits countless other skaters, including another legend of the sport, Rodney Mullen. A significant reason for this may be in part that, as Mullen himself points out, skateboarding is "the ultimate loner activity. There [are] no rules, no coaches, no teammates—you [skate] when and how you want to."[1] This seems to imply that the loner or outsider status which many skaters seem to have isn't merely some sort of cultural accident. There may be something inherent in (or intimately connected to) skating that fosters this sort of go-it-alone, independent standing.

If this is correct, then a philosophy that properly captures skateboarding culture needs to embrace the role of the outsider and the commitment to creating one's own style of self-expression, a commitment that can, in the cases of Hawk and Mullen, lead to greatness. And a view which captures each of these elements particularly well—and that skaters would be wise to embrace—is Zhuangzi's version of Daoism.[2]

Daoism is one of the oldest philosophies of ancient China, and Zhuangzi's book—titled simply the *Zhuangzi*—stands alongside Laozi's more famous *Daodejing* (the most translated work in the world next to the Bible), as a canonical text of this philosophical movement. Through various figures within the *Zhuangzi*, we find a celebration of the outsider and an emphasis on achieving one's own unique potential—one's *de* (德)—through creative expression. The *zhen ren* (真人) in Zhuangzi's philosophy—the true person—is one who, by marching to the beat of one's own drum while following the nature of things, that is, the *dao* (道), attains a mastery of a craft so exquisite that it can hardly be believed by others. As we'll see, the grace and ease with which skating legends such as Hawk and Mullen demonstrate as they casually rip through the air and masterfully complete a trick are examples of *de* on display.

Catching Cicadas, Wading in Waterfalls, and Popping Ollies

The first Daoist lesson the skateboarder should embrace is that the path to true greatness lies in following nature, rather than submitting to socially constructed versions of success. One of the common narratives in the *Zhuangzi* is the contrast between the overly cultured and sometimes pompous Confucius (a.k.a. Kongzi) and the comical characters he comes across in the forests who have eschewed societal conventions in order to pursue a more natural course. In one such story, Kongzi is traveling through a forest with his disciples where they come across a hunchbacked hermit who is catching cicadas with such ease that it astounds them. Kongzi asks the hunchback how he has attained such skill, to which the hermit replies: "Never mind how vast Heaven or Earth are, or the vast numbers of the multitudes of living beings, I concentrate my knowledge on catching cicadas."[3] In other words, "who really cares about anything else?—I've focused my energy on perfecting this craft, and that's good enough for me."

In another passage, Kongzi and his crew come across a man who jumps headlong into a waterfall thirty fathoms high whose rapids race "so fast that neither fish nor any other creature can swim in it."[4] Kongzi assumes that the man is committing suicide, so he directs his disciples to surround the bank so they can pull out the body. To their amazement, the man pops out of the river and continues to walk nonchalantly along the bank, singing a song while the water drips casually off his body. Kongzi approaches him, asking how he could possibly even attempt such a feat, to which the man replies quite simply that he follows the *dao* of the water without concern, thereby achieving his nature as a gifted swimmer.

The subtitle of Rodney Mullen's 2004 book, *How to Skateboard and Not Kill Yourself,* could easily be adapted to capture the philosophy of this swimmer. In it, Mullen reflects on how he attained such a graceful mastery of street skating through his countless hours of practice in rural Florida during his childhood. He recounts his marathon skating sessions with farm animals as his only company, practicing with his eyes closed and focusing all the concentration he could muster in order to master a trick.[5] Despite (or perhaps because of) this dedication, his father mercilessly implored him to give up skateboarding and do something "useful" with his life, even when he was proving himself to be a world champion skater. Mullen was undeterred, regardless of his otherwise noted respect for the naysayers.

In his 2014 TED Talk "Pop an Ollie and Innovate!" Mullen describes the child-like joy he experiences when skating and the freedom embodied therein that led to the creation of the ollie, the primo slide, the darkslide, and perhaps the most difficult trick he invented and perfected, the gazelle flip, which requires the skater to rotate the board one and a half times, kickflip, and complete a full backside rotation. The overarching theme of the talk is how "context shapes content," that is, how "the environment changes the nature of your tricks."[6] Like Zhuangzi, Mullen views perfecting one's potential as inherently linked to following *dao*, that is, the way of nature. Just as the cicada catcher follows the way of the cicada to catch them and the swimmer goes with the natural flow of the currents, he argues that excellence in skating entails a nuanced and deferential attunement with one's environment.

The word for one's unique potential in Daoism is *de*, which is commonly translated as "virtue," "power," or "efficacy." Zhuangzi tells us to "walk with *de* and travel with the *dao*, and you will reach the perfect end."[7] For Zhuangzi, we've all become a bit too unnatural due to our highly sophisticated civilization. Whereas the consummate Confucian is the cultured person who has read all the proper books and follows all the societal conventions—the rituals (*li* 禮)—to a T, the accomplished Daoist is one who follows their own path to perfection without worrying about what society may think. If the caricatured Confucian is the highly cultured, tuxedo-donning socialite on his way to the opera having finished his caviar, the Daoist is the punk teenager skating in the street on an empty stomach in his baggy pants rocking a Ramones shirt.

The term for one's unique nature in Daoism is *ziran* (自然), which literally means "self-so," that is, what you are naturally. And, as Zhuangzi makes clear, everyone's *ziran* is utterly unique. The person who achieves one's *de* does so by tapping into their *ziran*, thus achieving the highest end as a human being for Daoists, namely, the status of being a *zhen ren*, that is, a true person. This true nature can be perfected by masterfully catching cicadas, wading in waterfalls, or popping ollies, depending on the context and depending on the person, both of which mutually infuse each other. Regardless, proper growth as a human being means perfecting one's *ziran* by following the *dao* in order to achieve *de*.

The Creative Joy of Freedom

In addition to embracing nature and rejecting societal convention, a second Daoist lesson the skateboarder would be wise to take on is that to achieve a level of expertise that will allow one to maximize their creative freedom, one must dedicate themselves to their craft through regular, hard work (i.e., practice).

Just as Mullen walks through the creative joy that accompanies actualizing one's *de* in skating, Tony Hawk describes skating as a matter of joyfully achieving one's own potential. In reflecting upon the landing of his now famous 900 at the 1999 Summer X games, the two and a half revolution aerial spin in which he rotated 900 degrees and stuck the landing, thereby catapulting him to international fame, he states: "Skating is not about winning[;] it's about skating the best you can…. It's about pulling a trick after years of not being able to…. My landing the 9 wasn't equivalent to Jordan making a last-minute shot and crushing the other team. It was one skater landing a trick, and other skaters appreciating it."[8]

While there is an element of competition involved in skateboarding culture, the point for most isn't really to out-trick the other skater but rather to embrace one's own creative freedom and exhibit the graceful mastery—in Daoist terms, the *wuwei* (無爲)—that comes from years of practice. Such graceful mastery in skating requires a commitment to concentration and a simultaneous commitment to not caring what other people think, since, as Mullen says, "to get good, you have to throw your board around and fall"[9] and be okay going to school the next day with a jacked-up face which sometimes results from such falls.

Like Mullen, Hawk reflects on the work that went into his journey of becoming a household name, as well as how much he had to learn to not care about what the others thought of him: "By the time I was obsessed with skateboarding, it was a geeky fad that only weirdos and nerds continued to do…. I was the only skater in my school. I didn't look like anybody else."[10] Hawk describes how he'd race down to his local skate park as soon as the school bell rang and practice until the park closed day after day, trying to perfect a trick, only to challenge himself even further by perfecting an even harder one.[11]

Eventually, all the hard work put in by Hawk and Mullen led them to get so proficient that they could land tricks so gracefully that it comes off as if their performances are simply natural and spontaneous or even effortless. Daoists refer to such masterful grace as *wuwei*, which we can understand as effortless action that displays a mastery. Zhuangzi explains how *wuwei* is formed through a famous passage in which he invokes the analogy of a fish trap to explain what it means to engage in meaningful philosophical dialogue with another:

A fish trap is used to catch fish, but once the fish have been taken, the trap is forgotten.... Words are used to express concepts, but once you have grasped the concepts the words are forgotten. I would like to find someone who has forgotten the words so I could debate with such a person!¹²

Zhuangzi is attempting to describe how once one has mastered something, the tools the person used to master it are no longer necessary. Just as the fish trap is no longer needed once the fish is caught, there is no need to reflect intentionally and explicitly upon the meaning of words to engage in a meaningful dialogue with someone. Similarly, Mullen and Hawk have formed such a mastery of skateboarding that they can perform tricks in a seemingly effortless fashion such that they don't have to reflect explicitly on how to contort one's body to accomplish the trick, even if they did have to engage in such reflection before they perfected it. Put simply for novice skaters: getting good requires lots of practice.

Literally hundreds of hours are needed to achieve *wuwei* in a sport as complex as skating. Hawk, for instance, relays that he's done roughly 10,000 McTwists in his career, the inverted 540° backside spin coupled with a mute grab that takes skaters sometimes years to even attempt.¹³ This level of expertise—in which the skilled action relies upon non-reflective nonaction since it has been performed so many times—is an embodiment of *wuwei* (*wu* means "not" and *wei* means "action").

When one has reached the point of *wuwei*, one can engage in spontaneous freestyle skating that is akin to jazz improvisation. The Daoists refer to this as *xiao yao you* (逍遥游), which can be loosely translated as "carefree roaming" or "free and easy rambling." We can think of this as a sort of "trained spontaneity" that comes about when one has acquired an effortless competence in something. When skaters have formed a mastery of the craft to the point of *wuwei*, they can engage in *xiao yao you* and experiment, potentially inventing new tricks, thereby embracing their creative freedom. Mullen describes how he engages in something akin to *xiao yao you* when he skates alone in the middle of the night, thereby allowing him to enact his creativity. While it might seem odd that one of the greatest skaters in the world prefers to skate alone at 2 a.m., he explains his preference for skating solo as opposed to competitions as follows: "Everyone expects me to do certain things [in competitions]. It puts a ceiling on your progress. You're blocked by your pride."¹⁴ Whereas he found himself skating conservatively in competitions to ensure that he would win, his solo night skating sessions allow him "to crack open the barriers that people consider impossible, undoable [and] crack open a new skill set that will take you further."¹⁵ This commitment to creativity makes Mullen's skating a beautiful form of art. For Mullen, night skating gives him the opportunity to engage in *xiao yao you* and embrace total creativity, thereby displaying his unique way of flourishing as a skater and as a person—identities that he himself would never separate. This is a perfect example of *de* on display.

(Kick)flipping with the Flow

A third and final element of Daoist wisdom is one that the skater can enthusiastically endorse: skating (and similar enough pursuits) may lead to a better life. The way Mullen and Hawk describe how they feel when they are skating is very much aligned with Daoist conceptions of getting into flow. Perhaps the most famous story from the *Zhuangzi* that captures this is that of Cook Ding, who, when asked about how he became so skillful in the kitchen after doing it for several decades, replies:

> Now I practice with my mind, not with my eyes.... I see the natural lines and my knife slides through the great hollows, follows the great cavities, using that which is already there to my advantage.... An ordinary cook has to change his knife every month, because he hacks. Now this knife of mine I have been using for nineteen years, and it has cut thousands of oxen. However, its blade is as sharp as if it had just been sharpened.... When I come to a difficult part and can see that it will be difficult, I take care and pay due regard. I look carefully and I move with caution.

Zhuangzi describes Cook Ding's butchering as if he were engaging in a beautiful intuitive dance, as every movement is done with attentive grace and efficiency, a description that could accurately be used to describe a successful skateboarding run by Mullen or Hawk. The two features needed for one to acquire such a gifted mastery like that of Cook Ding are a high level of concentration as to what is needed, given the nuanced complexity of the situation and the ability to follow the natural curvature of the oxen he butchers, thereby setting himself up for success. Through time and attentive practice, Cook Ding is able to get into a flow state of *wuwei* in practicing his craft, and heighten his attention when coming across especially difficult cuts, leading to beautiful results.

Hawk's commentary on his own phenomenology of his early days of skating in the recent documentary *Until the Wheels Fall Off* also invokes the notion of getting into the psychological state of flow by following the environmental features in the context: "Freedom. I'm moving fast, but I'm in control and flowing. I could just cruise the landscape."[16] This notion of a flowing control is made possible by *wuwei*. Getting good at skateboarding was freeing for Hawk, as he began to form his identity around it. In the film, Hawk's family members describe how much Hawk changed for the better once he started skating as it built both confidence and generosity in his personality, which aligns with the Daoist notion that flow is essential for the good life.

Obviously, it makes sense that one would become happier once one has found their passion in life, especially for those who have an outsider mentality, but recent research in psychology has shown that getting into the state of flow is very much related to living a happy life, thus implying that the Daoists like Zhuangzi may have been onto something thousands of years ago. Mihaly Csikszentmihalyi, the world expert on the flow state, and his colleague Jeanne Nakamura who lives out in California with Mullen and Hawk, define flow as optimized "experiences during which individuals are fully involved in the present moment.... Viewed through the experiential lens of flow, *a good life is one that is characterized by complete absorption in what one does.*"[17] Some activities, argue Csikszentmihalyi and Nakamura, can be thought of as intrinsically motivating or—to use their language—"autotelic activity," which is a fancy way of describing activities that are rewarding in and of themselves (*auto* means "self" in Greek and *telos* means "end").

Autotelic activity can come in any form. For me, philosophy plays that role in my life, and I regularly tell my students that I'd be philosophizing even if I didn't get paid for it. Not surprisingly, this is precisely the way in which Mullen and Hawk describe their passion for skating, as they both kept up with their mastery even during the lulls in which it didn't prove lucrative to do so since skateboarding lost its popularity (this happened in the early '80s and early '90s). In a 2018 interview, Mullen, waxing philosophical in his own right, says "It's such a gift to be able to look at something and to love it for the sake of it. And nurturing and maintaining that, is one of the hardest tests."[18] Mullen continues to talk through the "visceral exhilaration" he experiences when skating that cannot be found anywhere else in his life. This explains, for instance, why people like Mullen and Hawk dedicate their lives to skating, despite the fact that both of them have been injured multiple times in doing so, and despite the fact that both had to embrace the outsider mentality as well.

The Usefulness of Uselessness

Philosophy and skateboarding have (on occasion) both garnered unfortunate reputations for being useless pursuits, captured in the age-old adage that "philosophy bakes no bread," similar enough to the admonitions from Mullen's father to do something "useful with his life." Mullen reflects on this at the beginning of his TED Talk. After showcasing some of his incredibly graceful tricks to the USC student audience, he says "So, that's what I've done with my life,"[19] implying at that initial stage of the talk as to its useless value compared to the great things the highly educated audience members presumably will go on to do. He ends the talk, though, with the parting words of wisdom that "there's an intrinsic value in creating something for the sake of creating it," thereby appealing to the joy of autotelic activity. In his public interviews, he radiates a sort of joyful wisdom as someone who has figured out the meaning of life. He followed his path and found success by being true to himself, thereby becoming a *zhen ren*, a true person. I think much of this has to do with marching to the beat of one's own drum and not really caring what others think. For Mullen, this meant pursuing skating even though his father saw no use in it.

This recalls a common theme in the *Zhuangzi* of the crooked tree that seems useless but whose very uselessness leaves it unscathed since it doesn't get cut down and have its energy be sapped by others. A carpenter comes across the tree and says, "Its trunk is so knotted, no carpenter could work on it, while its branches are too twisted to use a square or compass upon."[20] Thus, the crooked tree gets ignored, thereby allowing it to flourish and live a long life by growing in inexplicably odd ways, making it a true original, thereby showcasing the usefulness of uselessness.

In their own ways, Mullen and Hawk have done the same by displaying their undeniable *de* through skateboarding: they could have applied their intelligence (both were straight–A students) and work to the status quo out of the gates by taking corporate jobs; there's little doubt they would have been successful doing so. But they followed their nature, their *ziran*, thereby helping to form skateboarding into what it is today. From the Daoist perspective, this is the heart of wisdom, whether skater, philosopher, or otherwise: as Zhuangzi says, "my description of wisdom has to do with being wise in one's own *de*, nothing more."[21]

In the end, skateboarding is an art form, a lifestyle, and an aspect of one's identity for Hawk and Mullen. Through years of practice, and a willingness to embrace the outsider mentality, they formed such a graceful mastery in the sport that they casually complete tricks in ways that astound spectators. Zhuangzi's Daoist philosophy can help us understand their seemingly effortless mastery—their *wuwei*—showcased when even attempting the most difficult tricks. And embracing these Daoist notions may even help the skateboarder achieve similar heights.

Like the cicada catcher, the waterfall wader, and Cook Ding, Hawk and Mullen followed the natural way of things—the *dao*—in order to achieve their *de*, that is, their unique potential. They've gotten so good that they can maximize their creative potential with new tricks and embrace their joyful creativity through *xiao yao you*, that is, through carefree roaming, as exemplified most obviously in Mullen's penchant for night skating. In doing so, they embrace their true nature, their *ziran*, and show us what it means to be a *zhen ren*, a true person. It is appropriate to end, then, the same way in which we began—with a quote from Mullen that could as well have been found in the *Zhuangzi*: "Don't let anything poison your individuality. Break away and look in, not outward."[22]

Notes

1. Mullen, Rodney. 2004. *The Mutt: How to Skateboard and Not Kill Yourself.* New York: HarperCollins, 24.
2. Throughout the essay I utilize Pinyin as the romanization of the Chinese characters, since this system has been officially adopted by the Chinese government, as opposed to the older way of doing so that was created by Western missionaries who first traveled to China known as the Wade-Giles system. Thus, instead of Chuang Tzu, we get Zhuangzi and instead of Confucius we get Kongzi, etc.
3. Zhuangzi. 2006. *The Book of Chuang Tzu.* Martin Palmer (trans.). London: Penguin. 158.
4. *Ibid.*, 161.
5. Mullen, 1.
6. Rodney Mullen: Pop an ollie and innovate! https://www.youtube.com/watch?v=3GVO-MfIl1Q.
7. Zhuangzi, 113.
8. Hawk, Tony. 2001. *Occupation: Skateboarder.* New York: HarperCollins, 5.
9. Wilkinson, Alec. 2012. "Rodney Mullen Skates Central Park," *The New Yorker.*
10. Hawk, Tony. 2002. *Professional Skateboarder.* New York: HarperCollins, 1–2.
11. Jones, Sam (director). 2022. *Tony Hawk: Until the Wheels Fall Off.* HBO, 2 hr., 15 min.
12. Zhuangzi, 242.
13. Jones.
14. Wilkinson.
15. https://www.youtube.com/watch?v=i6Sla-RZ5Ts.
16. Jones.
17. Nakamura, Jeanne; Csikszentmihalyi, Mihaly. 2009. "The Concept of Flow," in *The Oxford Handbook of Positive Psychology*, C.R. Snyder & S.J. Lopez (ed.). Oxford: Oxford University Press, 89.
18. https://www.youtube.com/watch?v=i6Sla-RZ5Ts.
19. Mullen, Rodney. 2015. *Pop an Ollie and Innovate!*
20. Zhuangzi, 6.
21. *Ibid.*, 69.
22. https://boardandwheels.com/the-ultimate-skateboarding-motivation/.

Kierke-Grinding

Michael J. Regier

Among Danish philosopher and theologian Søren Kierkegaard's more famous ideas is his presentation of the leap of faith or leap *into* faith.[1] For Kierkegaard, faith affects the way we engage in our existence, and appropriating faith is a transformation he sees as vital, as it is through faith that we approach the world uniquely and assert our own selfhood. Rather than a passive faith, Kierkegaard advocates for a *radical* and *active* faith, one which at once accepts the riskiness of life and welcomes the challenges of the unknown—not unlike the radical attitude adopted when skaters leap onto their boards. Connecting Kierkegaard's leap to performing skateboarding tricks dramatizes the intensity of Kierkegaardian faith by highlighting its relevance to living life on the edge.

To show how *radical* (pun intended) Kierkegaard's conception of the leap of faith is, we need to understand what a life lived in uncertainty looks like. We actually see this illustrated by skaters—although Kierkegaard uses an account of *ice* skaters. However, despite a different type of skating, we find the same desire to perform tricks and push the limits of what one *thinks* they can do. This means that faith is not just a religious thing, and skaters like Tony Hawk confirm this. Hawk also talks about having faith, about trusting in yourself, and about not letting uncertainty or failure keep you from getting on the board—not just by yourself, but as part of a community where each member inspires others with their skills. Skateboarding illustrates how Kierkegaardian faith affects the way we interact with the world, understand ourselves, and form communities.

Kierkegaard's Leap of (or into) Faith

While Kierkegaard is closely associated with the concept of the leap of (or into) faith, it is not original to him. However, before we investigate where Kierkegaard draws this terminology, we'll first need to consider some background. The leap is discussed primarily in Kierkegaard's book *Concluding Unscientific Postscript to Philosophical Fragments*,[2] which he published under the name Johannes Climacus—pseudonyms being a common feature of his philosophical writing. This tome expands on a previous work published under the same pen name titled *Philosophical Fragments*, but it is much more focused on exploring human existence. For our purposes, it is simply important to note that Kierkegaard kept himself at a slight distance from this work because it is not explicitly Christian (as he was) and therefore, we should be cognizant that while we attribute these views to him, he himself kept them at arm's length. Understanding this, we can take for granted that faith is not *explicitly* theological in this work, and therefore one need not be religious to have faith—faith is *relational* (rather than doctrinal) for Kierkegaard and represents a disposition towards existence.[3] Of course, it seems natural to ask, what does "a disposition towards existence" mean, precisely?

Kierkegaard, in formulating his leap, draws on G.E. Lessing's dramatization of a leap over a ditch. Responding to this, Kierkegaard writes that Lessing's over-emphasis of the distance across the ditch is meant "to make the metaphor appeal to the imagination, as though even the least leap did not possess the property of making the ditch infinitely wide; as if it were not equally difficult for one who *cannot* leap *at all* whether the ditch is wide or narrow."[4] What Kierkegaard wants to draw our attention to here is that the requirement of the leap is already itself dramatic; one must already be *able* and/or *willing* to make the leap in the first place. This drama derives from the inherent uncertainty of the leap: there is a chance of failure, and so one may not even want to attempt the leap. This already reminds us of our first experiences with a skateboard: looking at the slim piece of wood with four wheels knowing that we very likely may fall off it. We may also have an inkling of what Kierkegaard has in mind here. Lessing's focus was on the physical dimensions of the ditch, but what Kierkegaard emphasizes is the individual's own perception of it, writing, "it not being the width of the ditch that prevents the leap, externally, but it being, internally, the dialectical passion that makes the ditch infinitely wide."[5] There is nothing *physically* keeping us from getting on the skateboard, instead it is our own fear of failure or of being bruised that holds us back from leaping or (perhaps in our case) skating.

We can now venture an answer to our earlier question: a disposition toward existence relates to the way we understand ourselves, the world, and how we act. Assuming a disposition of faith means adopting a willingness to embrace uncertainty, to embrace the *riskiness* of existence without shying from approaching life as ourselves; it allows us to traverse the boundary between assumed knowledge about our limits and testing those assumptions by actively pushing them. "But," Kierkegaard asks, "then what does it mean to take a risk? Risking is the correlate of uncertainty; once certainty is there, risking stops."[6] Faith, as a disposition, both grounds and requires a leap simultaneously: we must have faith that when we hop on the skateboard we can stay on, but also faith to overcome the fear that we may fall off when attempting tricks.

Kierkegaard was attuned to how tempting comfort and certainty are, and how difficult it can be to *start*—and any leap does indeed begin with a start. This is because, as Kierkegaard writes, "the leap is the category of decision."[7] The leap is active because it requires the decisiveness *to choose* to leap and the courage to leap regardless of a lack of certainty that we will stick the landing—mental fortitude is essential to faith. Thus, we find a transformation of one's relationship to existence, an internal change wherein the individual becomes a *single* individual in the sense that they embrace their uniqueness *despite* that uniqueness setting them apart from others. In a sense, it requires embracing becoming an outsider, which itself requires the courage of faith that being an outsider is not equivalent to being an outcast.

This is part of Kierkegaard's existential schema (his conception of self-becoming) which is made up of three "stages": the aesthetic, ethical, and religious. Each of these affects one's interest in existence. The aesthetic disposition embraces momentary passions and solitary self-definition, the ethical seeks universal order and an adoption of a generic or stereotypical sense of self mediated by social norms, and finally the religious stage appropriates faith and approaches self-becoming *with* others (more on this later) but without the guardrails of legitimized patterns of being. Rather than faith being merely belief in God, for example, it is the appropriation of an attitude toward existence wherein one directs their own self-becoming according to their own particular interests, desires, and passions (what Kierkegaard terms becoming "subjective") alongside and in relation to others (including God).

Prior to the leap, one can only attain a destabilized or generalized sense of self, because they are either prey to momentary whims or follow roads laid out for them by others. We may find here those who devote themselves to skating until they fail their first ollie and then give up and find a new passion as well as those who are risk-averse who may skate but without trying any tricks. Thus, it is in the moment of decision to return to the board and dedicate oneself to learning or overcome playing it safe that we make the leap, that we enter into the life of faith.[8]

The leap, we can say, represents the transition from a life of security to a life of risk; a dedication to pursue one's interests despite the potential for failure. Faith is the embrace of one's passion despite the uncertainty, and we find this not only when we try a kickflip and stick it but also when we try to replicate the trick and fail. From Kierkegaard's perspective, we do ourselves a disservice when we force ourselves to keep our feet flat on the ground, and it is only the anxiety-inducing freedom of the leap that frees us to dedicate ourselves to become who we can be, if we're ready to leap toward that possibility.

Kierkegaard's Ice Skaters

While Kierkegaard discusses faith as a leap, he illustrates the courage in the face of uncertainty that is indicative of faith in his book *Two Ages*.[9] The "two ages" of this work are the "Revolutionary Age," the period of the French Revolution, and the "Present Age," that period following the revolution when society was reformulated within the structures toppled by the revolution, now with the bourgeoisie in the place of the aristocracy. It is within this context that Kierkegaard presents us with two ice skaters, each representing dispositions encouraged by these oppositional ages. It is only natural to wonder: if Kierkegaard were writing in a contemporary context whether he would have used skateboarders on a vert ramp to illustrate his point. However, while the leap was explicitly about the acquisition of a disposition towards existence, here we find him more interested in the distinction between the life of certainty, comfort, and most importantly dispassion (hallmarks of the "ethical" stage), and one where individuals have passion and are willing to *dare*. Together, these will help further illustrate not only the life of faith Kierkegaard advocates but stress the *active* nature of that life.

First, Kierkegaard presents the Revolutionary ice skater.

> If the treasure every one covets lies far out on a very thin crust of ice, guarded by the great danger to anyone venturing so far out ... in a passionate age the crowd would loudly cheer the bold, brave person who skates out on the thin ice. They would shudder for him and with him in his perilous decision, would grieve for him if he meets his death, and would idealize him if he gets the treasure.[10]

With this in mind, Kierkegaard then discusses the Present Age's ice skater. Here, he notes that the crowd goes

> out and from their safe vantage point appraise with the air of connoisseurs the expert skater who can skate almost to the very edge (that is, as far out as the ice is still safe and just short of being dangerous) and then turn back. One of the skaters would be exceptionally skilled, and he would even be able to perform the stunt of making one seemingly hazardous swoop right at the very edge.[11]

These two represent the distinction between an individual with passion—faith being concomitant with passion here—and an individual who captures the *outward appearance* of faith but remains beholden to certainty.

To clarify this, our first ice skater is represented as possessing the faith to *try* to reach the treasure (following our previous discussion, we may understand the treasure as the skater's *self*); the skater is decisive and acts regardless of any uncertainty about the outcome. Pointing to the crowd, Kierkegaard emphasizes that there is something awe-inspiring about this skater, who has faith in the success of their venture, despite the danger of the thin ice. We can see parallels with an audience at the skate park, where the crowd is captivated in the moment as the board and its rider leave the safety of the ground. This is contrasted with the latter ice skater, who remains on the safe, thick ice and whose trick is more image than actual. There is no need for faith, no need for a leap, because the individual is prudent; there is no "pushing the envelope," so to speak, but a simulation of it. It is clear that it is the former ice skater Kierkegaard wants us to emulate; he is inspiring because he is an example that we too can succeed in our own ventures—the resoluteness of skating, whether boarding or on ice, is analogous to *any* risky venturing, in *giving ourselves over to uncertainty*. What faith provides is not only an impulse to act, as the second ice skater does indeed act, but provides the encouragement that we can strive beyond what we know and can achieve the treasure; faith allows us to trust in ourselves and our abilities to go beyond what is immediately achievable and serve as an example of this possibility to others.

Søren and Tony

Tony Hawk's discussion of the levels of skateboarding skills with *Wired* has a number of moments that show clear intersections with Kierkegaard's radical leap in faith.[12] Perhaps unexpectedly, we will start with the hardest trick he discusses: the 1080. Hawk admits that this is a trick that he not only has not done, but has not practiced, stating that he never felt comfortable with it.[13] We may think that means he lacks faith in himself, but an important part of Kierkegaard's conception of faith is trusting in yourself, and that means understanding your limits. We cannot leap *out* of ourselves with faith, but rather we must embrace who we are when we leap, and this includes those limits that make us who we are. However, it is a fine line between what we are comfortable with and being averse to risk. Faith opens us to risk as a way of revealing our limits and encourages us to see whether those limits can be pushed. Without that initial sense of faith, we would lack the courage to push beyond tricks that we know we can land safely—and Hawk notes many times the injuries he sustained in the process of learning himself through a decisive leap into learning and pioneering new tricks.

He is most clear about the role of faith when discussing the backside 180 ollie, where he specifically says that you're "going literally on blind faith" because you cannot see where you are going to land.[14] This is strongly reminiscent of the leap, where the decisiveness to leap negates the physical distance of what one is leaping over; one need not see where they will land to make the leap in the faith that they *will* land. And this, like Hawk says about the frontside pop shove-it is "more based on feeling than sight."[15] It's about trusting in yourself and allowing yourself to be in that moment in the resolution to leap, to leave the confines of what is certain. The distinction Kierkegaard is drawing, and which is highlighted by Hawk, is one of feeling versus knowledge, where faith connects to that sense of "feeling like I can" while knowledge interrupts this by suggesting one stick with what she *knows* she can accomplish.

This point is further clarified if we look at what Hawk has to say about the kickflip McTwist. He says of the first time he landed it that he "just made it happen. This trick I'd been testing and testing and testing, and I knew if I was ever gonna make it, it was gonna be this time with my contemporaries."[16] It was not that he knew it was going to happen at that moment, but that he felt like, in that moment, he could *make* it happen. Kierkegaard, as we found in our discussion of the leap, also sees this sense of "making happen" as a component of faith—it pushes the limits to reveal something new by transforming the way we approach the world: it is the *decision* to leap. His willingness to lose himself in the moment, to be decisive, is exemplified when he says he "made it happen."

Furthermore, faith does not have to happen all at once, it is not the successful landing of the trick itself, but is in the "testing and testing and testing" until that moment when you *make it happen*—the drama of the leap is not in the landing, but in the initial moment when the feet leave the ground—or, more accurately, when we *choose* to start trying. We also find a parallel to the ice skater when Hawk describes the elation of himself and his audience; it is exemplary that he achieved it and serves as an inspiration for his audience to engage in the same process.

Hawk's commentary on what is perhaps his most iconic trick, the 900, also clarifies the relationship between Kierkegaard's conception of faith and skateboarding. Most importantly, Hawk states that it is essential to know how to stick the landing, how to adjust and lean into it, but muses that "even then, you don't know if it's gonna work."[17] Again, we find this distinction between faith and knowledge: as much as we might know the mechanics, it's about the willingness to try to let our feeling take over in the moment of decision. He further states that you "gotta commit to the whole trick because otherwise you're gonna land on your back,"[18] something he has done many times, and, as we have stressed with Kierkegaard, we can suggest that faith picked him up and put him back on the board for another attempt.

Hawk helps to clarify another important facet of faith: knowing, or perhaps better stated, *becoming* one's own self. Rather than holding us back and keeping safely within a prescribed identity, faith encourages us to find who we are uniquely and individually—an ideal that is embraced by skaters. This, at times, has its own risks, and Hawk recognizes that he has "broken [his] ego many times" trying tricks.[19] But, as with the physical bruises, faith impels us to keep pushing to find who we are, and to act in accordance with what we can make happen even if our momentary failures make us look bad to our peers. What Hawk's interview illuminates is the significance of *realizing possibilities* (making things happen) and *becoming* in faith. Skateboarding captures these important elements of faith; when we land uncertain tricks, we discover something new about ourselves, about what we can do, and about where we can go from there—we don't have to stop after our first ollie, we can push toward a kickflip, some verts, or even a 1080.

Skaters, Outsiders, and Community

Faith, we can say at this point, has uniquely personal nature stemming from our own decisiveness to leap or not to leap into a life of uncertainty—this is especially true in regard to its role in revealing our own unique self as expressed through our actions (particularly those that push us to try new, daring things). This appears to be in line with skateboarding legend Rodney Mullen's description of skateboarding as "the ultimate loner activity. There [are] no rules, no coaches, no teammates—you [skate] when and how you want to."[20] Viewed from this perspective we may be tempted to say that faith has an isolating nature that only turns our gaze inward. However, while faith is indeed deeply personal and individualizing, it also, and very importantly, *opens us to others*. We have already had glimpses of this social aspect of faith: the crowd's awe at the ice skater, Tony Hawk's contemporaries being elated alongside him after he finally landed the kickflip McTwist, and his "bruised ego" that didn't stop him from continuing until he was successful. There is an (albeit unspoken) importance to the role of community in the life of faith, much as there is an importance to community in skateboarding; rarely does one find a skate park with only one skater honing her craft. Thus, to conclude our discussion of Kierkegaardian faith and its importance to skateboarding, we will place it into the context of the skateboarding community we belong to, as well as each of the other communities to which we belong.

While Mullen is right to note that skating is a particularly individual activity, you are alone on the board, and it is on your own *self* that, in the moment of decision when entering a trick, *chooses* faith over certainty. So too, Kierkegaard emphasizes, are we alone when we make the leap into faith—no one can make the leap for us, it is up to us to grasp our own faith. And while there is, therefore, a very keenly isolating element to faith, once we do adopt the disposition of faith, we also gain a greater appreciation for both our own self and the selfhood of others. We indirectly noted this when discussing Tony Hawk's recognition of his limitations, this does not infringe on who he is, and while he may have suffered a broken ego at times, he had a respect for the self he discovered through his actions. This also leads to a respect for others: Hawk doesn't expect *anyone* to do the tricks he does, but he'll encourage others to push to where *they* can go. This is an important element of Kierkegaard's concept of faith in his more explicitly theological works,[21] where the aim is to "upbuild" oneself and others through actions that are directed and supported through faith (i.e., love, care, and respect for one's neighbor). You don't watch Hawk, despair that you aren't him, and give up all hope of hopping on the board, you watch him and then get the bandages ready.

Faith, for Kierkegaard, is not only an internal change, but an external one as well—hence our continual reference to living the "life of faith." Faith, as a disposition toward existence, changes the way we relate to ourselves, our world, and other people, it makes us more courageous in manifesting our sense of self (*making* our self *happen*) and serves as an example for others to provide them courage to strive in their own ways. The other skaters watching Hawk complete a kickflip McTwist for the first time didn't lament not beating him to it but saw it as an inspiration. Similarly, one need not be inspired to skate by watching him complete it but can be inspired to strive toward the realization of one's own individual dreams. Faith, viewed in this way, provides the courage to be one's self and appreciate selfhood not as a competition with others, but as a cooperative endeavor *with* others. Like skateboarding, faith requires just that decisiveness and commitment to passion, and the leap, like even the most basic trick, starts and ends in that moment you choose not to bail.

Notes

1. "Into" is perhaps the better rendering as it captures the transformative power of faith that we will be exploring.

2. Kierkegaard, S. 2013. *Concluding Unscientific Postscript to "Philosophical Fragments."* Trans. A. Hannay, Cambridge: Cambridge University Press..
3. *Ibid.*, 273; it is both relational in the sense of relating to a certain idea, and relation to *others*.
4. *Ibid.*, 84.
5. *Ibid*
6. *Ibid.*, 356.
7. *Ibid.*, 84.
8. *Ibid.*, 213.
9. Kierkegaard, S. 1978. *Two Ages.* Trans. H. Hong & E. Hong. Princeton University Press. *Two Ages* is a commentary on a novel of the same name and is rather unique among his writings.
10. *Ibid.*, 71–72
11. *Ibid.*, 72
12. "21 Levels of Skateboard with Tony Hawk: Easy to Complex." https://www.youtube.com/watch?v=OOg-4mtA3Zo&ab_channel=WIRED.
13. *Ibid.*, Level 18.
14. *Ibid.*, Level 2.
15. *Ibid.*, Level 5.
16. *Ibid.*, Level 15.
17. *Ibid.*, Level 17.
18. *Ibid.*, Level 17.
19. *Ibid.*, Level 17.
20. Mullen, R. 2004. *The Mutt: How to Skateboard and Not Kill Yourself.* New York: HarperCollins, 2004, 24.
21. Cf: Kierkegaard, S. 1998. *Works of Love.* Trans. H. Hong & E. Hong, Princeton: Princeton University Press.

The Journey of the Stoic Skater

Glava Sofia

What does skateboarding have to do with ancient or medieval philosophy? You might think: not much. But consider the story of the Stoic skater, the skateboarder who's embraced Stoicism: the ancient school of thought which emphasizes personal virtue, rationality, and living in harmony with nature. According to the Stoic, happiness is achievable through understanding and accepting the natural order of the world.

Visualize the Stoic skater riding through the concrete expanse with a calm demeanor, welcoming falls and setbacks as chances for growth. This Stoic skater is not only achieving feats but is also implementing a philosophical frame of mind with every maneuver. As we consider the Stoic skater, it soon becomes clear that Stoic philosophy aligns with the challenges and successes of skating, unveiling unexpected connections between a contemporary sport and an ancient way of thinking.

The Stoic skater is a seeker of truth who navigates the city with a purpose that extends beyond stunts and tricks. In a world of constant noise and endless distractions, the Stoic skater is a testament to wisdom that is just as relevant today as it was centuries ago. By stepping onto the board and adopting a Stoic thought process, the skater embarks upon an exploration of the self, determination, and authenticity.

The Stoic skater is on a journey of aligning with nature, being present, and achieving harmony in the face of chaos. With every kick and push, the skater tunes into the rhythm of the world, embracing the imperfections of the terrain as a metaphor for life's ever-changing currents. The skater's commitment to endurance and perfection exemplifies Stoic values such as bravery, sagacity, and strength. The skater executes each trick with resolve, acknowledging that the journey is just as crucial as the destination; accomplishments are not merely noted but are considered significant milestones toward self-control. And the Stoic skater demonstrates the Stoic ideal of distinguishing between what can and cannot be controlled. Objective evaluations and criticisms have no bearing on their self-perception; instead, the skater is guided by an inner navigation, unmoved by external demands.

In the world of the Stoic skater, the fleeting nature of success and defeat serves as a profound lesson. Each tumble or unsuccessful trick reminds us of life's impermanence, highlighting the importance of seeking solace in the moment and exhibiting appreciation for the opportunity to ride. The Stoic skater employs a mental exercise to be prepared for future adversity, bolstering an inner fortitude both on and off the board.

Again, as we consider skateboarding through the lens of Stoicism, we encounter not just a sport but a moving philosophy. And, as we follow the journey of the Stoic skater, we can see that skating has more to do with ancient and medieval philosophy than we might have initially thought; we can see that skaters have a great deal to learn from those who came (a good long while) before them.

What Stoicism Is

Stoicism originated during the Hellenistic and Roman periods as a result of catastrophe. In 300 BC, a Phoenician trader, Zeno was sailing toward the port of Piraeus when his boat capsized, losing the ship's valuable cargo. Though he survived the wreck, Zeno arrived in Athens with essentially nothing. During his time there, he ended up studying under Kratis, a philosopher renowned for his cynicism. The Cynics could be thought of as the hippies of the ancient world; they lived with limited possessions, challenged authority, and ridiculed societal conventions. While Zeno admired their way of life to some extent, he believed that the Cynics lacked a comprehensive philosophy, which led him to establish his own school of thought.

Yet another group of thinkers at this time were the followers of Epicurus (341–270 BC) (i.e., the Epicureans) who emphasized the pursuit of pleasure and the avoidance of pain as the highest ideal. Epicureans secluded themselves within their garden. In contrast, the Stoics practiced philosophy out in public, often among merchants, priests, prostitutes, or anyone else who happened to be passing by. According to the Stoics, philosophy should be an engagement with the populace, directly tied to public life. The objective of this approach is to improve the quality of one's life by following the guidance of wisdom (which has been tested over generations and remains relevant still today).[1]

An important part of this wisdom is that true excellence comes from cultivating wisdom, courage, justice, and self-control, with these virtues forming the basis of a fulfilled life.[2] The Stoic worldview prescribes the attainment of peace through accepting the unchangeable aspects of existence and dissuades us from indulging in futile worries about external events or the behavior of others. By advocating emotional restraint, the Stoic highlights the ability to control emotion and to avoid being subdued by destructive passions. Stoicism teaches that living in harmony with nature entails accepting the impermanence that is inherent in all aspects of life. This perspective is reinforced by the doctrine of *memento mori,* a Latin phrase that translates to "Remember that you must die," an important reminder of our mortality. Self-reflection is a crucial exercise that fosters the development of one's character. Stoicism also emphasizes social duty, compelling us to fulfill our roles and responsibilities virtuously and to be just, compassionate, and dedicated citizens. As a philosophy that celebrates continuous learning and the ceaseless pursuit of wisdom, Stoicism argues that true freedom arises from the mastery of our desires, emotions, and judgments, transcending the external world's capriciousness and embodying the essence of a well-lived life. While what Stoicism teaches is important for living overall, it is also relevant for skating.

As the Stoic skater rolls through the urban jungle, the resonance of *memento mori* echoes with every kickflip and ollie, a constant reminder in the pursuit of tricks and triumphs. The ever-present sound of wheels on pavement becomes a meditative backdrop, inviting self-reflection on character and ethics. As the skater glides through the city, the reminder of mortality helps combat any temptation toward apathy, channeling the Stoic mindset to face challenges with commendable equanimity. And social responsibility extends beyond the concrete, prompting the skater to be a just, compassionate, and engaged citizen of the skating community.

As we can now see, by embracing Stoic philosophy's principles of continuous learning, skaters can approach each new trick as a lesson and a step toward wisdom. The art of skating parallels the mastery of desires, emotions, and judgments, forging a path to true freedom that transcends the twists and turns of both skating and life itself.

Embracing Nature and Asserting the Present

> "Happiness is to enjoy the present, without anxious dependence upon the future, not to amuse ourselves with either hopes or fears but to rest satisfied with what we have, which is sufficient, for he that is so wants nothing."
> —Seneca[3]

Seneca (4 BC–65 AD), a Stoic philosopher and statesman in ancient Rome, is most frequently recognized for his treatments of ethics, morality, and the transience of life. And, though the preceding passage was written centuries ago, it resonates even in the world of skateboarding. At its core, skating embodies living in the moment. It is a gravity-defying dance, a symphony of balance and motion that requires complete presence. Not unlike Seneca's philosophy of finding happiness in the present moment, skaters frequently describe a mental state referred to as "flow." This is the experience of time appearing to dissolve so all that remains is the steady sound of wheels on pavement, the wind blowing across your face, and a rush of adrenaline surging within. In experiencing flow, there is no past to mourn and no future to worry about. There is only the present.[4]

Just as Seneca warned against excessive concern for the future, skaters must achieve a balance in the present. It is natural to aspire to achieve ambitious aims, to desire and work to acquire new skills, and to imagine landing tricks of greater and greater difficulty. However, one must be cautious not to overlook the joy of the journey itself. The skater who only lives for the trick to come jeopardizes losing the pleasure of the ride itself.[5]

Skating is a sport which lends itself to the development of hopes and fears: the hope of landing a difficult trick; the fear of the various potential scrapes, bruises, and broken bones. But Seneca reminds us of the importance of avoiding the influence of subjective evaluations, unless explicitly necessary. The art of skating involves balancing these two forces. The skater must set himself audacious targets but also respect the inherent dangers of the activity and understand that sometimes, unfortunately, he'll have to hit pavement. Seneca's wisdom reminds us that to find balance in skating as in life, we must cherish each attempt, whether it ends in triumph or failure.

Additionally, the idea that we ought to "[find] contentment with what we have" applies to skaters as much as anyone else. The attraction of the sport is not restricted to the newest equipment or the most impressive skate parks. At its core, skating allows us to experience the pure pleasure of rolling through the streets as well as the companionship shared with friends at a nearby skate spot. The contentment derived from this activity promotes a profound sense of satisfaction that resembles Seneca's conviction that contented individuals lack nothing.

In essence, this ancient wisdom serves as a guiding principle as we navigate the world on four wheels. The synergy of skateboarding and philosophy teaches us to embrace the present, appreciate the journey, and find joy in the act of riding. This reminds us that the skate park of life is most enjoyable when we let go of future uncertainties and appreciate the beauty of the present moment.

Endurance and the Pursuit of Excellence

> "If you want to improve, be content to be thought foolish and stupid with regard to external things. Don't wish to be thought to know anything; and even if you appear to be somebody important to others, distrust yourself."
> —Epictetus[6]

In this brief passage, Epictetus (the first- and second-century Stoic philosopher) imparts to us yet another important lesson relevant to skating. The Stoic skater will manifest the ideals of perseverance and the unwavering pursuit of excellence. Epictetus urges individuals to adopt a mindset that prioritizes progress over all else. This requires a willingness to accept appearing foolish or stupid during the journey toward improvement. In the context of skating, this sentiment is particularly important for beginners. The journey of becoming an accomplished skater begins with unsteady knees, clumsy falls and, at times, the spectacle of stumbling. However, it is within these moments of vulnerability that genuine growth occurs. Learning to skate involves persistence, balance, and mastering tricks. This process requires embracing humility and recognizing that stumbles are a natural part of learning. This insightful philosophy takes on a compelling form in the context of the sport.

Moreover, Epictetus cautions against the desire for recognition and the need to be seen as knowledgeable. This message should resonate within skateboarding culture, in which skaters who conquer new heights and defy gravity may gain respect or even fame. Epictetus urges the maintenance of self-distrust. In other words, despite one's proficiency, there is always more to learn and another challenge to overcome. Pursuing excellence in skating, as in life, demands continuous inquisitiveness and a willingness to accept the uncharted and infinite path ahead.

At its philosophical core, skateboarding embodies the Stoic principles that Epictetus extols. Skating is a pursuit firmly grounded in endurance and an unwavering desire for excellence. Skaters, whether experienced or new to the sport, are confronted with the fact that progress often begins with moments that may make one appear foolish. However, this is where the beauty of the journey lies. The act of persevering through these challenges, humbling oneself, and embracing the potential for appearing foolish encapsulates a philosophy important to skating.

The parallels between skateboarding and Stoic philosophy are evident. Epictetus's wisdom reminds us that the pursuit of excellence requires endurance amid the trials, embracing humility, and a continuous hunger for improvement. This sage counsel echoes as we skate, guiding us to persevere, learn, and persist on our path toward mastery and excellence.

The Wisdom to Know What We Can and Can't Control

> "Some things are in our control, and others are not. Control what you can, and don't worry about what you can't."
> —Epictetus[7]

Epictetus again here gives us a piece of wisdom relevant for skating. In it, we are urged to undertake a thoughtful exploration into the essence of the sport, a domain where recognizing and appreciating the distinction between the controllable and uncontrollable is paramount. Epictetus recommends that we establish the boundaries of our authority.[8] Both in life and within skating, we encounter realms of control and non-control. The skater's platform is based on a series of choices encompassing tricks to attempt, devoted practice time, and the establishment of a robust mental disposition. These elements reside within the expanse of control, where the skater's individual will and determination hold sway.

The Stoic skater's guidance encourages us to establish the limits of authority. We experience areas of impact and areas of apathy in life, just as in skating. The skater has a myriad of options available to them—techniques to experiment with, practice sessions to attend, and a determination to cultivate a resolute mindset. These factors are within the skater's control and where their willpower and resolve flourish.

However, the final result of these efforts remains frustratingly obscure, susceptible to the unpredictable whims of fortune. The evaluation from fellow skaters, the capriciousness of the weather, and the skateboard's own (mental or physical) condition—these variables are not immediately under the skater's control. In skating, as in life, uncontrollable forces are inevitable and ever-present. Epictetus advises us to focus our energies where they will have the greatest impact. In skating, this means an unyielding commitment to refining our abilities, improving our techniques, and building resilience in the face of inevitable setbacks.

Conversely, the edict that we ought not worry about uncontrollable aspects should resonate with the skater. The path toward achieving skateboarding excellence is often riddled with unsuccessful attempts and setbacks, making it essential to acknowledge and accept this reality as a fundamental part of the journey. Epictetus would encourage skaters to let go of unnecessary worry regarding external circumstances and to concentrate on internal self-improvement and personal growth.

When viewed in the context of life's broader lessons, skating becomes a microcosm of vivid importance. By separating what we can manage (e.g., our efforts, attitudes, and choices) from what we cannot (e.g., external outcomes and circumstances), we can approach skating and life with calm and strength. The wisdom of Epictetus acts as a compass, guiding us in the world of skateboarding, as well as in the realm of Stoic philosophy. It helps us recognize that our power lies in mastering our response to the ride, rather than commanding its outcome. Thus, riding on the four wheels of a skateboard, we embark on a journey of self-mastery and acceptance.

Impermanence and the Transience of Triumph and Failure

"The universe is change; our life is what our thoughts make it."
—Marcus Aurelius[9]

Perhaps best known for his *Meditations,* Marcus Aurelius (121–180 AD) was a Roman Emperor and Stoic philosopher. In this now famous work, he observes that the universe is in a constant state of change; it is always evolving. Skating shares this fundamental concept of impermanence. Skaters understand that skate parks, tricks, and even their own abilities are always susceptible to change. Skate parks can experience alterations, weather conditions may impact the surface, and a skater's capabilities can either improve or decline. Despite this, victories and defeats in skating are short-lived. A skater can master a challenging maneuver after frequent efforts, relishing their success. However, they may fall while attempting an easier maneuver. This variability mirrors life's transience.

The latter segment of Marcus Aurelius's quote underscores how our worldview can significantly influence our encounters. In skating, one's mindset is (perhaps surprisingly) important. Approaching a new skating maneuver with confidence and a positive mindset increases the likelihood of success, while doubt and negativity can impede progress. The skater's thoughts shape how they perceive success and failure.

In addition, skating offers a unique opportunity to delve into the concept of impermanence, as mastering tricks involves a journey of learning and refinement, rather than a specific end goal. We realize as skaters that there is always room for improvement and that today's achievements can be surpassed tomorrow. This aligns with Marcus Aurelius's teaching that our thoughts shape our lives. The ability of a skater to adapt, learn from setbacks, and maintain a positive mental attitude all contribute to continual progress.

In essence, the adage from Marcus Aurelius serves to remind us of the perpetual metamorphosis of the universe and the transformative influence that our thoughts can have on our experiences. In the realm of skating, this philosophy prompts us to fully embrace fleeting opportunities, value every significant achievement, and perceive each setback as an impetus for improvement. Moreover, it accentuates the central role of our mindset in shaping our journey on a skateboard. Skateboarding illustrates the transience of the universe, with our ideas acting as the brushstrokes that depict its canvas.

Practicing Gratitude and Visualizing Adversity

> "Set aside a certain number of days, during which you shall be content with the scantiest and cheapest fare, with coarse and rough dress, saying to yourself the while: 'Is this the condition that I feared?'"
>
> —Seneca[10]

Here, Seneca emphasizes the importance of practicing gratitude and visualizing adversity. By consciously subjecting ourselves to a period of simplicity and discomfort, we attain a novel viewpoint on our anxieties and aspirations. In any given moment, this may spur us to ponder: "Is this the state I feared?" As a result, we develop an appreciation for the plenty and comfort that we habitually disregard in our daily lives. Within the realm of skating, this philosophical exercise assumes a distinctive dimension. Skating is a sport that often requires resilience and adaptability when the skater is faced with challenges. Skaters willingly put themselves at risk of falls and injuries in the pursuit of their passion. Each time a skater steps on their board, they must engage in a form of mental preparation for adversity.

For instance, consider a skater attempting a difficult stunt for the first time. Skaters may encounter falls, frustration, and physical discomfort when pushing their limits. However, with each successful attempt, skaters progress, which will ideally result in gratitude. Despite subjective feelings of achievement and overcoming fear generated by eventually landing a trick, skating promotes personal development and simplicity through fairly simple equipment consisting of a wooden board with four wheels. It allows skaters to hone their skills in a variety of settings, from empty parking lots to bustling city streets, and to derive pleasure from the activity itself rather than relying on extravagance. Seneca's method of embracing austerity and adversity is a reminder that pursuing one's passions involves encountering obstacles and discomfort, but such challenges offer opportunities for growth and resilience.[11] Skating encourages the appreciation of the journey and the head-on tackling of fear and hardship.

What all of this means is that Seneca's doctrine promotes the cultivation of gratitude and resilience through the voluntarily experiencing of simplicity and adversity. Skating offers a unique platform to adopt this ideology, since skaters frequently encounter challenges, envisage adversity, and find value in their pursuit of excellence. Ultimately, this practice improves not only their skateboarding journey but also their broader outlook on life.

The End of the Journey

As the sun sets behind the cityscape, casting long shadows across the familiar curves of the skatepark, this story comes to an end: a story that began with a skateboard and ended with profound wisdom. The journey of the Stoic skater is one of a seeker of truth and fulfillment, whose quest was not only to master the concrete obstacles along the path but also the obstacles of life itself.

Amid the hustle and bustle of the city, the Stoic skater embarked on a journey that illustrated how the timeless principles of Stoic philosophy informed every kick and push. This story was interwoven with the guiding principles of Stoicism, demonstrating its fundamental place in the skater's life. The skater recognized the fleeting nature of life's moments, much like the tricks they perfected. Every ride and every ollie pointed to the fleeting beauty of existence, ridden with grace and reverence. By cherishing the present, embracing the fleeting nature of each moment of the ride, and finding satisfaction in the simple act of riding, the skater learned the ultimate lesson of life's true power.

Just as the Stoic virtues of courage, wisdom and strength illuminated their path, the Stoic skater embodied these qualities with an unwavering pursuit of excellence. Triumphs and setbacks were not mere occurrences but profound milestones on the journey. By following the philosophy of Stoicism, the individual discovers the resilience to endure hardship and continually strive for self-improvement. The Stoic skater's ability to distinguish between controllable and uncontrollable factors reflects the principles of Stoic philosophy. The Stoic skater rode with honesty, guided by an inner compass, impervious to external pressures. Every fall and unsuccessful maneuver served as an opportunity to accept the fleeting nature of life. Similar to the Stoic practice of imagining hardship, the Stoic skater was prepared for the inevitable challenges, building a personal resilience that served him on and off the board. Stoic principles were not a theoretical abstraction but a guiding beacon that shaped every ride, every decision, and every fall. It became an integral part of their being, a silent ally throughout their journey.

As we reflect on the story of the Stoic skater, we acknowledge that the journey is not *just* about skateboarding, but about navigating life's complex paths with strength and wisdom. By embracing Stoic philosophy, the Stoic skater acquired the ability to skate with purpose, to see obstacles as opportunities, and to find satisfaction in the uncomplicated act of moving forward. Those inspired by this wisdom continue to navigate the complex terrain of life with a Stoic spirit, seeking meaning in the journey itself. The story of the Stoic skater is a testament to the continuing influence of philosophy in shaping and enriching our lives. It is a story of growth, resilience and wisdom, where skateboarding and stoicism come together to create a beautiful journey.

NOTES

1. Weiner, Eric. 2020. *The Socrates Express: Adventures in Philosophy*. Avid Reader Press, 2020, 325.
2. Booth, Mike. 2018. "Why Stoicism Matters." *The School of Life*. https://www.youtube.com/watch?v=vOj5KLcymgA.
3. Seneca. 1969. *Letters from a Stoic*. Campbell, Robin (Trans.). Penguin, 1969, 51.
4. Vogt, Katja. 2020. "Seneca." *The Stanford Encyclopedia of Philosophy*. Zalta, Edward N. (Ed.). https://plato.stanford.edu/archives/spr2020/entries/seneca/ .
5. G., Devin. 2022. "Can Stoicism Improve your Skateboarding?" *Devin G*. https://www.youtube.com/watch?v=BBwxQUEl900.
6. Epictetus. 2004. *The Enchiridion*. Long, George (Trans.). Dover.
7. *Ibid*.
8. Bonforte, John. 1955. *The Philosophy of Epictetus*. Philosophical Library, 125.
9. Kamtekar, Rachana. 2018. "Marcus Aurelius." *The Stanford Encyclopedia of Philosophy*. Zalta, Edward N. (Trans.). https://plato.stanford.edu/archives/spr2018/entries/marcus-aurelius.
10. Manela, Tony. 2021. "Gratitude." *The Stanford Encyclopedia of Philosophy*. Zalta, Edward N. (Trans.). https://plato.stanford.edu/archives/win2021/entries/gratitude/.
11. Holiday, Ryan. 2020. "Five Live-Changing Quotes from Seneca." *The Daily Stoic*. https://podcastnotes.org/the-daily-stoic/five-life-changing-quotes-from-seneca-the-daily-stoic/.

Skating Toward the Good Life

Emily Stefl

Critics of skateboarding often suggest that skating is an inherently harmful activity that jeopardizes the well-being of its participants. Skateboarding is a high-impact activity that often leads to injuries, ranging anywhere from minor scrapes and bruises to more serious fractures or head injuries. Such injuries can not only cause immediate physical harm but can also lead to serious long-term consequences. And, while skateboarding can be fun and exhilarating, it is often thought of as a short-lived pursuit.

Because of these concerns, it is often suggested that individuals should invest their time and energy in activities that have greater longevity and can be enjoyed throughout one's entire life, contributing to a sustained sense of flourishing and a life well-lived. In addition to these concerns, skating is often seen as rebellious and destructive, an activity in which skaters utilize spaces that are not explicitly designed for skateboarding and may challenge authority by skating in prohibited areas. In this regard, skaters are viewed as disruptive and reckless, ignoring established boundaries and exhibiting a lack of concern for public safety.

While these objections to skating and its impact on well-being aren't without merit, a closer examination of skateboarding as a whole reveals that it's actually well positioned to contribute to the good life and human flourishing. From the perspective of the Ancient Greek philosopher, Aristotle, the good life is achieved through the cultivation of virtues and the realization of one's full potential as a human being. Thus, the ideal skater is one that exemplifies Aristotle's view of the good life. By continuously striving for excellence, the ideal skater exercises their reasoning capacities, practices virtue, and realizes their potential.

Aristotle and Eudaimonia

A key concept in Aristotle's understanding of the good life is *eudaimonia*. Eudaimonia is often translated as "happiness" or "flourishing." In his most famous work on ethics and the good life, the *Nicomachean Ethics*,[1] Aristotle views happiness as being the ultimate goal and highest good of human life. For Aristotle, happiness is not merely emotional contentment. It is not a fleeting feeling or a momentary pleasure that can easily dissipate. Instead, happiness is a state of flourishing and living well, encompassing a holistic sense of well-being that is rooted in the fulfillment of one's potential and the cultivation of virtues.

Unlike other goods pursued as means to an end, Aristotle considers happiness to be an end in itself. This distinction becomes clear when considering goods like money, which is sought as a means to acquire *other* things such as material possessions or comforts. In contrast, a good such as love, is often considered an end in itself. Experiencing love enriches our lives with deep connections and joy, which is arguably valuable for its own sake, rather than being valuable for some other end. Aristotle posits that happiness is a self-sufficient end and valued for its own sake, rather than as a tool for acquiring something else. This is because happiness is the highest goal that all human actions and pursuits ultimately aim to achieve.

> We think happiness is most choice-worthy of all goods, since it is not counted as one good among many.... Happiness, then, is apparently something complete and self-sufficient, since it is the end of the things pursued in action.[2]

According to Aristotle, every human action and pursuit aims at some end or goal. The ultimate end is the highest good that is pursued for its own sake and not as a means to something else. However, there must be a final end or highest good that serves as the source of value for all other goals. The good of other ends derives from the inherent good of this ultimate goal. Thus, as Aristotle argues, the ultimate good, pursued for its own sake, is happiness.

The idea that happiness is the ultimate good for human beings ties into Aristotle's view of the *function* of human beings. As Aristotle uses the term, a function is a characteristic activity or role that is unique to a particular entity; the concept of function here is *teleological*, which is the idea that everything in nature has an end or goal, a purpose which it is driving toward. Everything in the natural world has a specific function that corresponds to its essence, and the fulfillment of this function leads to the highest form of excellence and flourishing for that thing. Thus, the function of a human being is "the soul's activity that expresses reason [as itself having reason] or requires reason [as obeying reason]."[3]

To achieve eudaimonia, human beings must fulfill their function, which is to live a life of rational activity. The complete fulfillment of this function requires that one acts and thinks in accordance with what is excellent (i.e., what is *virtuous*). Virtue is what makes us perform our function well:

> …every virtue causes its possessors to be in a good state and to perform their functions well … the virtue of a human being will likewise be the state that makes a human being good and makes him perform his function well.[4]

We must use reason well to guide our actions and decisions, which involves making choices that lead to the development of virtues and living a life of excellence.

There are two types of virtues that Aristotle is concerned with. The first type of virtue that Aristotle focuses on is *virtue of character*. Virtue of character is acquired through habit, since virtue is neither inherently part of our nature, nor does virtue go against our nature. Instead, we possess a natural capacity to cultivate virtue and reach our full potential through the practice of habit. Aristotle stresses the importance of practicing virtue from a young age, since virtue and vice are formed by good and bad actions:

> A state [of character] arises from [the repetition of] similar activities…. It is not unimportant, then, to acquire one sort of habit or another, right from our youth; rather, it is very important, indeed all-important.[5]

Practicing the right sort of habituation involves practicing virtue in the correct way. Virtue of character is a state that is a mean between two vices—excess and deficiency—which concern both actions and feelings. This mean between excess and deficiency is relative to us, and so we must use reason to practice virtue to the appropriate degree in various situations to avoid excess or deficiency.

Consider the virtue of courage. Cowardice can be considered a vicious state because it involves either an excess of fear or a deficiency of confidence. Imagine a skater who hesitates to attempt a simple trick because of an excess of fear. They may worry excessively about falling or getting injured, leading to a deficiency in confidence. The skater might miss out on the opportunity to improve their skill and experience the thrill of pushing their limits due to a fear holding them back.

Likewise, rashness is also considered a vicious state where there is too little fear or too much confidence involved. A skater who exhibits too little fear and too much confidence may act recklessly and attempt complex tricks without considering the potential risks. They might underestimate the difficulty of certain maneuvers or fail to take necessary precautions, resulting in negative consequences.

The virtue of courage lies in finding a balance between the excess and deficiency of rashness and cowardice. A courageous skater acknowledges fear, but doesn't let it paralyze them. They understand the risks involved in various tricks, take necessary safety measures, and gradually push their limits with a reasonable level of confidence. This balanced courage allows the skater to improve their skills and face challenges with a reasonable level of fear and confidence.

The second type of virtue is *virtue of thought*. In addition to forming habits that reach the correct ethical ends of action in various situations, it is important that we also use our intellectual capacities to form the correct means to accomplish these ends. Like virtue of character, virtue of thought is learned through experience. However, virtue of thought is concerned with grasping the truth. In particular, we try to grasp the truth about what actions will result in *virtuous* action, and consequently, what will promote living well. To do so, we must use what Aristotle calls *practical wisdom*.

Practical wisdom is defined as "a state grasping truth, involving reason, concerned with action about what is good or bad for a human being."[6] Before we decide on what to do, we deliberate about different ways to achieve an end. When we deliberate, we are expressing our rational calculation to pursue the best good that is achievable through action. Good deliberation is "correctness that reflects what is beneficial, about the right thing, in the right way and at the right time."[7] Practical wisdom is necessary to decide on what the correct means to attain an end is, and in Aristotle's case, the end will be what is virtuous and promotes happiness.

Eudaimonia centers on the cultivation of virtues through the exercise of reason. This holistic approach emphasizes both moral and intellectual excellence, urging individuals to live a life of rational activity and virtue. Ultimately, the good life is not merely about personal pleasure, but about a harmonious existence marked by ethical conduct and the pursuit of excellence in all aspects of life.

Skateboarding and Rationality

In order to achieve eudaimonia and live the good life, skaters should fulfill their human function of exercising reason and living a life of rational activity. However, rationality does not seem to be at the forefront for skaters. Again, skating is often regarded as a dangerous and reckless activity. The willingness to take risks is a distinctive feature of the sport and contributes to the excitement and thrill associated with skateboarding. This can lead skaters to ignore rationality and to instead act recklessly and put themselves in harm's way.

Some skaters may intentionally engage in reckless behavior simply for the thrill of taking risks. This might involve attempting dangerous stunts solely for excitement without considering the potential consequences. Skating has also been associated with disrupting public life, as some skaters use areas that are not designated for skateboarding, leading to conflicts with pedestrians and creating potential safety hazards in shared spaces.

Skaters also constantly face the risk of physical injury. Falls, collisions with obstacles, and unsuccessful landings can result in injuries ranging from minor cuts and bruises to more serious conditions such as sprains, fractures, or concussions. Moreover, many skaters choose not to use protective gear such as helmets, knee pads, or elbow pads. The absence of such safety equipment increases the risk of injury in the event of a fall or accident. By engaging in an activity that poses a high risk of physical harm, skating can be considered a failure in taking proper care of oneself.

Despite its reputation as a risky or even reckless activity, skating does provide opportunities for individuals to exercise their reasoning capacities. Skaters should exercise reason by evaluating the level of risk associated with attempting a trick, weighing the benefits of successfully landing the trick against the potential injuries or failures. This involves a careful and reasoned assessment of whether it is safe and appropriate to attempt the trick, factoring in their current skill level, the condition of their equipment, and environmental factors like the surface quality and potential obstacles that could get in their way.

Skating requires the mastery of different skate tricks and to be able to overcome the various challenges that come with skating, such as overcoming the fear of injury and to improve one's skills over time. Skaters should approach challenges with a rational mindset, employing problem-solving skills to overcome obstacles. This involves a strategic analysis of the terrain, understanding the physics of skateboard movements, and adapting to the evolving demands of the sport.

Skating rationally also involves recognizing the impact one has on society. The ideal skater should discourage recklessness by avoiding impulsivity and consciously evaluating the potential consequences of their actions. Consciously evaluating consequences requires prioritizing safety for oneself and others. This includes wearing appropriate safety gear, adhering to traffic rules, and considering the potential impact of actions on pedestrians and other community members. By making safety a priority, skaters contribute to a responsible and considerate skateboarding culture.

Furthermore, skaters should make an effort to respect public spaces where skating occurs, being mindful of local regulations, designated skate areas, and community guidelines. Skaters should actively contribute to maintaining a positive relationship between the skateboarding community and the broader public, respecting shared spaces and minimizing disruptions. The efforts to discourage recklessness and recognize the impacts of skateboarding on society showcase the rational exercise of reason within the skateboarding community. Through thoughtful decision-making, conscious evaluation of consequences, and a commitment to responsible behavior, skaters are able to exercise a rational approach to their passion.

In Aristotle's view, skaters who pursue the good life fulfill their human function of exercising reason. They actively participate in the fulfillment of their rational capacities, making calculated decisions that involve both skillful execution and prudent risk management, and lessening the recklessness that seems to be inherent in skating.

Skateboarding Virtuously

The complete fulfillment of our human function requires that we reason in accordance with what is virtuous. An excellent skater is one who reasons about skateboarding in a way that aligns with virtue, where the skater balances their actions and emotions between the vices of excess and deficiency.

At first glance, skating does not seem to be concerned with virtue. Some individuals skate purely for personal enjoyment and thrill-seeking, without a conscious focus on developing any virtuous qualities. While skating can be physically demanding and require skill development, it may not inherently promote virtue. Instead, the primary focus for skaters may be on developing physical skills and mastering tricks, rather than focusing on character development. Additionally, skating often involves risky or reckless behavior, such as attempting dangerous stunts without proper consideration for safety and others. These actions seem to contradict virtues like practical wisdom and temperance, which suggests that some skaters may prioritize excitement over responsible decision-making.

Contrary to its initial appearance, skating provides plenty of opportunities for individuals to practice virtue. Skating, by its very nature, places a strong emphasis on personal responsibility, requiring individuals to be accountable for their actions and decisions. Aristotle believed that the only actions that are praiseworthy or blameworthy are those which we freely choose to make, "Virtue, then, is about feelings and actions. These receive praise or blame when they are voluntary, but pardon, sometimes even pity, when they are involuntary."[8] By choosing to skate, skaters willingly assume responsibility for the potential consequences of their actions. The ideal skater in Aristotle's view is one who acts virtuously, where they find a balance that allows them to take risks while respecting safety considerations.

An important virtue that skaters should practice is courage. In seeking to expand their skills and achieve new feats, skaters must move beyond their comfort zones. Many tricks involve a level of fear and apprehension, especially when attempting more challenging and daring moves. Skaters often need to confront this fear and push through it to execute the trick successfully. As professional skateboarder Steve Cabellero has discussed:

> You're dealing with anxiety and stress and need to overcome those boundaries and those fears.... You allow yourself to overcome the fear and being uncomfortable.[9]

Skaters are able to develop the virtue of courage when they confront the fear associated with attempting challenging tricks.

Practicing the virtue of courage involves a thoughtful balance between the vices of rashness and cowardice. Rashness can be characterized by impulsive and reckless actions without due consideration. In skating, rashness might manifest as attempting highly challenging tricks without assessing one's skill level or the associated risks. Cowardice can be characterized by the avoidance of challenges due to an excessive fear of failure or harm. Cowardice might manifest as hesitating to try new tricks or avoiding obstacles out of fear. Practicing the virtue of courage requires striking a balance between these two vices. Courage in skating involves assessing risks thoughtfully, understanding personal limits, and embracing challenges with a measured enthusiasm. This balance fosters the virtue of courage that is grounded in thoughtful decision-making, while steering clear of the dangers posed by rashness and cowardice.

Skating also offers the opportunity to practice practical wisdom. Skaters who are rash and lack practical wisdom are not acting virtuously, which is what makes their actions bad. The virtue of practical wisdom is necessary in order to figure out the best way to achieve a goal and to perform actions that are virtuous. Practical wisdom in the context of skating involves striking a balance between risk and caution. Skaters often need to make quick, informed judgments about the level of risk and whether it's worth attempting a particular trick at a given moment. A skater who attempts a trick must have a certain degree of skill as attempting the trick carries with it a risk of injury. Skaters should recognize their abilities and assess the risks associated with different tricks or terrains. They should approach challenges with a calculated mindset, and make decisions that align with both their skill level and the demands of the situation.

Additionally, skating involves ongoing learning, experimenting with different strategies, and learning from experiences. Skaters should view setbacks not as failures, but as opportunities for learning; they should analyze the reasons behind challenges or falls, and use these experiences to refine their decision-making. The wisdom gained from setbacks contributes to the ability to navigate future situations with greater insight and practical judgment. Additionally, skaters should engage in reflective practices after each skating session, taking moments to contemplate the challenges faced, decisions made, and the lessons learned. This reflective habit contributes to the development of practical wisdom by deepening the skater's understanding and improving their decision-making capabilities.

Skating also provides opportunities for individuals to practice another important virtue, the virtue of friendship. According to Aristotle, the complete and highest form of friendship is the friendship of good people. The friendships of good people are built on mutual respect, shared values, and a recognition of each other's virtues. Friends in this category genuinely care for each other's well-being and are interested in the other person for their intrinsic qualities. Aristotle argues that friendships of good people are built on mutual admiration for each other's character and a shared commitment to personal and moral growth.

In the context of skating, individuals often support and encourage each other's progress, fostering a sense of virtue in the pursuit of excellence. The mutual support in attempting new tricks or navigating difficult terrain builds a camaraderie based on virtue. For example, skating requires courage to overcome fears and challenges. When trying to master a trick, such as a kickflip or executing a nose grind, skaters need to overcome challenges, such as timing, balance and precision. Skaters encourage each other to face and conquer these challenges, as professional skateboarder Brian Hansen has pointed out....

> It's always good to have homies there to help motivate you. It definitely helps when you're shooting photos or video with people you feel comfortable with; that really helps you get past the nerves.[10]

These shared experiences of facing such obstacles can deepen friendships, and can promote virtues like courage and perseverance as skaters collectively push their limits and grow in their skills.

Skating helps individuals fulfill their human function completely by providing opportunities to practice virtue. Through the intentional practice of skill, responsible decision-making, and the promotion of positive values in others, skaters not only enhance their personal growth, but also contribute to a virtuous skateboarding culture.

Skateboarding and Realizing Potential

Critics may still argue that skateboarding is a short-lived pursuit which focuses on immediate pleasure and satisfaction, rather than contributing substantially to the deeper and more enduring well-being that is associated with eudaimonia. Instead, it is suggested that the activities worth pursuing are those that have longer-lasting impacts on personal growth and life satisfaction.

First, it is important to note that Aristotle does not specify the type of life one should live. Happiness is inclusive in the sense that nothing is automatically ruled out as an acceptable way of living, so long as it does not involve immoral actions. In that regard, skating is an acceptable way to pursue the good life. Skating is a worthwhile activity that contributes to the pursuit of the good life by helping individuals to realize their potential, which can have a lasting impact on their overall well-being and personal development.

In Aristotle's view, when we strive for happiness, we are trying to realize our potential for good reasoning. The concept of potentiality refers to the inherent capacities or possibilities within an individual that can be developed or actualized. When we strive for happiness, we are aiming to fulfill our potential for good reasoning. However, human beings possess various potentialities, such as physical and intellectual potentialities. Skating provides the opportunity for individuals to actualize a multitude of these potentialities, which contribute to a flourishing life.

Skateboarding helps individuals to realize their physical potentialities. Skating requires the mastery of physical skills such as balance, coordination, and agility. The process of mastering new tricks and maneuvers pushes the boundaries of what the body can achieve. Skaters have the chance to actualize their physical potentialities, honing these skills to navigate and perform tricks effectively. Additionally, the more rational the skateboarder is, the less likely they are to injure their body so badly that they can't keep skating. These physical potentialities, once cultivated through skating, can contribute to a lasting sense of well-being and physical competence.

Skaters are able to realize their intellectual potentialities through problem-solving, risk assessment, and decision-making. Skating involves navigating complex environments and mastering intricate maneuvers. Different skate spots offer varying terrains and challenges. Skaters must adapt their approach to accommodate the specific features of each environment. This adaptability contributes to problem-solving skills as individuals strategize how to navigate and conquer diverse landscapes. Furthermore, skating involves a significant amount of trial-and-error. Individuals attempt tricks, learn from failures, and adjust their approach based on experience. This iterative process cultivates problem-solving skills as skaters analyze what went wrong, adjust their technique, and persist until they achieve success.

Skaters learn to assess risks and make decisions in real-time. Skaters frequently face situations where they need to weigh the potential rewards of a trick against the associated risks. This practice of calculating trade-offs develops a skill set that extends beyond skating, aiding in decision-making contexts where individuals must evaluate competing interests and potential outcomes. Skaters also find themselves making split-second decisions while performing tricks or adapting to unexpected obstacles. Skating helps develop the ability to make quick, yet thoughtful decisions, an invaluable skill which is applicable in various real-life scenarios where rapid decision-making is essential.

Skating serves as an avenue for individuals to realize and actualize a variety of their inherent physical and intellectual potentialities. Skating goes beyond the skate park, leaving a lasting impact on individuals as they realize their full potential.

Skateboarding and the Good Life

Skateboarding contributes to the good life by aligning with Aristotle's view of eudaimonia. As an activity that involves substantial risk, skaters often face a variety of challenges. In participating in such an activity, skaters are able to fulfill their human function by exercising their reasoning capacities and practice virtue. Skating also provides opportunities to realize a range of potentialities, which are important for living a flourishing life. As a result, skateboarding provides a unique avenue to pursue the good life and achieve eudaimonia.

Notes

1. Aristotle. 1985. *Nicomachean Ethics* (ca. 350 BC). Irwin, Terence (Trans.). Hackett Publishing Company.
2. *Ibid.*, 15.
3. *Ibid.*, 17.
4. *Ibid.*, 42.
5. *Ibid.*, 35.
6. *Ibid.*, 154
7. *Ibid.*, 163.
8. *Ibid.*, 53.
9. Dave. 2021. "Steve Caballero Interview". *Old Guys Rip Too*. www.oldguysriptoo.com/steve-caballero-interview/.
10. Men's Journal. 2019. "Conquering Fear with pro Skateboarder Brian Hansen." *Men's Journal*.

The Sound of One Deck Snapping

Seth M. Walker

> Shui-liao called on Ancestor Ma and asked, "What is the precise meaning of the coming of living Zen?" In reply, he got kicked over by Ancestor Ma, whereupon he was suddenly enlightened.
>
> —Chinul, *Straightforward Explanation of the True Mind*[1]

A cool breeze catches the hair fluttering over the bottom of your brow as you glide down the smooth asphalt. An earlier storm has left a musty aroma in the air, battling the smell of sweet, summer blooms appearing in and out of the neighboring hedges. The sun's radiance is slow to dry what remains of the damp morning; the puddles passing through your peripheral reflect the sudden change in the day's weather. The world seems utterly silent—the push of your foot struggling to break it—as you roll along toward a bright horizon.

Drawing similarities between various activities and meditative practice isn't exactly uncommon. And, something like skateboarding can certainly be just as meditative as walking, if you embrace it as such. With a statement like that opening this essay, you're probably thinking something like "Okay, I can see where this is heading: skateboarding is going to be likened to some sort of Csikszentmihalyi-like 'flow' experience or mindfulness practice, where you're fully absorbed in what you're doing to the point where it becomes capable of leading to enlightenment." But I'm not interested in any of that, regardless of whether that's a defensible analysis. For our purposes here, I could care less about how mindful your ride is or how meditative that pop shove-it feels to you. I'm interested in the moment when a handrail smashes into your groin because that earlier storm left it unpredictably slick later in the afternoon, when your head (helmeted, I hope) bounces off a curb because that radiant sun blinded you at just the right time, when that smooth asphalt is the *only* thing you smell—and taste—and when your tailbone is as suddenly cracked as the tail of your board tumbling off in the blurry distance—your agonizing howls having a much easier time breaking that silence than the foot you can no longer feel. I'm interested in the power and potential of *that* moment. And what that moment is capable of.

The instant leading up to a quick slide of a foot and flick of a board involves concentration, focus, and precision. But there's nothing more humbling in the moment that follows than *not* landing the attempted trick. And that fall—the slip, the crash—becomes a sudden jolt and disruption that can offer more than simply an opportunity to snarl at a blameless handrail or weathered curb. Disruptive moments like this can shift our perspectives in profound ways. And it's often through such moments when change *actually* happens.

Zen Buddhist traditions are known for their focus on the suddenness of awakening experiences through either "just sitting" or "silent illumination" meditative practices or the "direct pointing" of a teacher or teaching device. Often, the latter corresponds to the studying of *kōans*—seemingly paradoxical riddles of recorded interactions among various figures with the aim to bring about *kenshō*: the sudden, initial realization and insight into one's nature or being. And, interestingly enough, many *kōans* recount masters literally smacking their students into spontaneous moments free of disillusionment. When one's mind is freed from distraction and stubborn focus—when duality fades and opposition is unified—we inch closer toward *satori*: the much deeper resultant awakening experience. And, when a perplexing statement, story, or master's backhand isn't available, handrails and curbs can do just the trick.

We'll take a look at some of those *kōans* below as we consider the suddenness of *kenshō* more closely in the context of missed tricks, snapped decks, and shattered egos. But more broadly, we'll consider how such irritating and painful moments can similarly and abruptly knock us out of disillusionment and how they can extend to our broader lives as well: as opportunities, like any other *fall*, to learn more about ourselves and the world around us. Within such disruptive moments exists the possibility for awakening wherein dual modes of thinking fade in the wake of a more mindful mode of existence. And a bruised, bleeding shin can easily offer much more in this regard than just frustrated fuel for the next attempt.

Crashing into Kenshō

Kenshō is usually likened to the sort of awakening experience Siddhartha Gautama (the historic Buddha of around the 5th century BC) famously had while sitting under the Bodhi Tree and whose insight and teachings continue to persist today. It results from a direct understanding of oneself—seeing into one's nature. Now, this *seeing* has little to do with the sort of spatial skills needed to navigate a board more than a few yards. It refers to that illuminating, introspective moment that cannot be taught; it can *only* be met directly. According to Meido Moore Roshi, the knowledge associated with *kenshō* "arises from a fundamental, liberative shift in *the very manner* that one sees, apprehends, and knows."[2] In other words, *kenshō* is less an enduring experience than it is a complete and fundamental alteration to the way we *experience* experiences. *Kenshō*, Zen master Albert Low indicates, usually refers to "our first awakening to the truth that we are whole and complete." It is "the first intimation," he continues, "that dualism, which makes us feel divided against others, the world, and ourselves, and therefore causes us to suffer, is indeed an illusion."[3]

Postmodern theorists might recognize the affinity this has with notions of "deconstruction" wherein disruptive inversions of polarities result in a so-called "irruptive emergence." In other words, the world is often seen through a binary lens of oppositional concepts (good/bad, male/female, mind/body, skater/board, and so on), with one of the opposites always holding more power in those relationships. But in moments of disruption, the duality can be overturned—not simply in a way that inverts the dynamic and emphasizes the other, since such an inversion still maintains duality, but in a way that presses us to question our entire perception *of* reality. Such moments can result in powerful, monumental insight, as one is awakened to "the whole potential for the experience of experience itself."[4] And "irruptive" really is the best way to describe what we'll be discussing, as it implies a rushing *in* rather than an explosive *out*. We'll take a look at what can *emerge* amid those irruptions as well, as we consider how the abrupt sensation of feeling your lungs empty themselves as your back hits the pavement might be grounds for something illuminative too.

The thing is, we also *need* that pavement to get back up again. As Eihei Dōgen (1200–1253), the founder of the Sōtō school of Zen, explains in his main collection of works, the *Shōbōgenzō*, we cannot "doubt the moment of falling to the ground at the moment of getting up … those who fall down on the earth stand up on the earth; it is impossible to get up without using the earth."[5] Put differently, the ground need not be or become our rival. We're not battling the ground as we roll across its bumpy surface; it's implicated in the very act of skating, and this fundamental unity reveals itself the moment duality fades—when we see ourselves connected to more than just fresh grip tape.

A story about Musō Soseki (1275–1351)—generally held to be the one who established the practice of Japanese Zen gardening—describes an experience he had when stopping to rest while traveling: "he sat under a tree in the garden and went into a hut. In darkness he wanted to lean on a wall but there was no wall and he fell over."[6] He ended up laughing hysterically when he got up, and he immediately wrote a poem capturing his sudden enlightenment in that subsequent moment. Attaining enlightenment, Dōgen states, "is like those who fall to the ground and use the ground to stand up."[7] Slipping off a noseslide can become a useful first step toward *standing up*—indeed, when the ramifications of that disruptive moment prevail, it becomes clear that slipping and standing are simply part of the same practice. It just depends on how they're perceived and understood.

Knowing How to Fall

But hey, I know what you're probably thinking right now: "Come on. A bruised elbow and diminished sense of accomplishment hardly sound like a recipe for sudden awakening—more like stinging pain and an urgent cue to go grab a runaway board." And I'll agree: that's *one* way to think about them. But the impact of such things isn't *always* bad. What matters is how we understand and appreciate it.

In *zendos* (Zen meditation halls), the overseeing monk is often equipped with a flat, flexible piece of wood a few feet long—somewhere between a paddle and a baton—called a *keisaku*, or "warning stick." This is used to strike those meditating in the back when their attention is fading or when their posture is tiring. The sharp and sudden stimulation between the spine and scapula results in fatigue being relieved, the relaxation of the shoulders and diaphragm, the deepening of the breath, and a lowering of bodily energy. In other words, it's a useful tool for those engaged in what can be such a rigid act. But it can be a little confusing to consider a seemingly violent act useful in a meditation hall. It doesn't exactly *hurt*—no more than a missed ollie to the inner thigh, I'll tell you that! Moore even refers to it as a "compassionate" act for practitioners during especially lengthy meditation sessions and retreats, and he frames its use as "an excellent opportunity for us to cut through habitual delusion, tension, and spinning delusive thought."[8] The use of the *keisaku*, he adds, "essentially resets the body, breath, and energetic system—and thus our minds. It causes a sharp, instantaneous return to clarity: if we know how to receive the blows, they will in fact cause our usual dualistic, conceptual thinking to momentarily collapse"—perhaps even resulting in *kenshō*.[9]

That last point is important, too: *if we know how to receive the blows*. There's a profound difference in this context between reacting to a seemingly shameful smack in the back by someone walking around with a wooden stick (while you're trying to not think about the itch on your left cheek) and gratefully receiving an abrupt, helpful blow. The framing matters—here, and when we find ourselves on our backs, struggling to refill our lungs as we scramble off a flight of stairs. And just as the *keisaku* can be understood as a helpful tool rather than a harmful instrument, *if we know how to receive the blows*, then a similar "sharp, instantaneous return to clarity" from a missed landing might also help us loosen "our usual dualistic, conceptual thinking"—if we know how to *fall*. Learning how to learn from the fall is the next step, of course—about ourselves, our limitations, our expectations, our potential for growth, and the means to grow. And again, there's an important lesson as we come face-to-face with a ground freshly coated with the skin that used to be on our kneecaps: as Dōgen pointed out, we *need* it, and it has something illuminating to offer us if we can *see* it.

Twisted Noses and Missing Fingers

As noted earlier, one of the main ways of *pointing* people in that direction—especially in the Rinzai school—is through use of *kōans*. *Kōans* are often recognized by, and appreciated for, their perplexing riddle-like nature and idiosyncratic dialogues. But it's better to understand them as "public cases" (their literal meaning, from the Chinese *gōngàn*), or the recorded conversations and happenings between masters and students, to better grasp their function as an object of study: to help bring about moments of awakening by immersing oneself in the unpredictability and absurdities characterizing these exchanges—to knock one loose out of intense intellectual absorption or focus and back into the world in order to understand it *as it is* and ourselves *as we are*.

But you're probably wondering what these sorts of awakening-riddles have to do with that inevitable missed-landing, bloody nose, or broken finger. Well, *a lot*, actually—if we also think about falling as a perplexing moment filled with *irruptive* possibilities.

The *Bìyán Yuàn*—better known as the *Blue Cliff Record*—is a collection of one hundred *kōans*, commentaries, and verses compiled during the 12th century. Case fifty-three is particularly relevant here:

> Once when Great Master Ma and Pai Chang were walking together they saw some wild ducks fly by. The Great Master asked, "What is that?" Chang said, "Wild ducks." The Great Master said, "Where have they gone?" Chang said, "They've flown away." The Great Master then twisted Pai Chang's nose. Chang cried out in pain. The Great Master said, "When have they ever flown away?"[10]

The commentary associated with this case indicates that after Pai Chang's nose was twisted and Great Master Ma questioned him, an insightful, awakening moment followed. I'm sure his nose still hurt a little bit, too.

Another case, the third in the *Wumenguan (Gateless Barrier)*—a collection of forty-eight *kōans* compiled about one hundred years after the *Blue Cliff Record*—relays an exchange between Master Jinhua Juzhi and a boy in his company. One day, in the master's absence, the boy was asked about the meaning of the master's and the Buddha's teachings, and he responded by simply holding up a finger—just like Juzhi would do in response to those types of questions. Juzhi found out about this, of course, and he confronted the boy and asked how he responded to their questioning. When the boy held up a finger, Juzhi took out a knife and cut it off! The boy darted away in pain, but Juzhi called out and asked him to quickly explain the meaning of his and the Buddha's teachings. As the boy attempted to hold up his finger, he noticed that it was no longer there and became enlightened.[11]

See? Those types of injuries have a long history of leading toward *kenshō*. Of course, stairwells and half-pipes aren't exactly consciously fiddling with our noses or mangling (or removing!) our digits. But when we frame skateboarding incidents—or any kind of similar incident—as having the means to *point* us in the direction of discovery and insight, the suddenness of a fall's impact bears strong functional similarities and the potential for transformative rewards.

Feel That Fall

Up to this point, we've been considering the disruptive nature of falling and how that compares to certain Buddhist practices and the study of *kōans*. But it's not *just* about that disruption. There's an important introspective and contemplative element associated with it as well—what transforms disruption into that *irruption* I keep hammering at you regarding *kenshō*.

If you've heard at least one *kōan*, there's a good chance it was that catchy brainteaser about a single hand clapping. Hakuin Ekaku (1686–1769), one of the most important figures in the history of the Rinzai school of Zen, and known for his emphasis on *kenshō*, was reading through the commentary for case eighteen in the *Blue Cliff Record* when a line caught his eye: "A single hand does not make a random sound."[12] His inquiry, "What is the sound of one hand?" eventually became the famed, "What is the sound of one hand clapping?" But as Joan Sutherland Roshi points out, the literal translation is something more like, "One of a pair of hands makes a sound. Hear that sound."[13] The former, she states, is more like a riddle; the latter is "a bottomless well of a question."[14]

Let's tweak that a bit here:

An ambitious boardslide sends you tumbling. Feel that fall.

Yeah, I know. That sounds as easy as it *sounds*. But is it? *Kōan* examination—and more specifically, the introspection *kōans* encourage—isn't meant to just end after careful, reflective consideration of what was written down by some old Buddhists. *Kōan* examination is meant to lead to changes in the way we perceive and understand life and the world around us. And the point we're getting at here is: so can falling on your ass.

What *does* that fall feel like? Does a fall always feel the same? What can a fall teach us? Can the feeling of a fall be conveyed to another? What do we learn about ourselves and our limitations when we fall? What possibilities do we see? And how does our perspective change? Because the thing is, there's often another *kōan* found accompanying that lone hand that can be much deeper and far more important in many ways: "Who is the one who is hearing that sound?" And when it really comes down to it, *that* is the question behind *kenshō*.

Just the Beginning

But, as Hakuin also heavily emphasizes in his teachings, that awakening moment is just the beginning. He heavily stresses gradual practice and developing discerning knowledge associated with having this sort of realization. When we're suddenly jolted into these introspective encounters, when we start asking those deeper questions, and when we begin to see the world differently, the practice has really just begun. *Kenshō* pushes us to start considering *what now?* and *what next?* And post-*kenshō* practice—what we *really* mean by *kenshō*—is conditioned by that awakening moment: what we learn about ourselves necessarily shapes the aftermath of a fractured wrist or twisted ankle.

Remember Low's indication earlier, likening *kenshō* to a "first awakening" and a "first intimation" to the illusion of dualism? *Awakening* isn't the climactic endpoint; it marks a heightened sense of understanding and appreciation on our continuing path toward further realization (*satori*). With *kenshō*, Low adds, "the deeply engrained belief in the opposition between 'the world' and 'me' melts away. Because the age-old sense of separation dissolves, the anguish, despair, and fear that had accompanied it and had smothered and burnt throughout life is also dissolved."[15] That initial moment is filled with so much perceptive possibility rushing in to flood our awareness. It is, indeed, an *irruptive* first step.

But we can't, of course, simply glorify slipping off a board to the point where *that* becomes the goal or presume that every fall is somehow deeply transformative. When we're skating, we aim to land. And most falls are never as shattering to our understandings of reality as they are to our knees and elbows—even if we *know how to receive the blows*. If we're dedicated, we usually keep moving after we fall. We get back up when we're able and try another attempt. Persistence, often through the repeated assault or berating of a master, is also a common theme in those collections of bemusing cases. And, while those *kōans* generally result in that eventual *kenshō*, the point is that sometimes the gradual build-up is just as important as what follows. We might spend what seems like a lifetime falling while trying to land a frontside lipslide, but once we heed Dōgen's advice and learn how to receive that crash, then there's a lot more we have the potential to realize than simply how to adjust our timing and stance. And just *maybe*, we start to discern the interconnectedness between ourselves, our boards, and the ground each time we're shaken loose from those moments of intense concentration and focus. And then, just *maybe*, we might start to extend that discernment to other areas of our lives as well.

Now, get back to your mindful, flow-like ride. Just remember: when it's painfully or frustratingly interrupted, pay attention, and make sure you're looking *around* just as much as you are *inside*.

Notes

1. Clearly, Thomas. 1997. *Kensho: The Heart of Zen*. Boston: Shambhala, 27.
2. Moore, Meido. 2020. *Hidden Zen: Practices for Sudden Awakening and Embodied Realization*. Boulder: Shambhala, 11.
3. Low, Albert. 2006. *Hakuin on Kensho: The Four Ways of Knowing*. Boston: Shambhala, 43.
4. Clearly, viii.
5. Tanahashi, Kazuaki, ed. 2012. *Treasury of the True Dharma Eye: Zen Master Dogen's Shobo Genzo*. Boulder: Shambhala, 325.
6. Tanahashi, Kazuaki. 2024. *Gardens of Awakening: A Guide to the Aesthetics, History, and Spirituality of Kyōto's Zen Landscapes*. Boulder: Shambhala, 17.
7. Tanahashi, *Treasury*, 326.
8. Moore, 86–87.
9. *Ibid.*, 87.
10. Cleary, Thomas, and J.C. Cleary, trans. 2005. *The Blue Cliff Record*. Boulder: Shambhala, 309.
11. Gu, Guo. 2016. *Passing Through the Gateless Barrier: Kōan Practice for Real Life*. Boulder: Shambhala, 37, 42.
12. Cleary and Cleary, 120.
13. Sutherland, Joan. 2022. *Through Forests of Every Color: Awakening with Koans*. Boulder: Shambhala, 19.
14. *Ibid.*, 20.
15. Low, 12–13.

IV
Why Skate?

The Risk *Is* the Reward

Brian Harding

When you skate, one thing is certain: you're going to fall. You're going to fall in the beginning, as you learn to stand, roll, and eventually ollie. And you're going to continue to fall for as long as you skate. Or, at the very least, you're going to continue to fall for as long as you push yourself as a skater.

Since falling (along with a variety of other ways of failing) is inseparable from the pursuit, skating is an inherently risky activity. To get on a board and skate is to accept risk. Skateboarding has given me a wide variety of injuries: innumerable bumps and bruises, banged-up knees and elbows, broken toes, deep cuts (that left scars), and even a concussion. I'm fortunate to have not broken any major bones, but I've *seen* it happen. With all of this in mind, the goal I hope to accomplish here is to persuade you that the risks and possibly even injuries that come with skateboarding are not bugs but *features* of the practice.

Skating teaches us, in a very physical and direct manner, that one should risk pain and injury as the price of the achievement of a good. Note that I am not saying that skating is about risking pain and injury *per se*, only that such risk is a route to the good(s) skating offers. Moreover, while not itself a virtue, by teaching one to accept pain and discomfort for the sake of some good, it leads one *toward* virtue. The classical term for this condition is continence (*enkratiea*).[1] Typically, people seek to avoid pain or acquire pleasure, but the continent person does the opposite (acquiring pain or avoiding pleasure) for the sake of the good he or she wishes to achieve. Aristotle puts it this way: "the continent person knows that his appetites are base, but because of reason does not follow them."[2] In the context of skating, the continent skater knows that risk-avoidance is base, because he or she knows that to achieve many of the goods of skating (e.g., landing tricks, clearing gaps, improving over time, etc.) one must risk pain and even injury. To explain and defend this claim, I will offer some *phenomenological* sketches of the experience of skating (phenomenology being an approach to philosophy developed in the early 20th century which focuses attention on the analysis of experience) and argue that skating can teach us how to develop our moral character.

From the First Ollie to the Gap

The first trick one learns (after figuring out how to pump, turn, and balance) is almost always the ollie. Inevitably, the first ollie is exciting—even if the new skater only gets just barely off the ground. Why is getting such little air so exciting? At least in part, achieving such a minor skating victory gives us such a thrill because of the numerous failed attempts that preceded that first successful attempt. And, almost inevitably, those failed attempts come with a number of falls. The board sometimes shoots out in front of you as you fall backwards, landing on the unforgiving pavement. Even here, at the very beginning of your journey as a skater, falls and injuries can be common.

Your ollies will grow in height: from a quarter inch to six inches to a couple feet, from a real challenge to a trick you land regularly without much effort. This means two things. First, it is time to work on *new* tricks: kickflips, 180s, and so on. Second, you've got to start working on gaps. Gaps are an important, if not fundamental, element of street skating. You have to get off the flat ground and work on going up and down. First, you might try to ollie up and down curbs even though you'll experience some falls here as well. But eventually, success in landing these more involved tricks is not going to be good enough; it's time to hit the stairs: two steps, then three, and so on.

Sizing up that first set of stairs can be intimidating for a novice skater. The bigger the gap, the bigger the risk of injury. When I was a young skater, my friends and I often skated behind an elementary school near my house. It offered, among other things, a loading dock and a four or five step staircase. Loading docks are a bit easier as they only require that you manage the drop; distance isn't really an issue; you can just ride off while doing a small manual as you prepare to land. Stairs are a bigger challenge. A staircase requires that you handle both the height differential between take-off and landing as well as linear distance. To clear any kind of distance requires a degree of speed, which entails an increased level of commitment to the trick. If you're really committed to the gap, even bailing risks injury. In fact, there are at least *two* (closely related) forms of risk. There is the risk of failure (the chance that you simply won't land the trick), and there is also—perhaps more worrisome—the risk of injury (the chance that you'll really hurt yourself).

As we shall see, although these two types of risk are logically distinct, they are (in skating) phenomenologically inseparable: whenever a skater risks failure, he or she is also risking injury. That is, failure to land a trick is inevitably or inherently coupled with the risk of injury. Essentially every skater has had the experience of screwing up an even relatively simple trick and falling *hard*. So, while we can distinguish between the two forms of risk in principle, for the skater, they are often experienced (or to use the language of phenomenology, *given*) as the same thing. The gap is given as risky in both senses at the same time.

To see why, let's try a phenomenological exercise called "eidetic variation." Again, phenomenology is a variety of philosophy that focuses on the analysis of everyday experience as a way of approaching philosophical problems. Edmund Husserl, the founder of phenomenology, developed this method in an attempt to discover what is truly essential to an experience.[3] Without getting *too* technical, it involves imagining different ways an experience could be changed and asking whether it would still be the same thing given those changes. So, I can eidetically vary my image of a skateboard by imagining it with different graphics, different trucks and wheels, etc. And under such conditions it would still be a skateboard. However, if we vary it enough or in certain ways (e.g., by adding handlebars to it), it would no longer be an experience of a skateboard; it would be an experience of a scooter, albeit an imaginative experience.

With this in mind, let's try to eidetically imagine skating without risk to see if it would still be a worthwhile endeavor. Let's call our first attempt Eidetic Variation 1 or EV1. Imagine you were guaranteed to (a) land every trick you attempted so that (b) you never hurt yourself. Since EV1 completely removes the challenge and risk of skating, it is a far cry from skating as anyone normally experiences it. Under such conditions, there would be no satisfaction in landing even the most difficult trick, since success was guaranteed all along. This variation is missing both the risk of failure and the risk of injury.

Clearly, EV1 goes too far. Perhaps we can make it a bit more appealing in other variations. Let's try removing (a) but keeping (b), thereby reintroducing the risk of failure while still leaving out the risk of injury. Call this variation EV2. In it, since you might not land every trick or clear every gap, you risk failure, but since you will never be hurt, you do not risk injury. It's worth noting that EV2 departs fairly significantly from typical skating experiences where the risk of failure and injury are given jointly. The invulnerability that EV2 imagines us to have fundamentally transforms the experience of skating into something else, into some other type of experience. It may be worthwhile or interesting in its own right, but it isn't skating (at least, not as we know it). The point here is a phenomenological one. That is, this experience of skating (or, the way skating is *given* to the skater) would be transformed into something unrecognizable without the risk of injury.

That leaves us with one final eidetic variation. Imagine a scenario where (c) no tricks are landed, but (d) you risk injury every time you attempt a trick. Here, the risk of failure is 100 percent, but there is a chance that you don't injure yourself when failing. In fact, we don't have to imagine this variation; call it EV3. EV3 is essentially the experience of beginning skaters as they attempt to ollie.

This point can be reinforced if we note that this situation—not landing any tricks but risking injury—is the situation that confronts every skater as they attempt to improve themselves. I suffered my aforementioned concussion the first time I dropped into the bowl at Jeff Phillip's Skatepark in Dallas. I dropped in, fell, and banged my head on the wood (I didn't have a helmet; it was the mid-90s). Was this a pointless exercise? Not to my mind: more important than landing anything (or even successfully dropping in) was taking the risk that simply came with the attempt. The only way one can progress as a skater is to voluntarily increase the risks they take. Progress in skating is experienced as the successful navigation of increasingly risky maneuvers. Our three variations suggest that the *risk* of not successfully landing tricks and thereby hurting oneself is *essential* to the experience of skating. One of the great lessons of skating is that a skater *should* risk injury (in various respects or to certain degrees) for the sake of improvement. You will not improve as a skater if you don't take risks; something similar can be said of life in general.

On Certainty and Uncertainty

If the forgoing is correct, then skateboarding not only asks us to accept risk, but courts it as an important part of the experience of skating. The experience of skating is given as an experience of risk-taking. But of course, that's only half the story. There is an acceptable level of risk which skaters take, but part of what skating teaches is how to *gauge* risk. A beginning skater shouldn't attempt the same gaps as an accomplished skater. Consider the famous video of Danny Way dropping into a vert ramp from a helicopter. I have no reservation admitting that something like that is far beyond my skill set as a skater; it's something that I simply wouldn't try. There is a difference between *risk* of injury and *certain* injury. Lacking Way's skills, dropping in from a helicopter essentially guarantees failure and serious injury (for me, anyway).

This is perhaps an extreme example, but more mundane ones are all too familiar. While we might encourage the rookie skater to try a small gap, it would be irresponsible to point them toward a large staircase. While skaters should take risks, they must calibrate the risk and work themselves up incrementally toward greater and greater levels of risk. Many of those I skated with back in the day were more talented (or more practiced) than I was. I recall watching one friend at the skate park set up a chair on a 50-gallon trashcan at the top of a ramp so he could clear it. He didn't land it on the first try, but he did land it eventually. Nobody else at the park even made an attempt; for the rest of us, failure was certain.

The point is that skating asks us to thread the needle between certain failure and certain success; neither is good for the experience. Instead, skating requires risk and *uncertainty*. The gap is given to the skater as both threatening and enticing such that the skater says to himself "I *think* I can make it, and attempting to do so is worth the risk." When you're certain that you'll land a trick, there is a sense in which doing so doesn't even require you to try. When you're certain that you *can't* land a trick, you'll abstain altogether. Recall my experience of dropping into a bowl: I had been skating for a while and dropped in on most of the other ramps at the park. As such, the bowl seemed like the next logical challenge. It was not completely outside the realm of possibility that I would successfully drop in (at least, eventually). I was relatively sure I would fall any number of times *at first*. But there remained ramps (e.g., the 12-foot vert ramp) that I would not drop in on, feeling that I was not up to the task. So, again, skating involves us in an uncertain risk. And one accepts this risk as the price of pushing one's limits as part of what it takes to improve.

Relatedly, Aristotle's discussion of the virtue of courage in his *Ethics* includes the idea that courage requires exposure to the possibility of death for the sake of the noble.[4] However, he also claims that what courage requires varies according to the capabilities of each person. He does not expect all courageous people to act identically. For instance, a courageous octogenarian will manifest courage in a different way than a healthy, spry 21-year-old. Although I'm not claiming that risk-taking in skateboarding is (or entails) Aristotelian courage (for reasons to be clarified later), something quite similar can be said about risk-taking in skating.

As we've seen, skating requires exposure to the possibility of injury, but the appropriate level of risk-taking varies with the capability of the skater. And an important part of skating is learning how to evaluate one's own abilities and the corresponding level of appropriate risk to take. A fundamentally important aspect of this, as we have seen, is uncertainty. If you *only* attempt tricks you are certain to land, you are not skating seriously. At the same time, if you are only attempting tricks you are certain to *never* land, you are similarly wasting time. It seems that (what we might call) the golden mean is to attempt tricks that you *might or might not* land. As soon as one can land an ollie with little or no effort, it's time to move to the kickflip.

The Enduring Lesson of Skating

Thus far, I've tried to offer a phenomenological sketch of the experience of skating that highlights the importance of risk-taking. Risk, understood as both the risk of failure and of injury (because, phenomenologically they run together) is a major element of the experience of skating. In addition to this, the risks should be calibrated to one's ability, so that skating takes place somewhere between certain success and certain failure. At any given moment, that area of uncertainty is given differently to different skaters such that each must learn where that space is.

However, at this point, one might ask, why skate at all if it is so bound up with risk and injury? Aren't there better ways to spend our time? After all, what is going to happen when I try a gap and fail? It's pretty straight forward: I'll fall (and almost certainly onto a hard, unforgiving surface). Nevertheless, I want to claim that falling and hurting yourself while skateboarding *itself* is (or can be) good. Not only does skating require risk-taking, but the rewarding part of skating is more likely found in falling and hurting oneself than in successfully landing tricks. There are at least two reasons for this.

The first reason falling and hurting oneself while skating may be good is rooted in ancient moral philosophy. At various points in the *Nicomachean Ethics,* Aristotle notes that the majority of people are readily moved in one direction or another by the pursuit of pleasure and the avoidance of pain. In many instances, this isn't an issue: the morally correct thing may also be the most pleasant thing. However, this can present a problem when the morally praiseworthy path is also a painful one. As such, Aristotle suggests that one should accustom oneself to pain and discomfort, so that they are less easily influenced by the desire to avoid pain or seek pleasure.

Earlier, we referred to this as being continent. While continence is technically not a virtue—since the virtuous person would, according to Aristotle, find vice *per se* unpleasant—it is *on the way* to virtue. The distinction between the virtue of temperance or moderation (*sôphrosune*) on the one hand and continence (*enkrateia*) is subtle and doesn't need to be fully explained here, but one way of thinking about the difference is to imagine that in the temperate person, the appetites or desires agree with what practical reason (when it is functioning well) discovers to be good, while in the case of the continent person, he or she is pulled in two directions at once. The continent person knows what is good, but doesn't want to do it. There is an internal conflict in the soul of the continent person while the virtuous person is at peace with themselves. So, the continent person doesn't *want* to do the right thing for its own sake but forces themselves to do it anyway.

Cicero adds to this that continence must be developed by exposure to uncomfortable things; one must accustom oneself to discomfort.[5] But this is what skateboarding can do: by falling repeatedly, one accustoms oneself to pain and discomfort, learning to subordinate physical suffering to the higher intention of successfully landing the trick, eventually. It teaches us to try the gap that is a little scary, to push ourselves into an uncomfortable place. This is not a benefit exclusive to skating—it can be found in a variety of physical pursuits—but it is unlikely to be found in more mundane, less dangerous activities (e.g., e-sports, card games, etc.).

Second, not only does skating accustom us to risk and pain, it also teaches that risk, pain and injury are inseparable from many worthwhile pursuits. To skate, as we have noted, is to risk injury. The experience of clearing the gap is inseparable from the pain that accompanied the preceding failed attempts. I think that there is an important moral pedagogy here: to achieve anything good or worthwhile requires suffering. Too often we are encouraged to avoid risk and told that a life without risk or injury is preferable to one of suffering and uncertainty. Skating teaches us that this is false, that memory of risk and injury are part of the joy of success. To be sure, one could and should distinguish between kinds of pain or injury; one might say that skating teaches the acceptance of teleological injuries and pains that contribute to the achievement of some good, which is not to suggest that one should accept pointless injuries and pains that contribute to nothing. Skating, ultimately, is not about risking pain and injury *per se* but about accepting these risks as the price of the achievement of a good. It teaches us that the good we seek is *not* free and that achievement extracts a toll.

Earlier (when reminiscing about stairs and loading docks), I argued that the skater needs to commit to the gap. When dropping in on a ramp or bowl, you must lean into the fall; if you shrink away or lean *back*, you will bust. There is again an important lesson in this experience. Much of what we've said since then focused on risk and injury, but we would be remiss if we did not also highlight the importance of *commitment* to skating. To land a trick, clear a gap, or drop in, you must be committed. Often, one bails on a trick out of fear; the skater who bails decides that the risk isn't worth it. This should be distinguished from simply losing control on a trick; to bail is to intentionally abort the maneuver to minimize the risk of injury. To be sure, in some cases this is entirely justified, but it is equally true that the more you bail the less you develop as a skater. Commitment is required to develop one's skills, and it is commitment that allows us to persevere in the face of pain and injury. After falling, the skater must get back up and try again; the skater recommits to the risk of injury for the sake of skating. Here too skating teaches us: without commitment (in the face of risk) you will not succeed; skating teaches us to lean into that which makes us want to bail.

Saints and Skaters

The final important lesson from skating is that there is a link between the four important ideas we've considered thus far: commitment, risk, failure, and improvement. It is at least arguable that the last of these cannot be achieved without the first three. While we can separate them perhaps in principle, skating shows us that they are phenomenologically (i.e., in terms of how they appear in our experience) inseparable.

I haven't skated seriously in some time. I am not sure when (or if) I "quit"; I know that at some point I skated less and less frequently, and when my board would break, the time before I replaced it grew longer and longer. The time and effort I put into skating slowly turned toward other activities (e.g., rock climbing, backpacking, travel, obstacle course racing, etc.) which similarly enrich my life by making it needlessly difficult. That said, the lessons of skating—of taking risks, or even *seeking out* risk, as a key to growth and development in all and any areas of life—is one I have taken with me every day. Even writing this essay is part of the fruit of my skating: going to graduate school and then trying to get a full-time job teaching philosophy was pretty damn risky (as anyone familiar with the academic job market could tell you). Being comfortable with risk, and indeed recognizing that taking risks, failing, injury, and pain are inseparable from any pursuit or growth in one's life is a great lesson that I attribute to my time skating. But, if this is the case, it's worth asking: why does skating have such a bad reputation? Why did we have to adopt the mantra that "skateboarding is not a crime?" Why isn't skating recognized as a great teacher of virtue and embraced by schools and similar institutions?

To help us answer these questions, we can return to Aristotle who considers whether virtue can be taught. It depends, Aristotle argues, on the kind of virtue one has in mind. He distinguishes between intellectual and moral virtues: the intellectual virtues can be taught but the moral virtues cannot.[6] You can teach math or science in a classroom but not honesty or courage. Instead, the latter are inculcated by a kind of training or practical experience that forms one's character. In this sense, it is slightly misleading to speak of skating as teaching (as I have admittedly done throughout this essay). One learns *from* skating, not in the way one learns math or science, but in the way one learns to behave in one way or another. As I've argued, skating teaches continence. This, Aristotle makes clear, is not a virtue, but a step *toward* virtue. Moreover, since skating is not the *only* thing even a dedicated skater does, it is not the sole source of character formation in the skater; he or she exists in a complex web of practices and persons that will influence the development of the skater's personality and character. Skateboarding *can* teach us good things, whether we *in fact* learn the lessons skating offers is another question.

Thus, it's worth considering that, in *The Republic*, Socrates devotes a great deal of time to the praise of philosophy. Incredulously, his interlocutors ask him why the majority of people think that philosophers are weirdos or criminals if philosophy is so good (a question some may want to ask about skaters if we try to explain the virtues or benefits of skating). Socrates's answer is that while philosophy teaches good things, it is not the only teacher even the dedicated student of philosophy has, and often those other teachers can corrupt the young philosopher.[7] Something similar can be said of skating: skating teaches a good thing: continence. But it is not the only teacher the skater has, and these other teachers can inculcate bad habits. Moreover, since skating only occasionally takes place where skating is actually *allowed*, those other practices encouraged by skating involve law (or at least rule) breaking. And waxing, grinding, and sliding can damage property, if only mildly, so often that skaters are chased off the premises by security or police.

Skating may not be a *crime*, but it is often enough a misdemeanor. This being the case, it is easy to see why skating doesn't always lead to virtue. Again, Socrates makes a similar point in *The Republic*: the philosophical soul's desire to question and investigate traditional nostrums can also lead the philosophical youth to associate with less savory characters who will lead it astray.[8] Skating does not make one a good person, nor does it make one a bad person. Human life and development are too complex to attribute all good or all bad to just one source, but it is equally true that within that complexity, we can attend to the moral training contained within the practice of skating, even as we acknowledge that it is neither necessary nor sufficient for virtue. Nevertheless, all else being equal, skating is a rewarding activity, not *despite* but *because of*, its risks.

NOTES

    1. Aristotle. 1999. *Nicomachean Ethics*. Irwin, T. (trans.). Hacket, VII.1.
    2. *Ibid.*, 1154b, 10–15.

3. Husserl, Edmund. 1995. *Ideas Pertaining to a Pure Phenomenology and to a Phenomenological Philosophy: First Book*. Kersten, F. (trans.) Kluwer, 156–160; 1975. Husserl, Edmund. *Experience and Judgement*. J. Churchill, J.; and Ameriks, K. (trans.). Northwestern UP, 340–344.

4. *Ibid.*, Aristotle, 1115a—1115b.

5. Cicero. 2001. *Tusculan Disputations* King, J. (trans.). Harvard UP. As Cicero puts it in II.36: "the habit of toil renders the endurance of pain easier."

6. Aristotle, II.1.

7. Plato. 1997. *The Republic. Plato: The Complete Works*. Cooper, John (ed.). Hackett, 487b—489b; 491a—495b.

8. *Ibid.*, 492a.

Skate and Destroy Capitalism

THUNDER STORM HETER

Thrasher Magazine is an important archive of skate culture. Perhaps the most influential skateboarding magazine, it helped popularize (the now ubiquitous) street skating. Founded in 1981, *Thrasher* got its start just before the era in which VHS skate videos became a primary means of consuming skate culture. In part because of *Thrasher*'s photographs of the style, innovators such as Mark "Gonz" Gonzales, Natas Kaupas, Tommy Guerrero, and others, street skating boomed in the mid–1980s.[1] Young people across the United States consumed *Thrasher*'s photographs of amateur and professional skaters which led them to adopt a style of skating that could take place in nearly any urban or suburban environment. Earlier generations of skaters preferred ramp and pool skating while Gonz, Kaupas, and Guerrero were photographed skating ordinary city streets, as well as curbs, drainage ditches, and old parking lots. Kids from California to Kansas imitated what they saw in *Thrasher* and similar publications, while also building up local communities where they developed their own tricks and styles.

Thrasher's unofficial motto is "Skate and Destroy," but to "destroy" can mean several different things to a skater. Destroying terrain can simply mean to skate well and with aggression. But to "destroy" can also refer to the attitude some street skaters have toward the private and public property that make up their preferred spaces for skating. Street skaters often take the view that streets, park benches, curbs, and handrails *ought* to be skated, even (and sometimes especially) when city officials and private security guards treat them as unwanted vandals or trespassers.

Kevin Thatcher inaugurated *Thrasher* in January 1981 with an important editorial that set out the magazine's vision for skate culture. He queries, "[H]ave we, at times, lost sight of what skateboarding really is?"[2] As Thatcher saw it, skating has "unlimited possibilities." The skateboard is not only a "transportation device," and "a basis for a valid sporting activity," but also "a vehicle for aggressive expression."[3]

However, there is an ambivalence in Thatcher's description of skating as both a "sport" and a means of "aggressive expression." Some skaters take street skating to be a sport, fundamentally. That is, it's a form of competition with rules, winners, and cash prizes. For such skaters, there is no shame in being sponsored by for-profit corporations; they take pride in being paid to promote brand-name clothing, shoes, and skateboards. In contrast to this, other street skaters reject the idea that skating is a sport, preferring to see themselves as artists or rebels who couldn't care less about commercial success, formal competitions, or the latest gear. Appealing to this second type of skater, Thatcher makes the case that "thrashing is an attitude, a skate attitude. Thrashing is part of a lifestyle, a fast-paced feeling to fit this modern world…. Remember, there are tons of asphalt and concrete poured every day, so—GRAB THAT BOARD."[4]

Because skateboarding is a cultural phenomenon (i.e., a set of customs, collective ideas, and social attitudes toward the world) it is not surprising that there are conflicting ideas about what it means to be a skater. This conflict—between skating as sport and skating as spontaneous activity—is the subject of this essay. Understood as a sport, skating sits well with pro-capitalist sentiments about the importance of the marketplace and the neo-liberal idea that freedom simply amounts to purchasing power. Understood as a spontaneous activity, skating can be understood as *hostile* to capitalism and infused with tendencies toward anarchism: the political philosophy which rejects the validity of the nation state, rejects private property, and favors the creation of small communities that promote individual freedom. To navigate these different interpretations of skate culture, it will be helpful to draw on the work of the 20th-century French philosopher Jean-Paul Sartre. Sartre was a Marxist and anarchist philosopher who was highly critical of capitalism.

In *Critique of Dialectical Reason, Vol. 1*,[5] Sartre lays out a social theory that can help us understand how street skating culture is not monolithic but contains conflicting interpretations of what it means to be a skater. Sartre argues that any "society" (or culture) is a mix of different types of social assemblies (which he calls "groups" and "series").[6] Genuine groups, according to Sartre, foster social recognition and freedom, while serial social assemblies are alienating because they place individuals in external relations to one another, such as the relationship of one consumer to another.

The Skater as Anti-Capitalist Rebel: Vandalism and Sessioning

Sartre wrote nothing about skateboarding, but if he had, he would most likely have emphasized the contradiction between the spontaneous, anti-capitalist strain of street skate culture and the pro-capitalist, competitive strain. Sartre argued that one of the main effects of capitalist regimes, which is to say societies based on private property, was to alienate the citizens of society from one another.[7] Markets are impersonal, mass phenomena in which the consumer buys products to imitate other consumers. As an anarchist, Sartre rejected the legitimacy of the nation state, which he saw as a masquerade for the interests of the propertied classes. The antidote to capitalist alienation, according to Sartre, was the formation of spontaneous, decentralized groups which challenge the authority of the state and the institution of private property. One possible philosophical interpretation of street skating is to treat sessions as the kinds of freedom-enhancing groups written about by Sartre in the *Critique*.

Those street skaters who understand themselves to be anti-capitalist rebels and artists could point to the fact that street skating often involves vandalism and spontaneous sessioning. These two elements fit well with Sartre's notion of genuine groups. Spontaneous sessions, Sartre would argue, bring together individuals for momentary bonds of solidarity, not organized through a top-down structure, but through bottom-up spontaneous play. Sartre would also actually *praise* street skaters for their vandalism, which he would interpret as an attack on the capitalist institution of private property.

Vandalism (the deliberate destruction of public or private property) is one important element of street skating. Street skaters vandalize benches, handrails, curbs, ditches and other parts of the urban environment by painting, waxing, and otherwise physically modifying them in order to perform maneuvers such as "grinding" and "rail sliding." Grinding and sliding often chip concrete urban architecture, leaving it unsightly or unusable for its originally intended purpose. Not only do street skaters leave marks as they grind away concrete on benches, steps, rails, and curbs, they also manipulate "spots" by adding products like bondo and quickcrete to make obstacles more rideable.

Street skating also often involves trespassing on private and public property where skating has been explicitly prohibited. Skaters are known to clip chain link fences to gain entry into certain skating spots. Skaters also engage in vandalism by removing "skatestoppers" (metal L-brackets mounted in order to stop skaters from grinding). Skate-stoppers are commonly installed by cities to deter skating. By appropriating the billions of tons of concrete that make up urban and suburban spaces across the globe, many skaters implicitly challenge the capitalist institution of property by engaging in deliberate acts of property destruction.

Iain Borden, who has written extensively on skating argues that "skating is a critique of ownership."[8] While some street skaters think of themselves as anti-capitalists, many others are apolitical. For example, an anonymous editorial in the first issue of *Thrasher* describes street skating not as a political act but an artistic way of challenging conventional boundaries imposed by the city authorities:

> A curb is an obstacle until you grind across it. A wall is but a ledge until you drop off it. A cement bank is a useless slab of concrete until you shred it. A street is another downhill to be tucked…. You've got to give the street fair due, rolling is way cooler than walking. Don't restrict your boundaries, skate architecture is everywhere, grind every ledge.[9]

Another important element of street skating culture is the practice of "sessioning," or spontaneously joining with a group of fellow skaters to skate an obstacle. Tony Hawk notes that spontaneous skate sessions provided him with a sense of freedom that he never felt in team sports: "It felt free, liberating, boundless. I didn't have to rely on a team for my own success, nor did I have to adhere to a strict set of rules to play correctly."[10] While there are arguably many different types of skate sessions (e.g., some are competitive; some are not all that different from a football practice)[11] many sessions are anti-hierarchical. Professor Becky Beal writes, "The ethos of skateboarding resonates with me. It's fundamentally democratic: the participants are responsible for their own growth and development as well as the development of their friends' skill sets and the activity itself. Most skaters do not rely on coaches or a rule book; instead, skateboarders are the ones who construct the activity."[12] The type of skate sessioning that Hawk and Beal describe is one variation of how skaters make community, although there are also competitive, market-based forms of skating.

To get a better sense of spontaneous sessioning, consider a first-person (or "phenomenological") description of a skate session in my neighborhood.

> It's 5 p.m. on Wednesday. Gingi DMs me, "you tryna skate today?" I write back, "bet … where at?" After some back and forth we agree on a spot. "Wanna hit the curb behind Dunklebergers?" We agree to meet at the spot in about 20 minutes. The spot is a long, down-hill double-sided curb behind some businesses. When I arrive, I need to wax the curb. I pull out a block of paraffin wax and spend five minutes smearing it on the curb so that we can slide our skateboards on it. Gingi hits the curb first, with a frontside boardslide, a safe warm-up trick. The move involves turning the skateboard sideways on top of the curb and sliding as far as possible. He does not land the trick because the curb is waxed and too fast. His board shoots out from under his feet, but he has anticipated the fall, and he jumps deftly off the board. "I'll back you up," I say as I try the same maneuver, trying to calculate how slick the curb is based on Gingi's fall. I slide too fast and jump off my board. I let out a loud "whooo." Gingi responds with "yesssiiir" and pushes off with speed for a second attempt. As he ollies into the curb, the tail of his board makes a loud "snap," followed by the even louder sound of his wooden

board scraping across the concrete curb. This time he lands the trick, and I scream "yooooo!" and clap. Before I can push off for my turn on the curb, I see James and Lil John pull up. Then the session is on. I warn James "Its waxed up," as he pushes off and does an ollie to frontside tailslide. His maneuver is more difficult than the one I've been trying, and I'm stoked. "Yeah dude! Sick!" I roll back to the curb, trying to decide if I'll do an easy, safe trick that I know I can land or if I'll try a more difficult maneuver like the one James pulled. I go for a slappie to tail and though I pull the move, it is sloppy. James whistles in encouragement, but disappointed in myself I say "Ugh … that was garbage." Lil John jumps into the line-up, and as the best of all of us, he'll do a warmup trick that's harder than anything I could do on my best day. John ollies into a front blunt slide. We just look at each other and laugh, muttering "Oh my god…." It's Gingi's turn again. He turns his board backwards, snapping ninety degrees into a long boardslide, which he exits backwards. The session is heating up. We are feeding off of one another's energy to try harder tricks and to see who can slide the longest on the curb. I commit to a couple of long pushes toward the curb just as a blue CRV turns down the alley.

We are skating in a parking lot, so dodging cars is normal. The driver looks annoyed, so we move to the side and wave until they pass. For another hour, the four of us repeat the cycle of pushing towards the curb and sliding or grinding down it in various ways. Stoked by our friends, we try harder and harder maneuvers, and push faster and faster. There is no formal order of who will go first, or what trick will be performed. The session goes as long as everyone is "feeling it." We stop every once in a while to drink water or beer or to smoke tobacco or cannabis. There are no "winners" or "losers" in the session. We often fall and get hurt. We often yell or whistle or vocalize to encourage ourselves and others. The session is centered around the curb, which we treat like a sacred object, returning again and again, sometimes with mind-numbing repetition, trying the same move ten or fifteen times in a row. There are no rules for the session. There is no leader telling others how to skate. The session can dissolve at any time, for any reason—we sometimes get kicked out of this spot by the owners of the sewing machine store who share this parking lot with other merchants. Tonight, we do not get kicked out. John, James, and Gingi decide to drive to another spot, where they know there will be lights. I'm tired though; so, I push home.

The session just described might be interpreted by Sartre as a social group that temporarily binds individuals together in playful, artistic community. According to Sartre, the main elements of anti-capitalist social groups are spontaneity, rotating leadership, and recognition. Skaters who session are spontaneous because they select a spot to session based on personal desire and the feelings of other skaters in the group. They also utilize an urban environment which is dynamic: they navigate cars, pedestrians, weather, property owners, security guards, and police.

The order in which skaters take turns doing tricks or approaching obstacles is also spontaneous.[13] In many sessions, there is a norm of not "snaking" another skater (i.e., not cutting in front of them). The "no-snaking" norm is democratic; each skater should respect the others' use of the shared space. There is also a norm of taking "runs," which involves waiting for other skaters to perform their tricks and remembering who to go after. Another spontaneous part of the session is the choice of tricks each skater performs, as well as how they conceive of the obstacle to be sessioned. When one skater "backs up" another, they try the same trick out of solidarity. There can also be a friendly competition between skaters who want to see if they can match the tricks of others or perhaps offer a twist to the trick that was just performed.[14]

As Hawk notes, since there is no judge or coach dictating what tricks a skater should perform in the type of street session described above, skaters are free to create. The difference between a good session and a bad session usually consists in how the skater feels and how his fellow skaters feel. When and how a session ends is also spontaneous; sometimes skaters are "busted" by property owners or police. Some sessions end with skaters leaving together, while others end with skaters dispersing individually, sometimes running from police or security, and scattering so there is less likelihood of anyone being arrested.

According to Sartre, genuine groups do not have permanent leaders. Similarly, in many street sessions there are no permanent leaders; skaters take turns responding to tricks that other skaters perform. The goals of the session are in part dictated by the terrain. In the case above, it is the curb that organizes and solicits the skaters' boardslides and grinds. Each skater comes to understand the obstacle through the motions of the other skaters. They navigate each other's bodies, building on the energy of the session. As a session heats up, skaters might skate faster, try harder tricks and begin taking turns more quickly, sometimes almost doubling up on an obstacle. When skaters move faster, they also must navigate what to do when the skater in front of them crashes. The skater who crashes momentarily becomes the leader of the group, in the sense that by becoming an obstacle, they temporarily dictate a new "flow" of the session.

A third element of Sartrean groups is social recognition. In *Being and Nothingness*, Sartre coined the notion of the inter-subjective *look* (or gaze),[15] and he focuses on the "shame" that we feel when gazed at by another person. What makes a gaze freedom-affirming rather than alienating is that in some cases we freely allow others to gaze at us (and vice versa). That is, we both gaze, and we are gazed *at*. When skaters session, they invite the others in the session to gaze at them, to analyze their tricks and their style. Yelling out and vocalizing one's reaction to another skater's tricks is common and reveals a pattern of social recognition. The gazing in a skate session can be mutual. Not all sessions follow this pattern of mutual recognition. In some sessions, skaters may ridicule others for their style, their skill level, or even their race, gender or sexuality. In those cases, Sartre would say that the session has been hijacked by someone trying to become the voice, authority, and leader. The skate bully (like any kind of bully) gazes at others without being willing to be gazed at by them.

In addition to seeing some sessions as non-alienating groups, Sartre might interpret street skate culture as anti-capitalist because of the close tie between street skating and property vandalism. Many street skaters do not respect private property either in theory or practice. Although skaters may (or may not) be able to quote anarchist philosophers, those skaters who engage in vandalism and trespassing often do so with a sense that it is *their place* to skate on public and private property. Many street skaters have a deep suspicion of police and security guards. Even ostensibly "public" property such as sidewalks, streets, and parks are often governed by the logic of property ownership: they are heavily policed, and skateboarding is often made illegal.[16] Skating is made illegal either through the enforcement of anti-vandalism and anti-trespassing laws or through explicit criminal codes. For this reason, the phrase "skateboarding is not a crime" became a rallying cry for skaters in the late 1980s and early 1990s. In urban environments, legal skating is often relegated to publicly-owned skate parks, which themselves have elaborate rules and are monitored by police cameras and security guards.

Capitalist Strains of Street Skate Culture

Because street skating culture is complex, one should not ignore the fact that there are strong pro-capitalist elements of the culture. Some street skaters do not recognize themselves as anarchistic rebels but would see themselves as participants in a culture of competition, fame, purchasing power, and brand-names. Skate brands have become mega-businesses, at the same time that corporate-sponsored professional competitions have exploded in popularity.

As much as *Thrasher* promotes the idea of skating as a spontaneous "expressive activity" (in Kevin Thatcher's words), the magazine is also the publication of a for-profit organization and has become a globally recognized brand. At the same time *Thrasher* depicts skateboarding as a youth sub-culture, deeply tied to graffiti, punk, hip-hop, vandalism, and the do-it-yourself movement, it also stays afloat because of ad revenue and sales from subscriptions and merchandise. In fact, *Thrasher* was founded in part to promote skate equipment made by the Independent Truck Company.[17]

Thrasher also promotes the idea that skateboarding is a "valid sport" by its coverage of professional contests. Since its inception in 1981, which included a write up of the Gold Cup, depicting professional contests has been a constant feature of the magazine. While there are several different versions of formal contests for street skaters (e.g., the X Games, the Olympics, etc.) perhaps the most visible and dominant model of the professional street contest today is the Street League Skateboarding (SLS), founded by celebrity, entrepreneur, and former pro skater Rob Dyrdek.[18] SLS is a capitalist version of street skate culture in two ways. First, SLS is a for-profit corporation where competition takes place in privately owned indoor spaces. Second, and perhaps more importantly, SLS's scoring system offers a reductionist and commodifying vision of street skating.

In 1997, Dyrdek filed a patent application for SLS. A patent application is itself a form of the commodification of skating in that a patent is a way of claiming ownership over a product. Nevertheless, what is more revealing is *how* the patent envisions street skating. The SLS patent attempts to standardize judging techniques for the sake of making skating more appealing to non-skaters. Dyrdek claims that the lack of "organization" in traditional skate contests is a problem solved by the introduction of a standardized system of scoring tricks.[19] Of course, Dyrdek has tried to make the case that he is *improving* street skating competitions by ditching the individual run format in which skaters are given a few minutes to construct a run (a series of tricks on different obstacles across the park).

Runs are often judged on flow or how a skater links up tricks and takes advantage of multiple obstacles. Flow is about how a skater uses space, not about individual tricks. SLS replaces the run format with a trick-based format, where individual tricks are scored. SLS's scoring techniques break skating into its simplest components, rather than trying to comprehend a skater's overall style. In short, Dyrdek is attempting to standardize the style of tricks as well as the spaces where skating takes place. Such "organization" of skating is driven by the profit motive of making skating digestible to consumers who are not familiar with its culture. Dyrdek and others like him want to increase the number of spectators at SLS and similar events so they can line their pockets.

Admittedly, professional and amateur competitions have been an important part of skate culture since the 1970s. The difference in SLS, as clearly spelled out in Dyrdek's patent, is the attempt to standardize tricks and scoring, to replace runs with tricks, and to commodify skating. The commodified version of street skate culture offered by Dyrdek sharply contrasts with the spontaneous sessions discussed above. Not only are sessions not scored, they are based on spontaneous flow (i.e., how each trick or maneuver is related to every other trick or maneuver across time and space). A skateboarder's flow demonstrates how the skater understands the relationship of one trick to another and the relationship of the skater to space. A final clue to the bald capitalist nature of SLS is revealed by looking at the corporations that sponsor it, very few of which have any relationship to skateboarding including Nissin Cup Noodles, Nikon, Boost Mobile, G-Shock, Delta Airlines, Accelerator (energy drink), and Stanley.

Skate and Create

There is no single, demonstrably correct answer to Kevin Thatcher's question, "What is skateboarding really?" There are anarchistic, punk-minded street skaters who prefer spontaneous sessions, and there are sports-oriented entrepreneurial street skaters who thrive on shoe sales and SLS-style competitions. For the former type of skater, to "skate and destroy," means to vandalize and trespass in the name of one's art. For the latter type of skater, "destruction" is just a metaphor for aggressive skating, and does not indicate an anti-property, anti-police, or anti-state attitude. What we can learn from Sartre is that these two approaches to skating represent two different and largely incompatible worldviews.

These two types of skaters (or two interpretations of skate culture) tell us about a broader set of cultural struggles in capitalist societies like the United States. The anarchist seeks the social recognition found in spontaneous, leaderless groups that challenge property ownership. The capitalist prefers the anonymity of the market, the comfort of consuming brand-name products, and the sanctuary of privately-owned spaces. As a pro-anarchist, anti-capitalist philosopher, Sartre would say that street skate sessions are preferable to SLS contests because the former provide skaters with a short-term refuge from markets, consumption, and consumerism, while also contributing, in a small way, to an anti-state, anti-property politics.

Notes

1. Stacy Peralta states, "It wasn't until street riding came along in the late '80s that skateboarding, in my opinion, became what it is. Street skating really defines what skateboarding is—it brought it back to its original state, which is anywhere, anytime, anyplace there is concrete." See Mortimer, Sean. 2008. *Stalefish: Skateboard Culture from the Rejects Who Made It*. Chronicle Books, 166.
2. Thatcher, Kevin. 1981. *Thrasher*, January 1981, 5.
3. Ibid.
4. Ibid.
5. Sartre, Jean-Paul. 1960. *Critique of Dialectical Reason, Vol. 1*. Verso.
6. Ibid., 635–42.

IV. Why Skate?

7. *Ibid.*, 635.
8. Borden, Iain. 2001. *Skateboarding, Space and the City: Architecture and the Body.* Berg Publishers, 242. I have been heavily influenced by Borden's wonderful analysis of skateboarding, especially his book.
9. *Thrasher*, no author indicated, January 1981, 15.
10. Mortimer, Sean. 2008. *Stalefish: Skateboard Culture from the Rejects Who Made It.* Chronicle Book, 8.
11. Thank you to Josef Thomas Simpson for mentioning this important point.
12. Beal, Becky. 2013. *Skateboarding: The Ultimate Guide.* Greenwood, xi.
13. Borden, 124. Borden writes that in "the session format" there is an "informal queuing system."
14. The game of SKATE is one way skaters hold informal competitions among themselves. Like the basketball HORSE, skaters take a letter for every trick they cannot perform, until only one skater is left as "winner."
15. Sartre, Jean Paul. 1993. *Being and Nothingness.* Washington Square Press.
16. For example, in my own town, there are explicit laws forbidding skating on streets and sidewalks. See Borough Council of the Borough of East Stroudsburg 5-19-1992 by Ord. No. 972, approved 5-19-1992.
17. See Guevara, Milton. 2021. "Artists, Weirdos, Hellriders, and Homies: Thrasher Magazine Turns 40." *Morning Edition* on NPR.
18. Dyrdek, Rob. 2009. "Skateboard Arena and Method of Competition," U.S. Patent, W02009140664A2, filed 5-15-2009, published 11-19-2009.
19. "Over time, skateboarding went from amateur entertainment to a professional sport. Currently, skateboard contests are unorganized, and lack any understandable scoring system or performance statistics." See Dyrdek, paragraph 0006 [no page number in original].

The Serious Beauty of Skateboarding

John Becker

What is skateboarding, and why should anyone skate? When I ask these questions, I'm not looking for simple answers such as classifications of the activity. I am not asking whether we should think of skating as a hobby, a fad, a sport, or anything like this. These are surface level responses; what I have in mind is something deeper. In fact, I hope to go so deep that I'll be able to show that skateboarding can shine a light on what it means to be human.

The questions I'm raising are existential questions, questions which ask something about the nature of human existence. Existentially rich questions have captivated thinkers across every age and culture. All religious and philosophical traditions address such questions in one way or another. And, unlike the methodology of the hard sciences, there are no precise equations or formulas that can help us answers such questions. But this does not mean that they are meaningless or an unanswerable.

Perhaps unsurprisingly, I am not alone in drawing important parallels between skating, human nature, and religion. For example, Paul O'Connor, a sociologist of skateboarding, writes, "[w]ith hardly anyone noticing, skateboarding has become one of the most religious sports in the world." In his book *Skateboarding and Religion*, he argues that skateboarding and its culture have taken on a religious dimension insofar as they serve "as a central and meaningful motif in the lives of countless individuals who have committed years and sometimes decades to this demanding, difficult and sometimes dangerous pastime."[1] Put differently, skating (not unlike religion) gives people a meaningful and fulfilling orientation to their lives. For those of us who skate (or even know skaters), the all-consuming nature of skateboarding is readily apparent.

What I offer in this essay stems from my experience with religion, philosophy, and skateboarding. And, just as skating is deemed as a countercultural movement, I will draw from philosophical ideas that go against the contemporary narratives, being disruptive in their own way. First, I will very briefly discuss skateboarding's countercultural spirit as a way to introduce two contested ideas: Alfred North Whitehead's concept of beauty and Hans-Georg Gadamer's importance of play. In a consumeristic, hyper-capitalistic culture, these aspects are viewed as insignificant and unimportant, but each provides an answer to what it means to be human. And skateboarding helps us tap into them.

Counterculture Heritage

Counterculture is an idea that skaters should embrace, especially when it comes to skateboarding's inclusive and supportive culture. Professor Becky Beal has written extensively about skateboarding's countercultural and subcultural practices from a sociological and gender perspective. What she finds promising about skate culture is its ability in "creating alternatives [that] can serve as a blueprint for future interaction or social actions and cultural products, it can also inspire and give credence to the idea that there are social choices and that groups of people have the ability to creative alternatives."[2] While inclusivity has not always been the norm in skating, compared to other sports or segments of society, skateboarding has always been fairly progressive.[3]

What I want to highlight here is that skateboarding's dynamic culture has the power to create alternatives. But alternatives to what exactly? Skating can offer alternative possibilities that differ or are directly opposed to mainstream culture, often for positive reasons. Skaters express themselves differently because they view the world differently. It is in this countercultural spirit that I introduce my aim: skateboarding provides us a way to tap into human nature more deeply than mainstream culture. How does it do this? Skateboarding does this by prioritizing *beauty over function* and *playfulness over seriousness*.

Whitehead's Spin on Beauty

Humanity takes itself too seriously; we cannot truly entertain those most enjoyable aspects of our human existence if we are to be successful in our hyper-capitalistic world. If something *cannot* be quantified or monetized, our contemporary world seems to tell us, it does not deserve much attention. If something *can* be quantified or monetized, then that becomes the most important aspect of it. A prime example of this is found in the energy sector. Oil companies want to drill for oil in pristine nature preserves, despite the fact that critics argue that the land has worth in itself, beyond the utilitarian benefits of the fossil fuels it contains. Sadly, profits are continually valued over nature and beauty. The point here is simply that our modern world is primarily driven by profits, much to the detriment of a variety of other concerns. Monetary rationalization is frequently (if not universally) deemed more important than qualitative experiences.

The goal here is not to demonize (responsible forms of) capitalism but to demonstrate how lopsided our social and existential priorities have become. While nature and beauty have value in and of themselves, they also play a significant role in the human condition. What makes life worth living is not the accumulation of wealth but its alternative: the richness of our experiences. What gives rise to the richness of human experience? Simply put, it is the feeling of beauty in its various forms. Beauty (and the experiences felt by it) are what give life its lived texture. And, though beauty is complex and mysterious (because we can never give a universally agreed-upon definition of it), it's the type of thing we know when we see it (whether it be in art, nature, or humanity itself).

At the turn of the 20th century, mathematician and philosopher Alfred North Whitehead set out to defend the importance of beauty and its qualitative experiences. His philosophical system sought a holistic explanation of the universe, integrating seemingly opposite concepts: mind and matter, the objective and the subjective, etc. In this process, he argued that creativity and beauty are indispensable features of the universe. Creativity is the life force of the universe, constantly propelling the universe (and us along with it) into experientially rich and new contexts. It not only provides an understanding of our continuation into the future (e.g., ever-changing historical circumstances) but provides something more palpable: rich experiences that give rise to the way we understand value and importance. According to Whitehead, the feelings we experience when we encounter a beautiful landscape, a moving song, or even a steezy viral heelflip are concrete examples of the human response to beauty. These experiences elicit a bodily response that "fertilizes the soul" and breaks us out of our everyday life.[4]

What this means is that the beauty found in nature or forms of art (such as skating) can provide qualitative enthusiasm for life. This is not just a little extra added zest to human experience; it is a *necessity* for it. Our existence cries out to break from the ordinary expectations of society. Whitehead argues that "[h]uman beings require something which absorbs them for a time, something out of the routine which they can stare at."[5] It would be a mistake to think that a skate session is merely a break from the ordinary, a simple respite from our "real" lives to which we must ultimately return. The session cannot be thought of as something independent from our everyday duties. In contrast to this, Whitehead sought a holism and argues that we should be weary of compartmentalizing our world and experiences. When we are off the skateboard, we are affected by those intensities of experiences had on it (again, overcoming those on-off binaries). The world is a little different for skaters.

Skateboarding, then, cannot be viewed as just a leisurely hobby that we undertake to pass the time between the more serious, "important" moments in life. For Whitehead, the experiences of beautiful art forms infuse and rejuvenate our very being. And skateboarding, I would argue, is just the type of thing Whitehead has in mind here. The triumphs, struggles, and failures felt while skating revitalize our orientation to ourselves and the world. In line with skating's counterculture heritage, Whitehead reinstates the importance of art and beauty against claims that they are trivial. On the contrary, our experiences of art or beauty remind us of what it means to be human. Why else would we undergo such rich experiential intensities in the presence of art or beauty if they were merely trivial? This is a question worth taking seriously.

Beauty justifies itself by its immediate enjoyment. As Whitehead puts it, "[great art] is something which adds to the permanent richness of the soul's self-attainment. Its discipline is not distinct from enjoyment, but by reason of it."[6] Interestingly, Whitehead held together "discipline" and "enjoyment" in this last line and claims that discipline develops *from* enjoyment. In order to explain this further, we'll consider Hans-Georg Gadamer's thought on play as another way to support Whitehead's view and its application to skating and life.

Gadamer's Serious Play

Known for his work in hermeneutics (a branch of philosophy dealing with the nature of interpretation), German philosopher Hans-Georg Gadamer helps us interpret the dynamics between discipline and enjoyment or, to use his language, seriousness and play. To a "commoner" (read: a non-skateboarder), skating is not a serious undertaking. It does not help you climb the corporate ladder, nor is it a lucrative activity. But, as we saw above through Whitehead, skateboarding is a unique art form that revitalizes our souls and adds beauty to our lives. These artforms are ends in themselves, and we cannot get behind them (which is a claim I will return to in my ender).

With this in mind, we might again wonder why we skate at all. Why spend hours "disciplining" oneself to get a nollie flip on lock if doing so has no societal or financial gain? Whereas Whitehead would say that human nature naturally craves beauty and creativity, for Gadamer, it is quite simple. It is because "play itself contains its own, even sacred, seriousness."[7] Here again, the act of skating, as understood through the category of play, is compared to something religiously sacred, something literally "set apart" from the ordinary; this is simply what "sacred" *means*. The purpose of play or art is for the sake of itself, and therefore, it contains its own existential seriousness. Now, it would be worth unpacking how Gadamer comes to this conclusion.

What is the purpose of skating from a Gadamerian perspective? Play is an interesting concept because it serves its own purpose; that is, one plays for the sole purpose of playing. Unlike other human activities, play is not concerned with "serious" matters such as solving grave problems or working. In other words, there is no final resolution to play. Gadamer notes that "the child gives itself a task in playing with a ball, and such tasks are playful ones because the purpose of the game is not really solving the task but ordering and shaping the movement of the game."[8] The progression of "ordering and shaping the movement of the game" within skating has been absolutely mind-boggling. The purpose of play is not to accomplish it but to complexify it by, for example, adding more possibilities for getting a letter in a game of SKATE.

With this in mind, if there is nothing to solve in the act of skateboarding, then surely, one might think, there is some final form or finality that brings the task to a close. Not so fast. Gadamer continues, "[t]he movement of playing has no goal that brings it to an end; rather, it renews itself in constant repetition."[9] What a peculiar form of play! There are no "tasks" being solved nor is there a definite end to the activity. Bringing something to a conclusion is thought to be a rewarding task, yet skaters put themselves into an unending labor of love. This is the seriousness of play.

Skating has an objectiveless "objective," which again raises the question, why would anyone undertake an activity that has no real goals or an end? Why would anyone expend so much energy on such a seemingly pointless task? Gadamer, at first, retains the mystery to this quandary: "The player knows very well what play is, and that what [they are] doing is 'only a game'; but [they do] not know what exactly [they] 'know' in knowing that."[10] The allure of play or skateboarding is a mystery. In a very concrete way, it transcends logical thinking since we cannot adequately put into words exactly why we have such burning enthusiasm for it. Gadamer is certainly right when he proclaims that "[t]he real subject of the game (this is shown precisely by those experiences in which there is only a single player) is not the player but instead the game itself."[11] As it relates to skating, we might then say that we don't get a hold of skateboarding, but rather skateboarding gets a hold of us.

Yet, there still exists a mystery; why do we exert so much energy and spend so much time skating without any obvious reasons? What should we say to such a mystery? Here, the resonance with Whitehead becomes clear. Gadamer says that serious play is without a defined goal or end but then introduces an "A-ha" moment. He claims that it is also without effort. Oddly, "[Play] happens, as it were, by itself. The ease of play—which naturally does not mean that there is any real absence of effort but refers phenomenologically only to the absence of strain—is experienced subjectively as relaxation."[12] Here, we are given an answer—we perpetually exhaust ourselves skateboarding because *our labor is experienced as relaxation*. As with Whitehead, who re-introduces the importance of beauty, Gadamer re-establishes the importance of play, not as a time-wasting activity, but as a foundational aspect of human nature.

One could object here; skating is not without goals; it is *filled* with goals. Surely, we set out objectives every time we roll up to a spot with limitless possibilities. But these goals are utterly localized with only one thing in mind: self-enjoyment or Gadamer's *relaxation*. Within Whitehead's philosophy, self-enjoyment or satisfaction is a technical term because "the notion of life implies a certain absoluteness of self-enjoyment … the occasion of experience is absolute in respect to its immediate self-enjoyment."[13] Paradoxically, the goal is not so much the trick itself, but the self-enjoyment felt upon landing it. Yet, it is a fleeting enjoyment that requires constant renewal, like a never-ending story, or better yet, a never-ending line.

Once a trick is mastered, the potential combinations become endless, from stepping your game up to a new context (from flat ground to a double set) or added to a gnarly line, like in those mind-blowing Berric's clips ("Must be nice"). This rise of complexification leads to greater intensities of enjoyment done for its own sake. Worldly tasks lack this "existential" worth because it is contrasted to societal expectations, not personal enjoyment. Worldly tasks have ulterior motives. We'll see this point illustrated further in the concluding section.

The Ender

What we've considered throughout this essay is that beauty, art, play, and skateboarding are ends in themselves. This signifies something crucially important. To conclude, let me offer some existential observations in conversation with the ancient Greek philosopher, Aristotle. According to Aristotle, how to live well depends on what we hold as the highest good. This highest good is what orients our lives, what gives it meaning. How would you respond to this question? After deciding on the highest good, he asks us to decide where our notion of good would fall between two categories: Is our good *inherent or instrumental*? These terms are related to the distinction drawn above between tasks of self-enjoyment and worldly tasks. An inherent good is something that is, by its very nature, good. That is, there is no going beyond it for some deeper reason. Much like Whitehead's beauty or art, Gadamer's play, or Becker's skateboarding, it is undertaken for its own sake and serves its own purpose. In other words, it is its own end. For Aristotle, there is only one inherent good: *eudaimonia* (which means living well or is more loosely translated as happiness).

The greatest mistake we can make is to confuse an instrumental good for an inherent good. Consider the following example. Let us suppose someone remarked that having a career is the highest good. Certainly, having a career is important, but is it the *highest* good? According to Aristotle, having a career is merely an instrumental good. No matter how much you may love your career, it is ultimately undertaken in the pursuit of some other or greater good (e.g., money, security, having somewhere to go every day, etc.). Hence, having a career is a means to an end; it is not an end in itself. It is to be used—like an instrument—for another goal or for obtaining some other thing.

With this insight, Aristotle would also implore us to dig even deeper. Are goods like money (a good we pursue through our career) an inherent or instrumental good? Of course, money is also merely instrumental; it is a means to an end. We want money not because we want money (in and of itself), but because we want the things money can buy us. Cutting to the chase, ultimately, all instrumental goods are aimed at happiness (arguably, the one thing that is good in and of itself). Happiness or living well is the ultimate good, and it's something experiential that cannot be quantified. How far has our hyper-capitalistic world swayed us from this insight?

When the topic of beauty or play arises in a contemporary conversation, we often hear people respond with "beauty is subjective" or "beauty is in the eye of the beholder." Such responses are used to undermine the importance of beauty and the experiences it gives us. These platitudes suggest that beauty has little significance because it is "subjective." In true countercultural fashion, Whitehead turns this completely upside down. Art and beauty may be experienced differently by different people, but the strong impressions they make on us is a concrete fact of our human existence. If the notion of beauty and art is unimportant for life, then why does it move us so deeply? The only answer is that it is important by the mere fact that it resonates with what it means to be human. It reminds us that humans are experientially rich creatures who derive enjoyment from art in its various forms. Whitehead reminds us that "a living art, which moves on and yet leaves its permanent mark, can hardly be exaggerated."[14] I cannot think of a better description of skating.

Similarly, play or playfulness tends to carry with it negative attitudes: "Quit playing around!" or "Get serious!" Yet, Gadamer finds that acts of playfulness show us another side of human nature. Play absorbs us in the act where we enter an almost bizarre world: the seriousness of the world slips away, time seems to stop, social expectations are suspended, and the exhaustion of the act is experienced as relaxation. By examining what Whitehead and Gadamer have to say about beauty, creativity, and play, we can conclude that the act of skating is its own end. Skateboarding serves its own purpose. There is no going behind it to find some deeper purpose. Next time you are going out for a street session or cruising, remember that you are not merely "Going skating" or taking a break, but rather you are reinvigorating your soul by tapping into human nature.

Notes

1. O'Connor, Paul. 2020. *Skateboarding and Religion.* Palgrave Macmillan, 2.
2. Beal, Becky. 1995. "Disqualifying the Official: An Exploration of Social Resistance in the Subculture of Skateboarding." *Sociology of Sport Journal,* Vol. 23, No. 3, 252–267.
3. For example, watch Stevie Williams's documentary, *Being Stevie Williams,* which discusses the origins of DGK ("Dirty Ghetto Kids").
4. Whitehead, Alfred North. 1953. *Science and the Modern World.* Macmillan, 202.
5. *Ibid.*
6. *Ibid.*
7. Gadamer, Hans-Georg. 1975. *Truth and Method.* Seabury Press, 102.
8. *Ibid.*, 107.
9. *Ibid.*, 104.
10. *Ibid.*, 103.
11. *Ibid.*, 106.
12. *Ibid.*, 105. Phenomenology in this sentence highlights the lived experience of play: physically and mentally exhausting yet experienced as a form of "relaxation."
13. Whitehead, Alfred North. 1968. *Modes of Thought.* Free Press, 150–151.
14. *Ibid.*, 202.

The Girls Are Shredding It

Elly Vintiadis

I got my first skateboard at the age of 11 in the mid–1980s as a Christmas gift from my grandmother. It was the best gift I'd ever received, and in many ways, it shaped who I am today. It was a light blue plastic mini cruiser, the kind of banana board that's recently been enjoying a resurgence in popularity. I landed some of my first tricks on that board before moving on to a now classic (old school) wide Vision deck and finally to the mainstream popsicle doublekick that I still have today (I also have a longboard, but I'm useless on it).

This all took place in Greece and Italy where I was raised, both extremely patriarchal and conservative societies, even by 1980s standards, where skaters were few, and it was even more rare for women or girls to skate. More importantly, though I thought I followed what was happening in the skateboarding world, I had no idea that it was not just men skating. Looking back now, knowing what I know, it seems clear that women haven't skated nearly as much as men. And while the reasons for this are not hard to understand, none of these are good reasons for women to refrain from the sport. In fact, all of us, as well as skateboarding itself, can benefit if more women take up their boards and start skating.

A Forgotten Past

Like in many male-dominated sports, and extreme sports particularly, one could easily think (as I did as a young girl) that women did not participate in them hardly at all. Yet, women have been skating since the early days. In 1965, Patti McGee was the first woman to become a professional skateboarder, though she is rarely mentioned among the oldest or first skaters. In the same year, at 19 years old, she was featured on the cover of *Life* magazine doing a handstand on her skateboard. McGee was also the first woman to be on the cover of *Skateboarder* magazine, and in 2010 she was the first woman to be inducted into the Skateboarding Hall of Fame. Peggy Oki was the only woman on the Zephyr Skateboarding Team (a.k.a. the Z-Boys) in 1975, and in 1988 Cara-Beth Burnside was the first woman to be on the cover of *Thrasher*. Six years later, Burnside became the first woman to have her own signature shoe with Vans. In 1996, Elissa Steamer was the first woman to have a part in a major skate video, and she was the first woman to feature in a video game in *Tony Hawk's Pro Skater* just a few years later in 1999—the year that women's competitions were added to Slam City Jam, the North American Skateboard Championships.

In addition to these noteworthy and important examples, there have always been women skating and skating *well*, but their journey has always been uphill. Various factors have made it difficult for women to be part of skateboarding culture, and it took a lot of work and persistence from women to break down the all too many barriers that kept them on the fringes of the sport or outside of it altogether. Women's skating was considered second class and ignored for decades, and women were not being featured in the press or being sponsored by professional brands. Precisely because of this, Cara-Beth Burnside and Mimi Knoop created the brand hoopla in 2008, while Lisa Whitaker founded Meow in 2012 to support and sponsor female skaters. Even when women skaters were finally allowed to compete in the X Games in 2003, they got paid a staggering 25 times less than did the men (which led Burnside to organize a boycott in protest). To this day, female professional skateboarders are still not earning as much as their male counterparts.

However, skateboarding in general and women skaters in particular are today enjoying more popularity than ever before, so much so that the first all-female skate video was released by Nike in 2019. This is partly due to the changing social norms relating to gender, but what also acted as a catalyst for this change was skateboarding's inclusion as a medal sport in the 2020 (delayed until 2021) Summer Olympic games, thereby giving exposure to the sport as a whole but also importantly to women skateboarders. Women's divisions in competitions generally have started to appear more frequently, and the prize money for women's events has begun to increase. In fact, hoopla recently shut down because its skateboarders are now being sponsored by bigger, more broadly recognized brands (which previously seemed to have little or no interest in them).

The history of women in skating is relatively easy to find if one seeks it out, yet it remains largely unknown even by many skaters today. In fact, despite women's laudable contribution to the sport, skateboarding is still largely considered to be a male sport, and it is one in which women, for a number of reasons, remain significantly under-represented.

Why Don't Women Skate?

Even though women's skateboarding is the fastest growing demographic in action sports, women still skate much less than men. Is this because women are naturally worse athletes or worse skaters? There is no reason to think so. There is no physical requirement that acts as an impediment to women skating or excelling at the sport. In fact, skateboarding is as much about skill, style, and creativity than it is about physical strength. Rather, we can identify four major factors that have kept women on the fringes of skating that (though separate and distinct) are interrelated: gender roles and stereotypes, historic under-representation, women's lived experience in skateboarding, and prejudice.

The first factor that has played a role in keeping women back are ingrained gender roles and stereotypes that have made skating seem as if it is inappropriate for women. Traditionally, masculinity has been associated with risk taking, problem solving, physical prowess, independence, decisiveness, creativity, toughness, and strength. Femininity, on the other hand, has typically been associated with physical weakness, passivity, dependence, and emotionality. Men have been considered to be risk takers and problem solvers by their very nature, while women have not; men's bodies were taken to be naturally built for sports, while the bodies of women were not.[1] Since skating is an extreme, adrenaline-pumping sport that involves risk, right from the start, women are expected to be less adept at it than men. Indeed, that we use the language of "women skateboarders" itself seems to imply that we do so to distinguish them from *regular* or *normal* skateboarders (i.e., male skateboarders) as if women are not regular skateboarders. They are (at best) women who might also happen to occasionally skate.

Because of these gender roles and stereotypes, women who skate challenge most of the societal norms relating to how women should behave. Part of the beauty of skating is that it can be done independently; all you need is a board and an urban landscape or a ramp in order to skate street, freestyle, vert, or simply to just cruise around. The main characteristic of skateboarding is the freedom to be creative and to skate in whatever fashion you desire. Such freedom has rarely been given to women.

Skateboarding is also not a sport that is played in organized teams with coaches or rules. It began on the streets, and for a long time, it was associated with a subculture of troublemakers, antisocial behavior, and subversion.[2] This public perception of the sport makes it even more difficult for women to take up skating because divergence from norms, whether that means being part of a subculture or simply being creative (which involves finding novel ways of doing things, challenging the status quo, taking risks, being assertive, etc.), has been traditionally frowned upon for women.

Skateboarding is also a dangerous and rough sport that will inevitably lead to scrapes, cuts, bruises, and getting dirty (and possibly much worse). Boys are allowed and encouraged to play risky and physical games from a young age, while such activities have not been considered feminine. Girls and young women have all too often been taught to avoid such activities. Similarly, women have been conditioned to avoid the streets; street skating is not proper or safe and can be especially more dangerous for women than for men, even more so at night.[3] Because of this, women skateboarding have been perceived to be engaging in a masculine activity, and doing so can inevitably make the woman skater stand out—something that not everyone feels comfortable with, either because of internalized gender norms or because of the backlash a woman experiences when she engages in what is considered to be an activity that falls within the domain of men. Even I must shamefully confess that I stopped skating regularly when I was still an insecure teenager as my closest friend at the time, a girl, told me skating isn't feminine.

In addition to gender roles and stereotypes, a second factor that has kept women from skating is their under-representation in the sport. In fact, for a long period of time, skating didn't suffer from a mere under-representation from women; it had a complete lack of women's representation. Growing up, when we thought of skateboarders, we thought of men like Tony Alva, Rodney Mullen, and Christian Hosoi. We saw skaters represented on the screen by characters like Bart Simpson and Marty McFly, but there were no stories of women skaters to follow. The role models that were needed to break gender stereotypes and to help women feel comfortable to take up skating were simply not to be found in the '80s and '90s any more than they were to be found for the majority of skateboarding's history. The women who did skate did not get the exposure that men did when it came to magazines, skate videos, and sponsorships. As such, women who might have wanted to skate didn't know that other women were doing it. I vividly remember going to the skate shop in Greece and Italy during this period. There were no women working there; you would ask for a hoodie, a t-shirt, or a pair of shoes only to find that they didn't come in women's sizes. Though this has thankfully started to change, the sport remains predominantly male, and this only makes it difficult for women to start skating, to continue and advance in the sport, and to claim their space in it.

The two biggest skateboarding magazines, *Thrasher* and *Transworld Skateboarding* (which for decades have defined what skateboarding is, and thus could have been widely influential in the fight against the gender disparity in skating), rarely included female skaters. Since its beginning in 1981, *Thrasher* has only had three women on its cover: Cara Beth Burnside in 1988, Jamie Reyes in 1994, and Lizzie Armanto in 2017. Armanto was the first woman on the cover of *Transworld Skateboarding*, but this didn't happen until 2016. I recently came across some of my old issues of *Thrasher* from 1990 and 1991; I found only one photo of women in them, and they were a group of three fans at a skate competition. These days, there are occasionally special issues featuring women (or giving lip service to women in the sport), but there seems to be no genuine effort to be inclusive issue after issue. This gender disparity can also clearly be seen in the ratio of men to women on skate teams: Converse's Cons Skateboard team has one woman in 19, Nike has eight non-males in a team of 46, and Vans has seven women in 47.

In addition to gender roles and stereotypes, as well as underrepresentation, a third factor that has made it difficult for women to take up and stay in skating is women's lived experience in the skateboarding world. Studies have shown that girls need more support to take up skating than boys do and that women are more likely to take up skating and persist in it if they see other women skate. They're also more likely to stick with skating if male friends and peers support and encourage them.[4] Skate parks are a case in point.

It is common to see few or no women at a skate park. When women do make use of skate parks, they are always the minority, and it is all too common for a lone woman skater to be at the park among a group of boys. It is also a common experience for women to feel a heightened sense of uneasiness when compared to that of young men who feel emboldened to go to the park to start practicing tricks or ask for help.[5] To this day, because there is an assumption that skaters, and definitely *good* skaters, are men, there is a lot of pressure on women to be exceptionally good in order to be accepted into the group. It is as if women have to earn their right to be skaters; they must prove themselves and show that they have something to contribute to the sport when, of course, this is rarely if ever a requirement for men.

Women's lived experiences are often that they are outnumbered, judged, and observed. This feeling is so common that women will often only go to the skate park when it isn't crowded. They might go early in the morning and leave when the boys arrive, because they feel they are getting in the way.[6] This phenomenon is not unique to skateboarding culture: when claiming a physical space, there is a power negotiation, and, in generally male-dominated spaces, women feel self-conscious and lacking of entitlement to the space. Thus, they tend to occupy a smaller, marginal amount of that space.[7] It is precisely for this reason that the support of male friends and peers can be a force of legitimization of their presence.[8]

IV. Why Skate?

Beyond gender roles and stereotypes, under-representation, and women's lived experience in skating, the last major factor that has affected women's participation in skating is prejudice. The philosopher Miranda Fricker has shown how gender roles, stereotypes and social relations affect both the acquisition and the dissemination of knowledge, as well how testimony is received. In so doing, Fricker coins the term "epistemic injustice" for cases in which one is not taken seriously as a knower because of one's identity or social status.[9]

Something similar, in regard to *embodied* knowledge, is happening in skating, and possibly in male-dominated sports in general. Women are not taken seriously in virtue of their identity as women, because they belong to a group subject to prejudice. Not only are we undervalued as skaters while our abilities are questioned by male skaters, but often our motives are questioned, as if we cannot be skating because it is fun or because we are genuinely committed to the practice. We must be, so the prejudiced reasoning goes, someone's "groupie," or perhaps we are trying to prove something, to be cool, or to get attention from boys. The assumption that men will automatically be better skaters also all too often leads to patronizing behavior and hassle from men.[10] These common experiences of women can lead to a vicious cycle that tends to keep women away from skateboarding: you get better at skating when you practice with others, are mentored by them and so on, but for a woman to be accepted in a group, she must first demonstrate her worth by skating at a high level.

The unfortunate truth is that the skateboarding world is not always welcoming to women. In 2013, Nyjah Huston, a professional skateboarder, commented in *Thrasher* that "some girls can skate, but I personally believe that skateboarding is not for girls at all. Not one bit." And though, to be fair, while not everyone thinks this way, the skateboarding world can be very harsh on women. A perusal of the world of skateboarding on Instagram is indicative of the sexism and misogyny that women have to endure. Instagram has been a groundbreaking tool for women and non-traditional skaters all over the world because through it, anyone can gain visibility and promote themselves globally without relying on brands or sponsorships. Because of this, Instagram became a place where many skaters discovered a community beyond the gatekeeping of traditional media.

However, at the same time, it is clear from the sexist abuse and misogynistic comments online that diversity is not commonly accepted in the sport: women are criticized by men not only for their skateboarding skills but for their looks and what they wear, especially if they dare break with the normalized presentation of skaters and their baggy clothing. It is bad enough to skate as a girl, since embodying the traits of skaters is a challenge to traditional patriarchal gender roles, but for girls and women who do skate, there is a price to pay for those who do so without downplaying their femininity.[11]

Why Women Should Skate

Though the factors considered thus far help us understand why women haven't skated, none of them are good reasons for them to refrain from skating. If we think in terms of human flourishing, in terms, that is, of functioning well and developing as human beings, people need the freedom and opportunity to pursue ends that are important to them. Part of flourishing is cultivating virtues, and women—and, by consequence, the global movement for equality as a whole—can benefit from the cultivation of the virtues that skateboarding has to offer.

Skateboarding is about developing difficult to achieve skills: controlling a board, performing tricks, and putting together lines (i.e., a number of tricks performed consecutively). As such, it requires determination, self-motivation, discipline, perseverance, courage, endurance, and creativity. These virtues are developed when learning to ride a skateboard and in the process of constantly striving for improvement until one manages to successfully execute a trick (a process which can take months of practice to achieve). When finally succeeding to land a trick or a line, it is an incredible confidence boost. Especially when done with other women, skateboarding can be a tremendous tool of empowerment.

In many ways, this process resembles learning and working in philosophy. Looking back, I now realize that through skating as a young woman, I developed many of the tools that helped me become a philosopher, because the virtues that are developed through skateboarding trickle down to a number of other aspects of life. In the process, things that once were deemed impossible are revealed to be possible. By breaking gender stereotypes and motivating more women to pursue goals that they might otherwise have shied away from, skating can help combat what is called "stereotype threat" where a negative stereotype (e.g., that women can't skate as well as men) contributes to lowered performance. That is, social norms stop women from skating, but helping women skate can contribute to changing social norms.

It is important to stress that women shouldn't have to contribute something to the sport in order to be allowed in it, any more than men are required to contribute something to skating in order to be acknowledged as skaters. Still, one shouldn't ignore that inclusivity and diversity can have a positive effect on skateboarding itself. Obviously, if more people skate, it is good for the sport in the sense that it increases its market, thereby creating greater opportunities for the industry as a whole. But beyond this, inclusivity is not only about who participates in an activity but about the perspectives and ideas that the activity is opened to.

A good example of this involves one of the best skaters in the world, Leticia Bufoni, who was named by *Forbes* as one of the most powerful women in sport. Bufoni illustrates not only how inclusivity can bring new ideas into a sport and extend its boundaries but also of how counter-stereotypical examples can serve as role models, thus showing what is possible by changing the perception of what women are capable of. Among her other many achievements, Bufoni entered the Guinness Book of World Records (for a second time) when she combined skateboarding with skydiving as she performed the highest grind in history while jumping out of the back of a transport plane. Obviously, not all women who will take up skating will become champions or leave their mark on skating history to this same degree, but they will all contribute to changing social norms, and among them, there might be any number of skaters who can change skateboarding itself in new and exciting ways.

Space for Everyone

Things are much better than they used to be, but that doesn't mean that we should be satisfied with where they are today. Women should be given the space to skate. Firstly, because this is fundamentally a question of justice, in the sense that if they *want* to skate, women should be allowed to skate; it should be open and available to them. Of course, one could argue that there is nothing stopping women from skating. After all, as I said above, women have been skating for decades. Yet, if we think in terms of equality, then we must also think in terms of opportunity. And, the fact is that women do not have the same opportunities in skating as men, nor are they encouraged or supported when skating (making it much more difficult for a woman to take up skating and advance in it).

Though we are still not equally represented, and women skaters still receive less attention, less prize money, and smaller endorsement deals than men, brands are including women in their promotional materials and videos because there is now a market for them. For one thing, skateboarding is much more mainstream today than it was in the '80s and '90s because it is not only non-conformists or youthful rebels who take it up. In addition to this, because of the societal shift toward equality and diversity, women are less frequently actively discouraged from participating in previously male-dominated sports. And, because of user-generated content, women have a great deal more visibility than ever before—much more than when the two major skateboarding magazines all but defined skateboarding. Nevertheless, men still dominate the industry.

The truth is that not only does a skater learn best when they are around other skaters who have similar goals, but skateboarders also form a subculture that in many ways rejects accepted social norms, values authenticity, and whose members share an unspoken bond. Because of this, there is a bit of a paradox in the exclusion and marginalization of certain groups from skateboarding, because its very nature encourages diversity. It was this sense of community among people who loved skating that was one of the things that attracted me to it so many years ago, and it was this subculture that ultimately gave rise to women skateboarders despite the industry gatekeepers. In order to regain this sense of community we need to demolish the boys-club culture and see each other for what we are: not women or men (or anything like that or distinct from that) but just people who—in a world with a million different things to do for fun—have chosen to skate.

Notes

1. Wachs, F.L. 2005. "The Boundaries of Difference: Negotiating Gender in Recreational Sport." *Sociological Inquiry*, 75 (4): 527–547.
2. Lombard, K.J. 2010. "Skate and Create/Skate and Destroy: The Commercial and Governmental Incorporation of Skateboarding." *Continuum*, 24 (4): 475–488.
3. Paechter, C. Stoodley, L., Keenan, M., Lawton, C. 2023. "What's it Like to be a Girl Skateboarder? Identity, Participation, and Exclusion for Young Women in Skateboarding Spaces and Communities." *Women Studies International Forum*, 96:102675.
4. Atencio, M., Beal, B., and Wilson, C. 2009. "The Distinction of Risk: Urban Skateboarding, Street Habitus, and the Construction of Hierarchical Gender Relations." *Qualitative Research in Sport and Exercise*, 1 (2): 3–20; Paechter et al. 2023.
5. Paechter et al.
6. Atencio et al.
7. Carr, J.J. 2017. "Skateboarding in Dude Space: The Roles of Space and Sport in Constructing Gender Among Adult Skateboarders." *Sociology of Sport Journal*, 34 (1): 25–34; Rose, G. 1993. *Feminism and Geography: The Limits of Geographical Knowledge*. Polity Press; Reinhart, R. 2005. "'Babes' & Boards: Opportunities in New Millennium of Sport?" *Journal of Sport and Social Issues*, 29 (3): 232–255.
8. Atencio et al.
9. Fricker, M. 2007. *Epistemic Injustice: Power and the Ethics of Knowing*. Oxford University Press.
10. Paechter et al.
11. *Ibid.*

V

The Skater's Mind

Knowing How to Kickflip

JOSEF THOMAS SIMPSON

Any skater can tell you that at some point in your skating "career" someone will call out to you, insisting (or demanding) that you do a kickflip. In more polite moments, people without such boldness will instead ask if you *can* do a kickflip. Put differently, they're asking if you know *how* to do a kickflip. Equally likely, at some point after you have mastered the kickflip, you'll eventually be asked by a new skater (often in exasperated tones), "how do you kickflip?" Assuming you're in an accommodating mood, you may take a minute to help the struggling newbie. Your instruction might look something like this:

> First, hang your front foot heel a little off the heel edge of your board, just below the front trucks, with your foot slightly angled so that your toes are pointing a little toward the nose of your board. Next, as you snap your ollie, you are going to slide your front foot toward the nose while also pulling your front foot back toward the heel edge of your board (this is going to flip the board). Finally, after the board completes a full flip, catch it with your back foot, then your front foot, and land.

Nearly every skater over the last 30-plus years has received some version of these instructions fairly early in their time skating. Likewise, nearly every skater has failed utterly in attempts to follow these instructions in the first several dozen (plus) tries and has the shin scars to prove it. What has gone wrong? Why is it that we all struggled to follow these instructions early on? Or, more exactly, why is it that in following the instructions, we failed to do a kickflip until that moment when it just "clicked"? Believe it or not, both the instructions and failures highlight a rather interesting puzzle about the nature of knowledge: what is it precisely that we know when we know *how* to do a kickflip?

V. The Skater's Mind

Knowing: That a Kickflip Is a Trick, What a Kickflip Is, and How to Kickflip

To understand this puzzle about the nature of knowledge when it comes to knowing how to do a kickflip, we must first briefly look at some of the issues involved in regard to the concept of knowledge itself. The first thing to note is that we can distinguish at least three types of knowledge or ways we use the word "know." When your grade school teacher put a simple arithmetic problem on the board, say 143 + 81, and asked, "who knows the answer to this problem?" she was asking for your ability to recall certain facts. Similarly, when the same teacher asked you to spell "Wednesday" or what the capitol of your state was, she was asking you to recite particular facts. Philosophers call the content of these kinds of facts *propositions*.

The basic idea is that a proposition is a claim that can be true or false and is typically indicated by a "that clause." Your answer *that* 143 + 81 is 224 is a true proposition, a fact. But propositions need not be true; you may have answered that 143 + 81 is 124 (forgetting to carry the "1" as is common in early arithmetical education). Making such a mistake means you have put forward a false proposition. When you believe a proposition (i.e., think that it's true) and you have good reasons for thinking it is true and those reasons are, in fact, what makes it true, you have a bit of propositional knowledge, you know-*that* so and so (e.g., you know *that* 143 + 81 is 224, *that* the capital of California is Sacramento, etc.). So, one thing we can wonder about knowing how to do a kickflip is whether, in so knowing, you have a bit of propositional knowledge, whether you know a fact. Specifically, a fact or facts comprised of a proposition or propositions about how to do a kickflip.

But we use "know" in other ways, too. We say things like: "I know Aaron; we've been friends for years," or "I know how to kickflip," or "I know how to play the baseline of 'Tommy the Cat' by Primus." The former use of "know" communicates an *acquaintance* with the person. "I know Aaron" is another way of saying I am acquainted with Aaron. But notice, we need not know many of, or indeed any but the most trivial of, the facts *about* Aaron to be acquainted with him.

For example, in knowing Aaron, I might only know the following facts about him: his name, his address, that he has two daughters, that he seems like a cool guy, and that he is roughly six feet tall. Surely, *knowing* Aaron (by acquaintance) goes beyond merely knowing facts *about* him (i.e., having propositional knowledge about him). In any event, when we say we know how to do a kickflip, it does not seem like we are saying we are merely acquainted with kickflips. Why? Knowing kickflips by acquaintance is more like being able to identify a kickflip when we see a skater doing one, or being able to distinguish a kickflip from a pop shove-it or a heelflip. Whatever knowing how to do a kickflip turns out to be, it is not just about being able to identify a kickflip when we see one. After all, there are plenty of skaters and non-skaters alike who can *identify* a kickflip without being able to *do* a kickflip or without knowing *how* to kickflip. This leads to a third and final use of "know."

When I know how to do a kickflip or play the baseline of "Tommy the Cat," what do I know? Prior to considering this question, if you've never taken a course on the theory of knowledge (epistemology) or attended a lecture or read a book on the topic, you might have said that knowing how to do something is basically having the ability to do it. To know how to kickflip is to have the *ability* to kickflip.[1] Consider how odd it would be for someone to say they know how to kickflip and then admit that they've never actually landed one. It seems rather intuitive to conclude that they do not, in fact, know how to do a kickflip. Or, consider how strange it would be for someone, attempting to "demonstrate" their knowledge of how to do a kickflip, if they merely recited the instructions of how to do so (that we surveyed at the front of this essay). If you share these intuitions about such oddities, you are not alone. Many philosophers have thought that there is something unique in knowing *how* to do something. But, before we fully accept the idea that knowing how to do something is having the ability to do it, there are equally strong intuitions that knowing how to do something is *actually* made up of certain facts, that knowing how to kickflip just is knowing certain facts (i.e., having propositional knowledge) about doing a kickflip.

Are There Facts About How to Kickflip?

There are some philosophers who argue that knowing how to do something is just a special kind of knowing propositions, knowing facts. They say things like knowing how to kickflip is nothing more than knowing a *way* to kickflip where that way is made up of a set of propositions outlining the way to kickflip. They even go beyond this and suggest that ability is perhaps not even related to knowing how to kickflip. These philosophers are bolstered by the consideration of examples where know-how and having ability seem to come apart. That is, where there appears to be knowledge of how to do a thing without the corresponding ability to do it. Here are two such examples.

(1) Pat has been a skate instructor for 20 years, teaching people how to

164   V. The Skater's Mind

do complex skate tricks like the merlin twist. He is in high demand as an instructor, since he is considered to be the best at what he does. Although an accomplished skater, he has never been able to land the merlin twist himself. Nonetheless, over the years he has taught many people how to do it successfully. In fact, a number of his students have won medals in international competitions and competed in the Olympic games.[2]

(2) Jack is an Olympic-caliber skater practicing a backside 1260°. When one performs a backside 1260°, one rotates their body with their board three and half rotations. To date, only one known 1260° has been landed.[3] Still, Jack wants to land the second. Jack can land a 900° reliably, a 1080° about 65 percent of the time, but has never landed a 1260°. He knows that in order to do a 1260°, he must bonk his wheels on the coping out of the ramp at approximately 20 mph in order to get close to 30 feet into the air to give him enough time to complete three and half rotations before landing back on the ramp without bailing.[4]

Again, some philosophers argue that these examples show us that knowing how to do something and having the ability to do it are not the same thing. But what should we make of these examples? Do they show us that know-how is not, as we intuitively thought it to be, a matter of possessing the ability to do something? When we say that we know how to kickflip or play the bassline of "Tommy the Cat," are we only saying we know certain facts about those activities?

At this point, one might think I have oversimplified the issue. Why does it have to be so black and white? Why does it have to be a matter of only having an ability or knowing certain facts? To be honest, it doesn't, but these philosophers have thought that it does. So, those who argue that know-how is not about having an ability, have maintained that know-how is all and only about having some kind of propositional knowledge. Notice, however, these kinds of examples deploy highly refined abilities, typically involving very many coordinated movements at precise times in precise ways, not to mention the possession of particular concepts such as *bonk*, *coping*, etc. We might wonder whether they would have the same intuitions about examples that involve skills and abilities on a "lower" level.

Suppose instead of testing cases (1) and (2), philosophers tested the connection between know-how and abilities with cases involving simple undertakings like addition and subtraction, simple inference, attention, and the like.[5] In cases involving tasks such as these, I suspect that most people would be unwilling to attribute know-how when there is a lack of ability, or they would be unwilling to deny that there is a lack of ability when there is know-how. Consider how bizarre it would be to say that "Johnny knows how to add but does not have the ability to add."[6] Note, this is not to be read as "Johnny knows how to add but is unable to add *right now*" (due to being asleep or being thoroughly distracted trying to navigate the streets of New York City during rush hour). Nor should we read this as "Johnny knows what it takes to add but is unable to add." Knowing how to add *just is* having the ability to add. Likewise, for other very basic activities: knowing how to draw a simple inference is nothing more than being able to draw a simple inference; knowing how to balance on a skateboard just is to have the ability to do so. For our current purposes, we might simply say that to have an ability is to be reliable at succeeding in the goal of the ability when trying.

If there are instances of knowing how to do something that are abilities, this raises questions about our initial examples, (1) and (2) above. In each of them, the subject was attributed know-how without ability. But notice that the know-how at issue is highly complex. It is not the case that in each of the examples the subject possesses *no* relevant ability. Rather, the subjects in (1) and (2) are said to be experts in the general category of performance under which the specific tricks fall. It would be a mistake to try to build a case for the idea that knowing how to do something is nothing more than propositional knowledge of facts based on intuitions in these examples involving highly complex and technical tricks. It would be equivalent to testing whether young children have any propositional knowledge about mathematics *at all* based on intuitions about whether children have propositional knowledge of Euclidean geometry.

Just because our intuitions (even rightly) judge that young children cannot know that the area of a circle is calculated by squaring the radius and multiplying by *pi*, it in no way follows that young children are incapable of having *any* propositional knowledge about mathematics. Similarly, we should not base conclusions about know-how on intuitions regarding very complex activities. It in no way follows that because our intuitions (even rightly) judge that Pat knows how to do a merlin twist or Jack knows how to do a 1260° backside air even though neither have the *specific* ability that *all* knowledge-how is propositional.

First, this is because, as we have seen, many instances of know-how entail abilities as we've here discussed. Second, there are very many abilities that Pat and Jack, in cases (1) and (2), *do* possess that are not only related to the tricks in each case, but constitutive of them. In other words, it is literally impossible to do a 1260° or a merlin twist without the ability to balance on a skateboard, balance on a skateboard switch stance, ollie, air over the coping on a vert ramp, backside air on a vert ramp, and so on. These "lower" level or less complex abilities are part of the whole of complex tricks. Pat's expert skating ability surely plays a constitutive role in his knowing how to do the trick. To conclude that know-how is not an ability based on (1) and (2) is akin to coming to the very end of a chain every previous link of which contained an ability necessary to the subsequent link and deciding to ignore everything before it.

Suppose we ask Pat, "do you know how to ride a skateboard if you don't have the ability to balance on a skateboard?" and then, "do you know how to ollie if you don't have the ability to ollie?" followed by, "do you know how to do a front-foot impossible if you don't have the ability to do a front-foot impossible?" and so on. We can make these questions as detailed in each step as we would like, but it seems like the answer to the questions about (especially) the less complex things like riding and ollying, would simply be "No!"

No, Pat does not know how to ride a skateboard if he doesn't have the ability to ride a board. But then, even if we (rightly) judge that Pat knows how to do a merlin twist even though he doesn't have the ability to do one, it would be mistaken to conclude that abilities play no constitutive role in knowing how to do a merlin twist. This is even more apparent in less complex tricks like a kickflip.

Knowing how to ollie and knowing how to slide one's foot in the correct manner is constitutive of knowing how to kickflip by flipping the board and landing on it. Likewise, knowing how to snap my tail by depressing the tail of my board with the right timing and sliding my foot forward in the appropriate way is constitutive of knowing how to ollie, which is constitutive of knowing how to ollie while sliding my foot in a slightly different way. And this, of course, is constitutive of knowing how to kickflip.

By similar reasoning, knowing how to do the far more advanced tricks such as a merlin twist or 1260° backside air is constituted by very many lesser abilities. It is implausible in the extreme that Pat would know how to do a merlin twist and teach it without any kind of ability to skate whatsoever, let alone an ability to skate expertly. The most we can draw from the intuitions about (1) and (2) then, is that *some* instances of knowing how to do something do not entail (and thus are not constituted by) the *specific corresponding* ability to do that thing. However, to infer from this that all instances of know-how are instances of propositional knowledge is unwarranted. To reiterate, such intuitions do not motivate, let alone commit, one to the irrelevance of ability for know-how.

Of course, none of these implies that propositional knowledge is not involved in knowing how to do something; it is only to maintain that in some instances of know-how, what we know is not a (set of) proposition(s). To be clear, to know how to kickflip or play the baseline of "Tommy the Cat," we do obviously know some facts. The fact that, to do a kickflip, I must know, for example, that the object in front of me is a skateboard, or that skateboards need wheels, trucks, etc., is clear. The real question is whether knowledge of facts makes up my knowing how to kickflip. From what we have seen, it does not. Put more precisely, there are not (a set of) instructional or *regulative* propositions that make up (or are constitutive of) my knowing how to do a kickflip.

The Intelligence of Skaters

So, what? Why does it matter that know-how is not propositional knowledge of facts, but instead constituted by abilities of the knower? I think it matters most because when we think about know-how as an ability, it allows us to say something important (and true!) of skaters that is quite honestly neglected. To see this, we must take into consideration one of the first clear defenses of know-how as ability which comes from the 20th-century philosopher Gilbert Ryle in an essay entitled, "Knowing How and Knowing That." In it, Ryle wanted to "exhibit part of the logical behaviour of the several concepts of intelligence, as these occur when we characterise either practical or theoretical activities as clever, wise, prudent, skillful, etc."[7] In other words, he sought to correct the mistaken idea that skillful behavior is not intelligent behavior by arguing that skillful behavior is a kind of knowledge and thus can and should be characterized as intelligent. As he puts it, "there is no gap between intelligence and practice corresponding to the familiar gap between theory and practice."[8]

So, if knowing how to do a kickflip is constituted by having the ability to do a kickflip, then there is a kind of *intelligence* in skating. More exactly, although skaters are often thought of as adrenaline junkies, vandals, etc., since having the ability to do these complex and dangerous tricks is properly understood as *knowing* how to do them, then, in every trick, skaters are manifesting intelligence. If so, perhaps in addition to calling tricks smooth, awesome, sick, and the like, we can also, we *should* also, call them smart!

Notes

1. Of course, having an ability is also affected by circumstances. We would not say that you don't know how to kickflip if you can't do a kickflip in an active war zone with bombs dropping or if you are currently underwater, for example. The circumstances matter to the appropriateness of ascribing an ability to someone.

2. This example is adapted from an example by John Bengson, Marc A. Moffett and Jennifer C. Wright. See Bengson et al. 2009. "The Folk on Knowing How." *Philosophical Studies*, Vol. 142. Springer, 387–401, here 391.

3. Mitchie Brusco at the 2019 X Games in Minneapolis.

4. Bengson et al., 392. Bengson et al. use the example of an Olympic caliber figure skater attempting a quintuple salchow.

168   V. The Skater's Mind

5. See Bengson and Mofett for a fuller discussion about ability-based concepts and know-how. Bengson, John, and Mofett, Marc A. 2006. "Know-How and Concept Possession." *Philosophical Studies*, Vol. 136. Springer, 31–57.
6. *Ibid.*, 37.
7. Ryle, Gilbert. 1945. "Knowing How and Knowing That: The Presidential Address." *Proceedings of the Aristotelian Society*, 1.
8. *Ibid.*, 2.

Gleaming the Cube or Destroying the World[1]

Mukasa Mubirumusoke

The opening of the Lost and Found segment of the Fall 2002 issue of *On Video* titled "Why Style Matters" is punctuated by John Cardiel's simple but important observation, "Everybody has style, everyone!"[2] Indeed, everyone does have style, but why it matters and why it is subject to obsession and debate within the skate community probably follows from the way it ties the uniqueness of an individual's skating to an aesthetic judgment only tangentially related to skill. Generally, style refers to how a skater appears when they skate. Evaluating a skater's style can range from pleasure and inspiration to repugnance and even offense. A cursory definition of style is that it is the singular way a particular skater's body contorts and responds to their maneuvering and, simultaneously, is observable as a totalizing embodiment or inhabitation of the skater's relation to their skateboard and to their environment. You can recognize the distinctiveness of a skater's style in a way that's similar to noticing that everyone has a certain way they walk, or because a skater's style can be unique in a way comparable to an individual's signature.

This cursory definition of style should sound intuitive, but it is far from complete. And it is perhaps surprisingly the focus on the individual that leads this definition to be unsatisfactory. Style's relation to skating is not reducible to how a skater looks on their board despite our initial inclinations about the topic. There is an entire world, an entire context, necessary to properly frame the question of style in regard to both what it is and why it matters. The importance of this context (or framing) can be helpfully expressed using a branch of philosophy known as phenomenology.

170   V. The Skater's Mind

Phenomenology: Worlds, Bodies, and Habits

Phenomenology is a branch of 20th-century European philosophy founded by Edmund Husserl. Though he was a trained logician, Husserl was inspired by the structures and foundations of consciousness and experience. When we think about consciousness, it is natural to wonder about its cause (e.g., is it divinely inspired or merely the result of evolution and complex neurobiology?). Husserl points out that while religion and science may have their own explanatory value in regard to this issue, they provide little insight into how we experience consciousness more generally. To get to this general level, Husserl insists we adopt what he calls the natural attitude, exploring consciousness from the perspective of our immediate experience.

One of Husserl's first observations is that in our immediate experience, we are conscious of a world. However, when Husserl is using this idea of a world he is not talking of a specific place like Earth. Rather, our consciousness, our immediate experience of being conscious, always takes place in a context and the simplest constituents of that context are the familiar dimensions of space and time.[3] Any experience you've had or could imagine having takes place in space and time.

Secondly, the world and the things that make it up are available to us as conscious beings. This amounts to experiencing the world around us as vaguely familiar; we are not constantly looking around in a state of confusion. Instead, the world we experience feels available for our use and exploration, to be perceived directly or indirectly. For example, you may have been absolutely in awe when you saw your first skate park. Maybe you thought, "What are those rails on the ground, and what about the curved banks around the edges?" And yet, even amid its marvelous, novel, or, perhaps, menacing presence, the objects and people of the skate park were accepted as being of this world, as available to understanding, if only in a limited manner. This is all to say that experience seems grounded in some sense of familiarity so that even when we encounter new things and people, they are never completely beyond comprehension.

Philosophers after Husserl took up this phenomenological approach and refined, redefined, and expanded upon it. French philosopher Maurice Merleau-Ponty made some particularly insightful innovations that are helpful to approaching skateboarding specifically. He understood that consciousness is not something merely in our head; it is something we do with our bodies.

When we experience the world, we experience our consciousness of the world through our bodies. This seems clear when we reflect on simple tasks we do every day (e.g., walking, typing, driving, etc.). If I'm hungry, I might decide to go to the kitchen with the task or goal of looking for something to eat. If I'm an able-bodied adult, I stand up from my desk and walk to the kitchen, conscious of my goal of finding something to eat. Perhaps I'm thinking of the Chinese take-out leftovers I know are awaiting in the fridge. Both the thought of leftovers and my legs moving toward the kitchen are part of the same task: my walking body is as much of an extension of my goal of getting something to eat as wondering how many spring rolls are left in the container. I do not need to isolate my thoughts and actions to get my body to move as if it were some foreign object. Instead, my body and my thoughts work in concert to complete this task. Any failure of this coordination would be jarring, like a foot falling asleep or missing a step on a staircase. These exceptions only prove the rule.

Embodied consciousness means that our minds and bodies are not two foreign things that come together through brute cognitive force. Rather, they inherently work together like your fingers and your hand. Our bodies are essential to our experience of the world, or as Merleau-Ponty puts it, "[the] body is the pivot of the world."[4] This, of course, does not mean that we don't need to learn the bodily motor skills that we will come to habituate or that such learning won't entail difficulty. We learn to walk, type, and skate in a way that constantly renews our bodily orientation.[5] But learning the motor skills of any different "bodily" activity requires the same habituation process as seemingly purely cognitive tasks like solving math problems. Sometimes we even see the body intrude on seemingly exclusive cognitive skills like when trying to recall a phone number by typing on an imaginary keypad.

Importantly, these habits of mind and body, or simply consciousness, operate in the background. We do not need to call upon them with explicit intention. In fact, we often struggle to do so when we are focused on a specific task. I cannot constantly be telling my body to sit as I type these words, nor can I try to individuate every little muscle in my body to move in concert so that I reach a steady jog. Instead (when, for instance, I am trying to reach a steady jog because I am late for class), I am looking ahead so that I do not crash into a parked car while trying to remember if I locked my front door. My body is habituated in a way that a world where running to class is an available task. These sorts of tasks require my body to work in the background with habituated surety. Attempting to get to class on time is part of the wonderful, horrible life of a chronically late embodied consciousness.

Why Style Matters in a "Skate World"

Surely, you can already imagine how embodied consciousness applies to skateboarding: once you learn to balance and push with confidence, the mechanics of these tasks often fade into the background of whatever skate task you have in mind. However, before entertaining skating in depth, let's return to this idea of a world. We know that our experience is always contextualized, that there needs to be a background/foreground dynamic in order for one's experience to cohere. This is the idea of a world. Now, while there is the world of everyday experience that is contextualized by places like home, time markers like sunrise, and mundane goals like waking and brushing your teeth, there are also more curated worlds, such as the world of work.

Consider the example of a chef. The kitchen is the physical environment where the chef's activities of prepping, cooking, receiving orders, washing dishes, etc., take place. Working at a restaurant is, in a way, its own little world. But there may also be a world of love where the chef and the chef's romantic partner have rituals like walking their dog, watching television, holding hands, and the like; their love world is primarily situated in their apartment. According to Merleau-Ponty, these worlds have a style.[6] Specific worlds present themselves in certain ways so that the same task in different worlds with different styles demands different approaches. For instance, it makes less sense to the chef to rush through preparing a meal at home in the love world, even though at work it is imperative. The chef's world of work is characterized by a style of efficiency and speed that may not be applicable in the love world.

The world of skateboarding, however, is very peculiar. This follows from the fact that the "worldiness" of skating is founded and grounded by purposefully transgressing the vague horizons that outline a "world" in the phenomenological sense. Skateboarding, at its core, is a style rooted in transgressing limits, disposing of old horizons, destroying the phenomenological conception of the world as a legitimating context. The skate world is created and expanded through its fundamental antagonism with the limitations of its context. "Skate and destroy" is not just a pithy slogan that fits nicely on a sticker or t-shirt; it is indeed an ethos, the style of the skate world.

In some ways, this may be intuitive. Skaters are often perceived as having a rebellious, punk rock sort of attitude. Skaters break property, injure their bodies, and have a problem with authority. Admittedly, it may at least seem as if this characterization is a facade, especially nowadays with the acceptance of skateboarding into mainstream culture, the hegemony of popular big-name brands in footwear and clothing, and the introduction of skateboarding into the Olympics. However, no matter how homogenized, popular, adopted by mainstream media, abducted by big brands, or constrained by Olympic judges that skating may find itself, in the end, it necessarily challenges the experience of a limited world.

Gleaming the Cube or Destroying the World (Mubirumusoke)

The skate world begins with legend: surfers attached skates to planks of wood and rode them around their southern California neighborhoods when the surf was flat. They used banks and backyard pools to imitate the movements of carving a wave. Importantly, however, they were not supposed to be there. The pools and drainage ditches obviously weren't waves; yet, they took their makeshift shred sleds and made an activity out of ingenuity, imagination, skates, and wood. This evolved into a skate world of ramps, handrails, stair sets, parking garages, urethane wheels, titanium trucks, magazines, skate shops, baggie pants, tight pants, drug abuse and recovery, monuments and museums, ice baths and Tylenol, skate parks and curbs.

But is skateboarding really that different because skaters take advantage of spaces or equipment that were used in an unintended way? Would not skateboarding simply fall into the category of things like stick ball, street football, bucket drummers, and countless other activities that often take place in alternative environments or with adapted equipment thereby remaining somewhat parasitic on their original activity? Why is skateboarding not just expanding the horizon of surfing; why is it not only as rebellious as using a waste basket as a hoop?

Well, at some indeterminate point in time and space, with some vague conceptual inception, skateboarding realized that its out-of-placeness was in fact its essence. What was assumed to be a relocation from water to asphalt, was no longer *essentially* an imitation, it was *essentially* a transgression. A transgression against surfing, sport, leisurely activity, transportation, and world building altogether. Skateboarding became more than an activity; it became an attitude, an ethos. It is a style where wrong will always be right, despite pressures to conform from the landscape, society, and even skateboarding itself.

To be sure, worlds, in the phenomenological sense, are constantly interrupted by transgressions. For eons, humans looked up at the planets and saw divinities. French conceptual artist Marcel Duchamp looked at a urinal and saw a fountain. In a similar way, skateboarding embraces the surreality of the former, and this is why many have analogized skating with art against sport. However, while similar to the surrealist temperament, the dimensions of skateboarding transgression reach beyond the limits of fine art.

Skateboarding *inhabits* and *embodies* a disposition, an attitude, where normative, legal, physical, and even self-imposed cultural limits do not slip into the background easily precisely because they are targets of attack. Even skate parks are not safe. Its static nature may seem satisfactory to some extent, but the skate park pales in comparison to the dynamism of skating obstacles that were not meant to be skated, with people who may

174   V. The Skater's Mind

or may not appreciate your presence. Fundamentally, all horizons of the skate world are targeted to be ripped from the background and dissected in the foreground because skateboarding is always on the attack, always seeking to destroy. There is no terrain, board, body, music; no norms of tricks, gender or racial politics, that are not vulnerable.

Don't misunderstand; skaters are human. They live in the modern world and, therefore, have and will continue to operate and perpetuate many of the normative values (mentioned in the passage above); they'll even deploy tribal instincts unique to skating itself. From how to push to gender norms, from what to skate to what music to listen to, from how to dress to how to flick your kickflips. A sometimes-shameful cultural conservatism in skateboarding exists and always will. And yet, unlike the majority of other world-making activities, the compulsion to transgress these norms, the skate and destroy attitude, remains rooted and essential in a way that makes any constitutive rules of engagement that outline and distinguish different cultural values and worldly experiences as always *questionable*. No comply is not just a trick or a skate shop on 12th—it's the foundation of the precarious world of skateboarding, whether skateboarders know it, acknowledge it, or want it. Policing authenticity, gender, or skate tricks will fail just like any other form of policing (especially skatestoppers).

If not mastery, what about progression? Can't progress characterize the way skateboarding "transgresses" in a perfectly recognizable sense? In fact, "progression" can be found in any sport, field, or activity. Consider basketball players like Dr. J, Steph Curry, or even those found on *And1 Mixtapes*. One could argue that Dr. J's acrobatics and Steph Curry's marksmanship transcended the worldly experience of the basketball of their time. Meanwhile, the handles of Hot Sauce deconstruct the concept of dribbling all together—an element of progress disguised as art. The expanding horizon of a particular world is part and parcel to the phenomenological experience.

However, even this progressive reimagining of long distance shooting and bouncing the ball off the defender's head still takes place within a sport framed by specific goals. While Curry's shooting and Hot Sauce's dribbling may take advantage of certain rules and transgress certain norms, the interpretive framework of the basketball world remains wedded to a larger set of rules and goals imbedded in the identity of basketball, like scoring points or tricking the defender. Meanwhile, try to ask those Fancy Lad dudes about progress; there is no transcendental father to their style. In skating, a brutal slam can be just as "valuable" as a make, ask Heath. This is skateboarding. Skating does not have "infinite horizons." Rather, it is the immediate intervention of the vertical and the relentless demands of the radical that problematize any new horizon.

Admittedly, this skate and destroy style might sound simply like a marketing campaign. With the evolving techniques and technologies of the culture industry, skateboarding seems more and more homogenized and mundane. However, even in the Olympics, while we saw national teams and jerseys, training, and scorecards, we also saw eccentricities that were of a different flavor than the weird haircut of a swimmer or sprinter that would often stand in for counter cultural rebellion: whether it was Andy Anderson's freestyling routine during the park event or (perhaps more indicative of the skate and destroy ethos) the women's park camaraderie with their "competitors." There is no bigger middle finger to the feigned Greco-Roman gladiator mentality they try to cultivate at every spare moment in the Olympics than the women skaters hugging and high-fiving each other after their runs. This is why style matters. Of course, maybe this sort of camaraderie won't be present at the next Olympics, or maybe it will. Either way, "skate and destroy" as an ethos, as a style, will always find a way to defy the gravitational pull of the many worlds that attempt to keep it grounded.

Return of the Mack: Style Recontextualized

Like I said before, style, as it is traditionally understood, would seem to have less to do with a skate world and everything to do with that particular person and how that person, by the grace of God and a bit of skill, looks on their skateboard. Actually, grace is often evoked to describe the most vaunted styles: whether it be that of Audrey Hepburn or Brad Cromer. They both have style, the former on the big screen or the red carpet, the latter on his board. The way his knees bend when he pops, the way his arms move in the air, and the way his body seemingly comes to a complete stop halfway through a frontside flip and then lands gently as if he has clouds for insoles: these all demonstrate that Cromer has style, good style, great style, exceptional style.

Or, consider Mike Carroll; suppose he's doing a feeble on a ledge. The board is touching the ledge, obviously, and he looks down and forward spotting the board and landing at the same time. His right arm is by his right leg, the left is up toward the heavens, palms up: style. Hopefully, in this image in your head, he was goofy footed and while you might initially think his stance has nothing to do with style, in fact, a person must stand on their board and be comfortable riding for some of your intuitions about style to form. Therefore, acknowledging a "natural" stance might seem to be the first clue into thinking about style in a different sense, a person cannot have style unless they have a stance in which they feel comfortable, a way of riding the board they naturally inhabit.

The "naturally inhabited" stance of a skateboard takes us back to the discussion above about the body and consciousness, or specifically the way the body and consciousness are tethered together. An individual skater's style, while it can mature, is nascent from the very beginning of the skater learning to balance and ride. Their style reflects a relation to their body that corresponds to the way in which they feel comfortable riding their board in a specific stance. Moreover, inasmuch as skateboarding is a habituated practice, just like those skills developed to operate a car or to sign your name, the more you skate and participate in the rituals of skateboarding (e.g., pushing down the street) the more your style reinforces itself. You start to naturally in*habit* your skateboard.

The spectrum of describing or evaluating a style for different individual skaters is literally innumerable, though common metrics include how controlled a person looks on the board or how inhibited; how graceful or smooth they look, how chaotic or undisciplined. These characterizations may correspond to their arm movements (or lack thereof), their head, how deep their knees bend, how they may lean, how they point their index finger before popping a trick, how they stick their tongue out, or where they place their feet.

This, however, is only style at a glance. In fact, there are other metrics of style, and now, once again, this analysis moves further away from the movement of a skater's body. These other metrics are often in the background of (or secondary to) normal discussions and intuitions, but they are crucial to our mosaic of skateboarding inhabitants. For instance, how tight are the skater's trucks, do they skate fast like Clem, do they skate cellar doors like in a Static video? What type of tricks do they decide to do, and where do they decide to do them? What do they wear and what music does it look like they listen to? These attributes are essential to the discourse of style in skateboarding and yet they displace the movement of the body itself from its initially singular position. That is because when someone describes style as "how someone looks on their board," while their first thought and the foreground of their mental picture may be the skater's body, just as important to the idea of style is the skate world that provides context.

No matter how hard we want to intuitively home in on the body as the locus of style for skateboarding, style is always contextualized, and it cannot be appreciated and recognized without the queues one gets from the ever-disruptive boarders of the skate world. One may object, "But wait, I can tell a skater's style not only from an image, but just by their silhouette." This is true. I'm sure it would not be too difficult to identify a dangly Jimmy Wilkins backside air cloaked in shadow. Nevertheless, identifying a silhouette is an abstraction that could never give the full experience we often attribute to the idea of style and that we reflexively fill in when we see a skater.

Actually, let's stick with photography for a second. Photography has been an essential dimension of skate culture from its inception, and we often make declarative judgments about a person's style from just a photo. However, you cannot imagine a skate photo completely ripped from the context of the skate world. The person will be somewhere, doing something, and that place and that maneuver are always contextualized as skateboarding, as taking place in a skate world, and only in this context does it make sense to talk about the skater's style. This observation is probably not groundbreaking, but that is precisely because at stake is the ground upon which something like style can be made legible. That a skater's style depends on the context of skating is so commonsensical that it seems silly. However, that is often far from someone's mind when they are thinking about Gino's lean after that shove-it (you know the one). But the context of that lean matters: the LA school yard, the NY music, and his gear all give us the skate context that makes that lean look so right even if it's indicative of a relatively ungraceful dismount. When Cardiel says, "Everyone has style," he is also saying that they are skateboarders and that they belong to the skate world.

At this point, it's worth asking how the skate world, inasmuch as it is rooted in a playful antagonism with horizons, reflects on the question of style. Well, the very uniqueness of everyone's style and the "imperfections" that highlight that uniqueness wink at the skate and destroy ethos. In the Olympics, when a diver enters the water with a large splash, or when a gymnast teeters upon their landing, they lose points. And, of course, this type of thing is true for skateboarding in the Olympics. There is a difference though, when you are at home challenging the score for a diver, you probably would say, "Wait, no, that was perfect; the splash was not that big. They didn't measure it right." However, when skateboarders see Ishod's hand drag as he rides away from a hardflip they can rightfully argue that this "imperfection" made the trick better, more stylish. Imperfection and displacement are not just acceptable or legible in questions of style; they can, in fact, underline it.

The End (Sorry No 900)

The skate and destroy attitude begins with the impulse to make a world in a place where you are forbidden, but most importantly to make this world together with those who want to come along. Architects, city planners, and private owners have attempted to slow skaters down, but

V. The Skater's Mind

there are no breaks on a skateboard (sorry rollerblading and BMX). Skateboarding necessarily tempts the forbidden, the protected, and the private with unmitigated raw hospitality. Nothing is off limits; everyone and everything is welcome. That's kind of our style.

NOTES

1. Thanks to Travis Clow for his editing, skateboarding, and friendship expertise. Also Mont, Dan, Pete, Taylor, Fletcher, Carter, Perry, Coyne, Hogan, JCal, Jose, Laybold, Droy and Clem RIP, Eastern Boarder, No Comply, my parents, your parents, the couches, the music, the friendships, and most importantly, the kickflips.
2. Cardiel, John. 2001. "Lost and Found: Why Style Matters." *On Video Magazine*.
3. Husserl, Edmund. 1982. *Ideas Pertaining to the Pure Phenomenology and to a Phenomenological Philosophy: General Introduction to Pure Phenomenology*. Kersten, F. (trans.). Springer, 53.
4. Merleau-Ponty, Merleau. 1945. *Phenomenology of Perception*. Landes, D.A. (trans.). Routledge, 84.
5. *Ibid.*, 143.
6. *Ibid.*, 197, 345, 425, and 477.

The Skater's Eye

Brian Glenney

"Two hundred years of American technology has unwittingly created a massive cement playground of unlimited potential. But it was the minds of 11 year olds that could see that potential."
—Craig Stecyk

The tennis ball hit her eye. Out it popped right from the socket and bounced off her racket, mid-swing, rolling to a stop on the green court, dangling a retinal appendage. The ER surgeon, gazing at her white surgical bandages, smiled and said, "I have good news, an eye donor just arrived!" A few months later, playing tennis with her sight fully restored, she started to notice that this new eye had taken on a life of its own, lingering over the curbs, stairs, and handrails at her country club. She finally called the surgeon after she became uncontrollably fixated on a fence sign that read, "empty pool, stay out." The surgeon, after a thorough examination, consulted the donor's records. "I have bad news," he said. "The eye donor was a *skateboarder*."

This fictional story, first told by Don Redondo in the September 1987 issue of *Thrasher Magazine*,[1] introduces the concept of the "skater's eye."[2] As skate scholar Sander Hölsgens writes, the skater's eye is "a capacity to, instantaneously and without (much) reflection, gauge whether a space is skateable."[3] If you skate, you may have noticed a similar lingering attention and urge to skate seen spots in the city. Like Stecyk's epigraph suggests, a skater's eye transforms the city into a skater's playground.[4]

The urban alchemy of a skater's eye provides evidence that skating is what the philosopher L.A. Paul calls a "transformative experience,"[5] an experience with radical, enduring, and diverse psychological changes.[6] This fits with the argument that skaters transform urban architecture from mundane utility into an arena for creative and risky adventure, redefining what is possible not only for a city, but also for its citizens, particularly those who skate.⁷ With all of this in mind, I want to make the case that a skater's sideways view of the city, a unique "stanced" orientation that is either right-foot-forward (goofy) or left-foot-forward (regular), generates much of the skater's transformation.

Transformative Experience

L.A. Paul defines a "transformative experience" as something that provides a kind of knowledge that not only changes how to understand the world, but how it is valued and what is believed about it. Paul's examples of becoming a parent or a vampire (tongue-n-cheek) show that transformed lives are so unique that no other experience can help prepare for what it is like to have one. And, once this new life happens, there's no going back. A new life changes both what is known and what *matters*. In one sense, having a transformative experience could be an improvement on life. However, according to Paul, there's another sense that raises some problems for choosing such a new life. For instance, if parenting is a transformative experience, then parenting is impossible to rationally choose—you don't know what to expect when you are expecting.

If I'm right about skateboarding as a transformative experience, then this is a problem for would-be skaters as well. No one can rationally choose to be a skater because no one can really know what it is like until they skate. A parent's undying affection for a child or a vampire's insatiable urge for blood is not possible to know before becoming a parent or a vampire. So too, a skater's impulsive ability to see playful possibilities in the city and urgency to skate them can't really be known before first stepping onto a skateboard. However, once they do, the would-be skater experiences an unexpected shift in their values and priorities toward new ways of knowing.

There are a few transformative experiences that come at you when you skate. You've no doubt found your natural stance: you push left foot-forward—you are "regular" footed, or you're "goofy," right foot-forward.⁸ Maybe you've discovered your uniquely tuned "ear" and love for the sound of skating, a sound that everyone else hates and even complains about.⁹ And again, you've developed this "eye" for street spots; like Redondo's transplant recipient you can't help but urgently gaze at red painted curbs, down ledges, and bent over poles. No one else has any desire to hang around these unwanted often polluted spots, what some people call "grey spaces,"¹⁰ but you can't stay away. What's more, when you skate these spots, you do so in an interactive way, trying tricks that "fit" the spot.¹¹ You find yourself caring for these spots: waxing them and fixing cracks.¹² Before you know it, these little transformations add up to a changed identity. Like a sailor finding their sea legs, you're a skater with street legs—your body is tuned to the city.[13] You are transformed!

A tricky part of being transformed is trying to explain all this to others who don't skate—to those who can't see a street spot or don't care if they do. That said, the fact that explaining this is difficult (at best) just might show how transformative skateboarding really is, changing what you know and how you find meaning. If you want to be a skater, read on. But you've been warned: it takes one to know one.

The Skater's Eye

If you are an artist, designer, or landscaper, you might have an analogous "eye" for design. A "designer's eye" fixates on how spaces are seen by others, an eye that almost automatically knows what it is like "in" a space. A skater's eye is like that, except it is fixated on what it is like to be "*on*" a space. This fixation urges a skater to not only skate but to think about the space as if it's theirs for the taking. In other words, a skater's eye urges a skater to use someone else's private property for their own use. This way of thinking often shifts what skaters believe, with many holding radical political and social views like anarchism[14] and the belief that property can't be "owned." What's more, this political outlook urges many skaters to hold social values of inclusivity and diversity regarding race, gender, and orientation,[15] as well as all kinds of disability.[16]

As I've been arguing, a skater's eye reveals to its owner a new urban world. Skaters can see a spot invisible to others among a vast array of banal architecture, a bit like how an expert birder can identify a bird in the woods which a novice can't even see. Some of these skate spots, like "Wallenberg," become pilgrimage sites.[17] Others, like "Southbank" in London, become protected heritage sites.[18] But most spots, like San Francisco's "Hubba Hideout," are eventually destroyed by their city, removed like yesterday's trash. Their legacy is celebrated by skaters in name, stories, images, and videos, cultural achievements not possible without the skater's eye that first discovered them. And the videos and photographs that are carefully studied by skaters develop in them a kind of "cinematic" skater's eye that furnishes their mind with a uniquely grounded knowledge of urban architecture.[19]

Philosophers of the Street

Adept onlookers, like the French public intellectual David Abiker, describe skaters as *philosophes du bitumen*, philosophers of the streets.

V. The Skater's Mind

And like the ancient Greek philosopher, Socrates, who was banished from the streets of Athens for sharing his knowledge, so too are skaters. "No Skateboarding" signs, security, surveillance, and skate stoppers act like sticks to beat skaters away from the city,[20] while skate parks that recreate urban architecture are built to entice their willful exclusion.[21] But skaters, not unlike Socrates, would rather drink hemlock than submit to their banned status. The streets to a skater are like the sea to a sailor.

Skateboarding is a crime, but this scofflaw status bestows an allure of notoriety, one that even onlookers like Abiker notice: "'Let's make them a skatepark' sing the neighbors. Fools! That will totally extinguish the charm of skateboarding, for all that is attractive about skating is taking hold of a territory that was not made for it."[22] Why all this urgency to skate a street spot, you might ask? Chris "Cookie" Colburn, a pro skater, says, "the skater's eye adapts to your levels and desires over time. Your choice of spot and how you skate it individualizes the skater, making them unique." Colburn even explains how some spots will "speak" to the skater, "the spot talks to them, telling them how to skate it." Skate spots thus encourage authenticity. They provide a way to "know thyself" (*gnothi sauton*), the most important moral value to ancient Greek philosophers, known as the Delphic principle. How a skater sees the city makes them who they are.

The skater's eye also helps to see how other skaters see and express themselves. Sky Selig, another pro, told me that "a skater's eye is really personal to the skater and that's what makes skating with others so cool, and why skate videos are a topic of excitement: you are experiencing another person's vision and expanding upon your own." Videos of street skating are the most important feature of the skate industry—they make or break a skate company or crew.[23] These videos provide evidence of skateboarding's collective memory and imagination—we really skate when we watch another person skate, a kind of "phantom body" skating, as Thom Callan-Riley argues in his PhD dissertation.[24] He's right! When I watch a video by the skate company Heroin, I mentally skate through Ira Ingram, aka "the curb killer." In my mind's eye, I imagine clandestinely skating a barrier whenever I watch Canada's famous "Barrier Kult" crew. What's more, the curbs and barriers in my neighborhood come alive and spark with an urgency to skate them. I wonder whether these phantom sessions are possible if I didn't skate?

If someone never actually skated, could skating in a video game give them a transformative experience? Could they acquire a "virtual" skater's eye? Sheehan, a video game player who doesn't even own a skateboard thinks so. "Play 'T.H.P.S.'[25] long enough and you'll notice your perspective on reality change. My brain instinctively looks for good rails to grind, places I could get air or make a slick transition."[26] Long-time skater and writer for *Thrasher Magazine*, Wez Lundry, thinks Sheehan is full of shit. "You do not have a skater's eye. You do not know what it feels like. Video games don't hurt when you fall, and that's why this is insulting. Beat it kook."[27] Only real embodied skaters know what skaters know. For Lundry, if you haven't felt the screaming pain of a shin absorbing a spinning board or a hip flattening on the pavement from a fall, how could your theories or ideas on skateboarding matter to those who have? Just as you wouldn't take parenting advice from someone who has no kids, you can't trust ideas from people about skateboarding if they don't skate. Why? Skateboarding is a transformative experience.

The Quixote Quandary

Those who skate may nod in agreement at these descriptions of the skater's eye and related transformative aspects of skating. But there may still be reason to remain skeptical. After all, becoming a skater isn't like having a religious conversion. For some, skateboarding isn't a lifestyle at all, but rather a sport or leisure act like running or swimming, or it is just for transportation across campus. For others, skateboarding is a fleeting stage of life, something that you transform *out of*, say, by becoming a parent. And maybe this is because the skater's eye is superfluous and illusory: seeing a skate spot is more like Don Quixote seeing windmills as giants.[28] If so, skating a spot is as ignoble as Quixote stabbing a windsail thinking it is a giant's arm. Grow up!

Non-skaters force skaters into a Quixotic quandary: How do you convince someone of the reality of something you know they cannot see? Non-skaters may have *concern* for skaters. From the perspective of Don Quixote's sensible sidekick, Sancho Panza, the skater's eye is delusion-inducing, making the skater's actions outlandish, or worse, disturbed. The non-skater might even echo Sancho's practical appeal, "what you see over there isn't a skate spot, that's private property, and what seems to be a hubba is a concrete handrail to support pedestrians walking up and down stairs." But there's still our skater's side, a child-like insistence that the battle is real, shouting to the Sanchos of the world "thou are not versed in the business of adventures!"[29]

Skate Phenomenology

If Sheehan's virtual skater's eye cannot help a non-skater idealize the change that a skater undergoes when skating, then maybe a sci-fi story might walk us, or roll us, down an imagined transformative path. Think of the Transformers; Optimus Prime (my favorite Autobot) really transforms from a robot into a semi-truck. Or consider L.A. Paul's vampires, shapeshifting from an ambling human to a flying furball: vampires really know what it's like to be a bat! These fictional accounts help imagine a novelty that empowers the skater's eye: a bodily shift from walking to wheeled motion. Feeling your body glide sideways is something that must be experienced to be understood, and there's no amount of walking or running, or swimming or even flying that can prepare you for the floaty experience of your body rolling on a board.[30]

Phenomenologists are philosophers who study what it is like to walk, fly, and roll in hopes of gaining insight into the structure of our conscious experience of reality. They argue that your body isn't stagnant, but includes its possible actions and activities, what they call "bodily space."[31] To a phenomenologist, if you skate, then your bodily space is reshaped by your *actual* body becoming wheeled, not just a phantom, imagined, or virtual body. When you *feel* your actual body glide, suddenly your possible actions and activities include bolting eye-cry fast down hills and flying gut-drop high in the air. And if your actions and activities actually change, then *you* change: your priorities, values, and even personality transform. You are different in a way that no one can know unless they experience rolling about fast, high, and "fly."

The skater's eye is fundamentally shaped by their bodily space—all the potential actions and activities as well as their transformative impact on the world. I bet that this is why skate spots are hidden to those who don't skate; they don't have a skater's rolling bodily space. But this comparison also shows a difference. Sci-fi "Transformer" transformation is distinct from anything humans can undergo—skaters don't grow wheels like transformers. Riding a board does not change a skater's body any more than a groundskeeper riding a lawnmower. Do groundskeepers get a "mower's eye"? If we claim that a skateboard changes a skater's bodily space, then it seems like we have to accept that a "mowers eye" is also a thing. That is, unless skateboards are somehow different than lawnmowers.

From a Stepping Gait to a Stanced Glide

So far, I've argued that the transformative experience of being a skateboarder converges at the point of the skater's eye originating in the feel of gliding sideways—a new bodily space. The skater's eye provides a unique knowledge of where to skate a city and an urge to do so that may be analogous to vampiric blood lust with an almost parental care for these spots. An ambling pedestrian simply cannot share the skater's rolling glide that gives them their unique set of potential actions: a bodily space phenomenology that, as I will now argue, is different from other ways of being sideways due to its "stanced" orientation.

Walk yourself and your board up a hill. Roll down. You've transformed your walking gait to a very fast glide. It's a new feeling. It's transformative. It's different from mowing your lawn because it categorically transforms the possible actions you can do. Why? Your glide is sideways. What's more, this orientation is either a regular or goofy stance, an orientation that is so dominant that skating "switch stance" (i.e., with an opposite orientation) feels and looks like a right-hander writing left-handed.[32] Even though skaters don't grow wheels like a Transformer, they grow a stance, a nearly unknown achievement of human evolution.

Being sideways is uniquely human. Being stanced is unique *among* humans. There are lots of sport activities that include a sideways orientation, from javelin and baseball throwing to bat and golf club swinging. But sideways sports are oriented around handedness, not stance—golfers and batters think of themselves as right or left-*handed* not regular or goofy-*footed*. Stance is also different from sideways orientation in that it affects not only internal balance,[33] but also external preferences like what waves a surfer would catch.[34] Some surfers and skaters have a talent for switching their stance, landing demanding tricks switch stance in a state of unbalance, a glide different from riding backwards, or "fakie," further complicating a skater's repertoire to the casual onlooker. And if stance influences both internal and external factors then it affects a skater's bodily space, and thus their skater's eye and therefore their knowledge and beliefs about the world. A stanced bodily space makes skateboarding transformative in a way that's very different from mowing the lawn, or javelin throwing, or bat swinging, or even Transformer transforming.

The Birth of Stance

Stance is seriously understudied. We don't know when stances were first discovered, much less when humans first discovered that their body could move in a sideways orientation. We don't even know when surfing, an activity that predates skating, incorporated a sideways standing orientation. Most early surfers laid on their belly or sat on their boards. Those that stood did so face-forward like a skier.[35] Standing sideways when surfing was not normalized until the early 20th century. And it took another fifty years before anyone talked about having a "stance," with the first written record in 1962 of a surfer being "goofy-footed,"[36] well after skateboarding had risen in popularity.[37]

Could it be that skaters discovered stance? Imagine a savvy 11-year-old "sidewalk surfer" on their 1950s homemade board suddenly discovering a natural goofy stance, telling their friends about it, and the rest is history.[38] On the other hand (or stance), you can imagine a pre-history discovery of stance; did Peking man throw a spear goofy? Today throwing is no doubt a "handed" activity, but what if stance predates handedness in human evolution? After all, those who have discovered their stance find it as natural as handedness, making these primitive roots less surprising. If so, stance fills a missing link in the story of human evolution, up there with evolving opposable thumbs, starting fires, and running.[39] We may even speculate that the attentional resources cued by primordial hunting awaken when a body moves in a stanced orientation, adding potential evolutionary evidence to the claim that skateboarding is a transformative experience.

What Is It Like to Be a Skater?

Skateboarding is a transformative experience. The skater's eye makes it so, a gaze grounded on a skater's uniquely stanced knowledge with meaning and values that permeate a life course.[40] Even if you haven't skated for decades, you may still find skate spots popping out like a 3D *Trompe-l'oeil* painting, tweaking the meaning of a city's architecture from a metropolis of commerce to a skate spot hunting reserve. If you want a skater's eye, then get a board and skate. But be forewarned, it can be as painful as a tennis ball in the eye.[41]

Notes

1. Redondo, D. 1987. "The Skater's Eye." *Thrasher Magazine*. September Issue.
2. Sometimes the term "skater's gaze" is used in scholarly work instead of skater's eye. This can be confusing if a reader associates it with the "male gaze," an encultured sexualized looking that has seriously bad vibes. The male gaze denotes a theft of subjecthood that turns a person (often a woman) into an object. By contrast, when a skater eyes a spot, they imbue it with meaning, even reverence. See O'Connor, P. 2018. "Handrails, Steps and Curbs: Sacred Places and Secular Pilgrimage in Skateboarding." *Sport in Society*. 21 (11): 1651–1668. Thus, when a scholar uses the word "gaze," it has an opposite meaning to a "male gaze" connotation, referring to the allure or fascination of a skate spot, endowing a spot with subjecthood and giving care. See McDuie-Ra, D., and Campbell, J. 2023. "Preparing Surfaces for Shredding: Skateboarding, Repair, and Care Across Scales." *Area*.
3. Hölsgens, S. 2021. *Skateboarding in Seoul: A Sensory Ethnography*. University of Groningen Press.
4. The skater's eye is not limited to sight, particularly as there are very accomplished

skaters who are blind, such as Dan Mancina, who is pro for Real Skateboards. Also, the feel and sound of the material surfaces are partial determiners of a spot. See Glenney, B., Boutin, M., and O'Connor, P. 2023. "The Sonic Spectrums of Skateboarding: From Polarity to Plurality." *The Senses and Society*. 18 (3): 207–233. Others have argued that the skater's eye includes the sense of balance and other motoric sensory abilities: see Nowodworksi, P. 2023. "Balance as a Skater's Duty? Sensual-Trained Action as an Expression of Scene Affiliation in Skateboarding." *The Social Meaning of the Senses: The Reconstruction of Sensory Aspects of Knowledge*. Eisewicht, P., Hitzler, R., and Schäfer, L. (eds.). 99–116. Sanders Hölsgens has convincingly argued that culture influences the tuning of a skater's eye. Hölsgens, S. 2024. "Learning to See or How to Make Sense of the Skillful things Skateboarder do." *The Routledge International Handbook of Sensory Ethnography*. Viannini, P. (ed.). Routledge. For instance, because South Korean skate culture is different than European skate culture, South Korean skaters may have a differently calibrated skater's eye. *Ibid.*, Hölsgens, 2021.

    5. Paul, L.A. 2015. "What You Can't Expect When You're Expecting." *Res Philosophica*. 92 (2): 149–170.

    6. Chirico, A., Pizzolante, M., Kitson, A. Gianotti, E., Riecke, B.D., Gaggioli, A. 2022. "Defining Transformative Experiences: A Conceptual Analysis." *Frontiers in Psychology*. 13: 790300.

    7. Borden, I. 2001. *Skateboarding, Space, and the City: Architecture and the Body*. Berg.

    8. Some regular footed skaters, like pro skater Bill Danforth, push with their left foot, called "Mongo" by keeping their back foot on the board, a pushing style that is ridiculed unless it is done in "switch stance," a stance opposite to the skater's natural stance. At one time, being goofy footed in surfing was ridiculed, a bit like how being left handed was in many American schools, resulting in a social constructed prevalence for right-handedness. See Muirhead, D. 1962. *Surfing in Hawaii: A Personal Memoir*. Northland Press.

    9. Glenney, et al., 2023.

    10. O'Connor, P., Evers, C., Glenney, B., 2023. "Skateboarding in the Anthropocene: Grey Spaces and Polluted Leisure." *Leisure Studies*. 42 (6): 897–907.

    11. Glenney, B. and Mull, S., 2018. "Skateboarding and the Ecology of Urban Space." *Journal of Sport and Social Issues*. 42 (6): 840–855.

    12. The suggestion that skaters care for spots mentioned here and advocated by McDuie-Ra and Campbell, may come off as a strange irony to those familiar with the common "skate and destroy" ethos. After all, skateboarders leave scratch and wax traces on virtually all obstacles they skate to the chagrin of property managers worldwide. To those who do not skate, these scratch and wax traces appear as cases of destruction, a perspective that enthralls most skateboarders as these marks are a feature of their identity. The look of these marks leaps out in sharp contrast to a skater' eye, which sees these traces as care insofar as it makes the space better for skating. For more on how the skate and destroy ethos is a kind of spot care. See: McDuie-Ra, D. and Campbell, J. 2023. "Preparing Surfaces for Shredding: Skateboarding, Repair, and Care Across Scales." *Area*.

    13. Glenney, B. 2023. "Polluted Leisure Enskilment: Skateboarding and Ecosophy." *Leisure Sciences*. 46(8): 1212–1236.

    14. Borden.

    15. Willing, I., and Papalardo, A. 2023. *Skateboarding and Change*. Palgrave Macmillan.

    16. Nikolaus Dean is just finishing his dissertation at University of British Columbia on skateboarders who have physical disabilities: from blind skaters who use a cane to amputees who sit on their boards, adding to the incredible diversity of skate movement.

    17. O'Connor, 2018.

    18. Magdin, R., Webb, D., Ruiz, P. 2018. "Resisting Relocation and Reconceptualising Authenticity: the Experiential and Emotional Values of the Southbank Undercroft." *International Journal of Heritage Studies*. 24 (6): 585–598.

    19. McDuie-Ra, D. 2021. *Skateboard Video: Archiving the City from Below*. Springer Nature.

    20. McDuie-Ra, D., and Campbell, J. 2022. "Surface Tensions: Skate-Stoppers and the Surveillance Politics of Small Spaces." *Surveillance & Society*. 20 (3): 231–247.

V. The Skater's Mind

21. Glenney, B., and O'Connor, P. 2019. "Skateparks as Hybrid Elements of the City." *Journal of Urban Design*. 24 (6): 840–855.

22. My translation. "leur des pistes! > couinera le riverain. Surtout pas, ça casserait le charme; car tout l'attrait du skate, e'est d'occuper un terrain pas fait pour ça." Abiker, Dr. 2022. "Le Skate, ça fait u bruit. Je me dis cela en passant par les escaliers." Available at: https://www.instagram.com/p/CZ1ZeXar7n7/?igshid=MTc4MmM1YmI2Ng%3D%3D.

23. D'Orazio, D., 2020. "The Skate Video Revolution: How Promotional Film Changed Skateboarding Subculture." *The International Journal of Sport and Society*. 11 (3): 55–72.

24. Callan-Riley, T. 2018. *How beautiful it can be: Exploring Collective Memory and Collective Imagination in Skateboarding*. Dissertation. The Bartlett School of Architecture, University College London.

25. T.H.P.S. is short for a famous video game, Tony Hawk Pro Skater.

26. Sheehan, J. 2023. "What I Learned about Cities from 'Tony Hawk's Pro Skater.'" *The New York Times*, 11 October.

27. Lundry, W. 2023. "Skater's Eye." Available at: https://www.instagram.com/p/CypPqKvsn4Z/?img_index=1.

28. Cervantes, M. de. 1866. *Don Quixote de La Mancha*. D. Appleton & Company.

29. *Ibid.*, p. 59.

30. Gliding sports are discussed in a recent paper by Loland and Bäckström, though it does not mention skateboarding for some reason. I think of rolling and gliding as having an equivalent phenomenology. See Loland, S. and Bäckström, Å. 2023. "Into the Glidescape: An Outline of Gliding Sports from the Perspective of Applied Phenomenology." *Journal of the Philosophy of Sport*. 50(3): 365–382.

31. Merleau-Ponty, M. and Landes, D.A. 2012. *Phenomenology of Perception*. Routledge.

32. Alexandre, M. 2022. "Skateboarding Stance and Handedness: A Brief Analysis of Relationship, Proportions and Influences." *arXiv* preprint arXiv: 2310.11460.

33. Anthony, C., Brown, L., Coburn, J., Galpin, A.J., Tran, T.T. 2016 "Stance Affects Balance in Surfers." *International Journal of Sports Science & Coaching*. 11: 446–450.

34. Furley, P., Dörr, J., and Loffing, F. 2018. "Goofy vs. Regular: Laterality Effects in Surfing." *Laterality*. 23 (6). Routledge: 629–642.

35. Moser, P. 2008. *Pacific Passages: An Anthology of Surf Writing*. University of Hawaii Press.

36. Muirhead.

37. Borden.

38. Watch the 1966 skate documentary *The Devil's Toy* and you can actually feel this time of vibrant discovery of self through skating.

39. Zaraska, M. 2021. "The Evolution of Throwing." *Pastimes*, 15 July.

40. The French word *"regard"* seems to best capture the concerning or caring look of the skater's eye.

41. Thanks to Levi Glenney, Joshua Heter, Neil Moloney, and Josef Thomas Simpson for helpful editorial comments. Special thanks to Chris "Cookie" Colbourn and Sky Selig for proving insightful comments and ideas about their skater's eye.

Skateboarding Glossary

A number of these entries have been adopted and updated from the *Skateboarding Master Class*'s "Guide to Skate Lingo." See https://www.masterclass.com/articles/guide-to-skate-lingo.

Aerial: a trick in which all four wheels of the board leave the surface the rider is skating on (e.g., ramps, walls, flat ground, etc.).

Backside: a trick which is executed with the skater's back facing the ramp or obstacle. Also, the act of the skater rotating the back of their body in the direction they are riding.

Bail: the act of deliberately abandoning a trick during some part of its attempted execution.

Boardslide: a trick which includes sliding the underside of the board between its front and back trucks along an obstacle such as a rail or a curb.

Bonk: a short nose grind which involves a quick tap of the board's front truck on an obstacle.

Coping: a protruding edge which runs along the lip of transitioned pools, bowls, or ramps.

Drop in: the act of transitioning from a flat platform (or, in extreme cases, from ledges and helicopters) into a steep decline or downward trajectory.

Fakie: the act of riding in one's normal stance while rolling backward.

Flip Trick: any trick in which the board is rotated or flipped along its lengthwise axis.

Frontside: a trick in which the skater's front faces the ramp or obstacle.

Goofy-foot: a skating stance in which the right foot is the lead foot.

Grip tape: adhesive-backed sandpaper bound to the top of a skateboard to give the skater traction.

Half-pipe: a ramp made of a flat bottom with concave transitions leading to vertical surfaces on either side.

Skateboarding Glossary

Handplant: a trick which requires the skater to do a one-handed handstand while their other hand grabs and holds onto their board.

Heelflip: a flip trick executed in the middle of an ollie in which the skater uses their front heel to flip their board 360° along its lengthwise axis.

Kickflip: a flip trick executed in the middle of an ollie in which the skater uses their front toe to flip their board 360° along its lengthwise axis.

Ledge: any elongated block with edges on which a skater can do slides or grind tricks.

Line: a set of tricks performed consecutively. Also, the route a skater plans to skate.

Lip: often built with coping, the edge of any transition which a skater rides.

Lipslide: a slide in which the tail of the board goes up and over the obstacle, and the skater's board slides between the front and back trucks.

Manual: a trick in which a skater balances on either the front or back wheels of their board without the tail or nose of the board touching the ground.

Mongo-foot: a skating stance in which the skater pushes with their front foot and keeps their back foot on the board.

Nollie: a variation of the ollie where the skater uses their front foot to pop the nose of the board against the ground.

Nose: the front of a skateboard, from the front truck bolts to the tip of the board.

Noseslide: a slide on an obstacle using the underside of the nose end of the skateboard.

Ollie: a trick in which a skater's back foot is used to pop the tail of the board against the ground while their front foot lifts the board up into the air.

180: a trick in which the skater rotates their board, body, or both of these 180°.

Rail: the edge of the skateboard. Alternatively, a handrail or any other object made to mimic or serve as a handrail.

Regular-foot: a skating stance in which the left foot is the lead foot.

Session: a time during which skaters get together at a spot for the purpose of skating.

Sketchy: a term used to describe the poor execution of a trick.

Street: a style of skateboarding constituted of riding on largely flat-ground surfaces within urban environments (and which often includes tricks, grinds, etc.).

Switch stance: the opposite footing from what a skater normally uses; a regular skater's switch stance is goofy-foot, and a goofy skater's switch stance is regular-foot.

Tail: the rear of the skateboard, from the rear truck bolts to the end of the board.

Tailslide: a slide on an obstacle using the underside of the tail end of the board.

360: a trick in which the skater rotates their board, body, or both of these 360°.

Trucks: the front and rear axle assemblies which connect the wheels to the deck and allow the board to turn.

Varial / shove-it: the spinning of the skateboard along its plane or vertical axis.

Vert: a style of skateboarding constituted of riding on (nearly) vertical surfaces such as half-pipes, pools, or bowls.

About the Contributors

John **Becker** is a lecturer of religious studies at CSU Long Beach. He has several publications in the areas of process philosophy, comparative religions (Buddhism-Christianity), and religious pluralism. Skateboarding dominated his pre-academic life as he was first a part of the Philly Crew (Phillips Ranch, California) and was later sponsored by Trinity Board Shop. He is in talks with CSU Long Beach to offer skateboarding classes.

Matthew J. **Cull** is a postdoctoral research fellow at Trinity College Dublin. They work mainly in transgender and feminist philosophy, and their publications have appeared in venues such as *Philosophical Papers*, *Feminist Philosophy Quarterly*, *Disputatio*, and *Social Epistemology*. Their steeziest trick is a smooth, high-popped no comply. Their first book, *What Gender Should Be*, was published in 2024.

Bradley **Elicker** holds dual appointments in the Department of Philosophy at Rowan University and Saint Joseph's University. He has published recent essays in the *Journal of Applied Philosophy*, the *British Journal of Aesthetics*, and *Philosophy & Literature*. His initial exposure to skating was a used VHS copy of 1990's *Board Crazy* which was also his first time being exposed to bands like Mudhoney and Nirvana.

Brian **Glenney** is an associate professor in philosophy at Norwich University. He works in both the fields of philosophy of perception and skate studies, where he has co-edited several books and written many journal articles. His recent focus concerns the ecology of skateboarding, a fit with Guattari's ecosophy. He has not stopped skating since he got his first board in 1986, a pink Lance Mountain Future Primitive.

Brian **Harding** is a professor at Texas Woman's University. He started skating sometime in high school and continued through college. He mainly skated in parking lots and loading docks around Denton County, Texas (with occasional trips to Jeff Phillips' Skatepark in Dallas). He used to work at a skate shop and swimwear store and to this day considers it one of the best jobs he ever had.

Joshua **Heter** is an associate professor of philosophy at Jefferson College. He is the co-editor of a number of books on popular culture and philosophy, including *Punk Rock and Philosophy: Research and Destroy* (2022) and *Post-Punk and Philosophy: Rip It Up and Think Again* (2024). He skated in his youth with friends, gaining an enduring appreciation for skateboarding.

About the Contributors

Thunder Storm **Heter** is the author of *Sartre's Ethics of Engagement* (2006) and *The Sonic Gaze: Jazz, Whiteness and Racialized Listening* (2022) and the editor of *Creolizing Sartre* (2023). He started skating in 1986 and still skates regularly. He learned to skate in Southeast Kansas on homemade half-pipes, brick streets, and drainage ditches. His favorite completed trick is a frontside rock-and-roll at The Proud Ramp in Fort Scott, Kansas.

William Giovanni **Jiménez Senzano** teaches philosophy at Fordham University and the City College of New York. As a teenager, he fell in love with skateboarding after watching *Almost: Round Three* on DVD and playing *Tony Hawk's American Wasteland* on the PlayStation 2. He can be found skating around Thomas Jefferson Skatepark in East Harlem, being outdone by kids half his age who have never even heard of DVDs.

Mukasa **Mubirumusoke** received his PhD in philosophy from Emory University and is an assistant professor of Africana studies at Claremont McKenna College. His work has been published in a number of outlets such as the *Journal of Speculative Philosophy*, the *Journal of Political Theology*, and *Philosophy Today*. He enjoys kickflips and friendship. If you'd like to skate, he'd probably be down.

Hector **Quintero** is a philosophy graduate student at San Diego State University. He studied philosophy and anthropology at Arizona State University. His research explores metaphilosophy and the history of philosophy. Using *Tony Hawk's Pro Skater* for the Nintendo 64, Hector has spent countless hours mastering virtual skateparks and performing tricks he could only dream of. This allowed skateboarding to carve out a special place in his heart.

Michael J. **Regier** pursues research in continental philosophy (especially) perspectives on ethics within the existentialist, phenomenological, and hermeneutic traditions, while also dabbling in rhetoric and argumentation, historiography, and narratology. Previous research interests include Kierkegaard's ethics. Michael received his first (and only) skateboard second-hand and broke it in half on a sidewalk artlessly attempting to land an ollie into a grind.

Casey **Rentmeester** is a professor of philosophy at Bellin College. He is author of *Heidegger and the Environment* (2015), co-editor of *Heidegger and Music* (2022), and author of numerous peer-reviewed journal articles and book chapters. His son, Bennett, just received a skateboard for his seventh birthday so he can channel his inner Rodney Mullen; the results are yet to be determined.

Josef Thomas **Simpson** teaches philosophy and coaches under-resourced students at Catholic University of America. He skated long before he knew about philosophy. He started with a cheap, Bruce Lee–themed K-Mart board that snapped his first day skating. That was quickly replaced with a Bones Brigade Mike McGill board (with Bullet 63m wheels) that he rode at Pipeline Skatepark and on all the half-pipes he and his older brother built.

Glava **Sofia** earned her bachelor's and master's degrees from the University of Ioannina in Ioannina, Greece, where she is a PhD candidate in the Department of Philosophy. Her work has recently been published in *Philosphein*. Though she only somewhat recently got into skating, she has always admired skaters, having

About the Contributors 195

passed by them in her neighborhood park and stopped to watch them for sometimes hours.

Emily **Stefl** received her bachelor's degree in philosophy from the University of Oshkosh and her master's degree in philosophy at Virginia Tech. In addition to philosophy, skateboarding has been a big part of her life. She started skating in 5th grade and stll continues to this day. She has mastered numerous tricks, but her favorites are probably varial heelflips or frontside boardslides.

Elly **Vintiadis** is an assistant professor of philosophy at Deree—the American College of Greece. Her main areas of research are the philosophy of mind and psychiatry. Her latest publications include *Brute Facts* (2018), *Animals and Us* (2020), and *Philosophy by Women* (2020). Elly started skating when she was 10 and spent the next decade street skateboarding in Greece and Italy. Skating is still a big part of her identity.

Seth M. **Walker** received his doctorate in religion at the University of Denver. He studies remix theory, Buddhist philosophy, and popular culture. His work has appeared in a number of academic volumes such as *Punk Rock and Philosophy: Research and Destroy* (2022) and *The Routledge Handbook of Remix Studies and Digital Humanities* (2021). He vividly recalls the first time he attempted a heelflip—so can his scarred right shin.

Index

Abiker, David 181–182
Adams, Jay 26
aesthetic experience 54, 56–61
Alva, Tony 26, 152
Aristotle 101–104, 106–110, 121, 125–126, 128–129, 146–147
Armanto, Lizzie 153
art 47, 147
Athens 92, 182

backside 87
bailing 89, 122, 127–128
Beal, Becky 134, 142
Best, David 62
Birdhouse Skateboards 47
boardslides 117, 134–136
The Bones Brigade 29–31
bonks 164
Buddhism 112, 116
Bufoni, Leticia 156
Burnside, Cara-Beth 150, 153

California 1, 26, 54, 59, 61, 79, 131, 162, 173
Callan-Riley, Thom 182
capitalism 26, 28–31, 132–134, 137, 139–143
Cardiel, John 169, 177
Christianity 83
Cicero 127
Colburn, Chris 182
Confucius 74–75
Converse 153
coping 164–165
counterculture 1, 144
critical social kinds 28–30
Cynicism 92

Daodejing 73
Daoism 73, 75
Darwin, Charles 55
De Certeau, Michel 48, 50, 52
Dembroff, Robin 28–30
Dewey, John 54–61

dropping in 27, 124–125, 127
Dyrdek, Rob 138

eidetic variation 123–124
Epictetus 95–96
Epicurus 92
epistemology 163
eudaimonia 102–104, 109–110, 147

fakie 19–21, 185
flip tricks 18
Fricker, Miranda 154
frontside 19–20, 87, 175

Gadamer, Hans-Georg 144–146, 148
gatekeeping 44, 154, 157
Gonzales, Mark "Gonz" 131
goofy-foot 19, 175, 180, 185–186
grip tape 1, 113
Guerrero, Tommy 131

half-pipes 57
Hawaii 58
Hawk, Tony 20, 25, 30, 58, 73–74, 76–80, 82, 86–89, 134, 136, 150
heelflips 143, 163
Heroin (skate company) 182
Hölsgens, Sander 179
hoopla (skate company) 150
Husserl, Edmund 123, 170
Huston, Nyjah 154

Independent Truck Company 137
intellectual humility 41–43
Irvine, Michael 46, 48

Jackass 27

Kaupas, Natas 131
kickflips 7, 19–20, 67, 75, 85, 93, 108, 126, 161–164, 166–167
Kierkegaard, Søren 82–89

Index

Knoop, Mimi 150
Kratis 92

Lessing, G.E. 83
lines 19, 146, 155
lipslides 118
London 181
Lords of Dogtown 26
Los Angeles 49
Lundry, Wez 183

manuals 18, 20, 63, 66
Marcus Aurelius 97
Marxism 132
McFly, Marty 152
McGee, Patti 149
McTwists 20, 77, 87–89
Meow (skate company) 150
merlin twists 164–166
Muir, Jim 26
Mullen, Rodney 73–81, 88–89, 152

New York City 165
Nike 150, 153
nollies 19–20, 55, 145
noses 19, 108, 161
noseslide 114

O'Connor, Paul 141
Oki, Peggy 27, 150
ollies 18–20, 55, 66–67, 75, 84, 93, 99, 114, 121–126, 134–135, 161, 165–166
Olympic Games 2, 9, 63, 138, 150, 164, 172, 175, 177

Paul, L.A. 179–180, 184,
Peralta, Stacy 26, 46
phenomenology 78, 121, 123, 169
Philadelphia 52
philosophy of science 8
Plan B Skateboards 50
poseurs 3, 37–44
Primus 162
pump track race 63, 68
punk rock 37, 137

Redondo, Don 179
regular-foot 19, 180, 185
Reyes, Jamie 153
Ryle, Glibert 167

Santa Cruz Skateboards 46
Sartre, Jean-Paul 132–139
The Search for Animal Chin 30
Seattle 51
selling out 26–32

Seneca 93–94, 98
Simpson, Bart 152
SKATE (game) 12, 63, 145
skate parks 47, 50–52, 94, 97, 137, 153, 173, 182
skate videos 27, 47, 108, 125, 131, 150, 152, 156, 181–182
Skateboarder (magazine) 150
Skateboarding Hall of Fame 150
skatebumps 49–50, 174
Slam City Jam 150
Socrates 2, 129, 182
sponsorship 26, 31, 41, 132, 137, 150, 152
Steamer, Elissa 25, 150
Stecyk, Craig 179
Stoicism 91–100
Street League Skateboarding 138–139
street skating 1, 46, 49–50, 64, 69, 74, 122, 131–139, 152, 182
Suits, Bernard 8–11
surfing 15, 26, 54, 58–61, 173, 185
switch stance 19, 23, 165, 185

tails 19, 67, 112, 135, 166
tailslides 66–67
teleology 79
Thatcher, Kevin 131–132, 137, 139
Thrasher Magazine 47, 50, 131, 134, 137–138, 150–154, 179, 183
Tillman the Skateboarding Bulldog 25
Tony Hawk's Pro Skater 150
Toy Machine Skateboards 50
Transworld Skateboarding 152–153
trucks 1, 123, 161, 166, 173, 176

Until the Wheels Fall Off 78

vandalism 27, 51, 133, 137
Vans 150, 152
varials 19
vert skating 12, 16, 85, 124–125, 151, 165
virtue 41, 75, 92, 99, 101–110, 121, 125–129, 155

Warshaw, Matt 58–59
Whitehead, Alfred North 142–148
Wilkins, Jimmy 76
Wittgenstein, Ludwig 22

X Games 12, 63–67, 70, 138, 150

Zen 111–116
Zeno of Citium 92
Zephyr Skateboarding Team 26, 150
Zero Skateboards 47
Zhuangzi 73–81